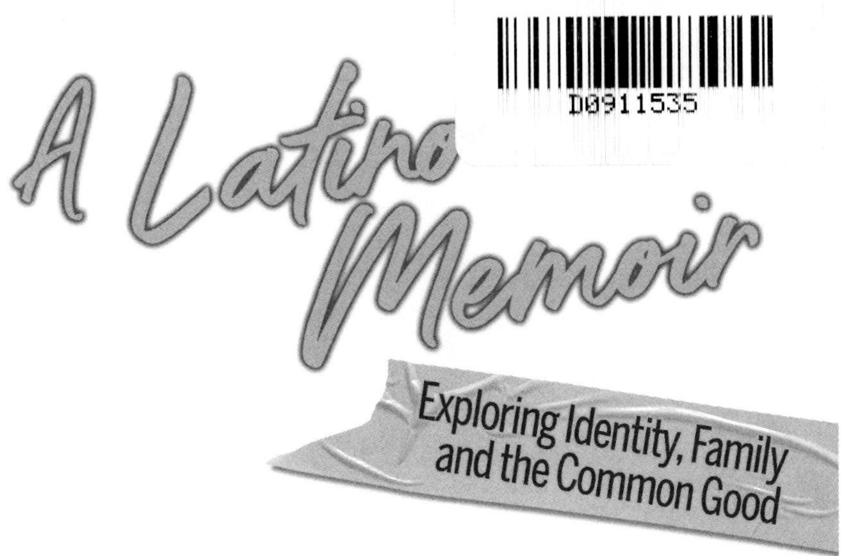

Gerald Poyo

Arte Público Press
Houston, Texas

A Latino Memoir is made possible through a grant from the City of Houston through the Houston Arts Alliance.

Recovering the past, creating the future

Arte Público Press
University of Houston
4902 Gulf Fwy, Bldg 19, Rm 100
Houston, Texas 77204-2004

Cover design by Mora Des!gn

Names: Poyo, Gerald Eugene, 1950- author.
Title: A Latino memoir : exploring family, identity and the common good / Gerald E. Poyo.
Description: Houston, Texas : Arte Público Press, [2019] | Summary: "In a bumpy, anxiety-producing plane ride across the Straits of Florida to Cuba in 1979, graduate student Gerald Poyo knew his life would either end that day in the World War II-era prop airplane or change forever. He survived the trip, and his ten-day visit solidified his academic research and confirmed his career as a history professor. In this wide-ranging examination of his relatives' migrations in the Western Hemisphere—the Americas—over five generations, Poyo uses his training as a historian to unearth his family's stories. Beginning with his great-great grandfather's flight from Cuba to Key West in 1869, this is also about the loss of a beloved homeland. His father was Cuban; his mother was from Flint, Michigan. Poyo himself was six months old when his parents took him to Bogotá, Colombia. He celebrated his eighth birthday in New Jersey and his tenth in Venezuela. He was 12 when he landed in Buenos Aires, where he spent his formative years before returning to the United States for college. 'My heart belonged to the south, but somehow I knew I could not escape the north,' he writes. Transnationalism shaped his life and identity. Divided into two parts, the first section traces his parents and ancestors as he links their stories to impersonal movements in the world—Spanish colonialism, Cuban nationalism, United States expansionism—that influenced their lives. The second half explores how exile, migration and growing up a 'hemispheric American, a borderless American' impacted his own development and stimulated questions about poverty, religion and relations between Latin America and the United States. Ultimately, this thought-provoking memoir unveils the universal desire for a safe, stable life for one's family'—Provided by publisher.
Identifiers: LCCN 2019029044 (print) | LCCN 2019029045 (ebook) | ISBN 9781558858794 (paperback) | ISBN 9781518505676 (epub) | ISBN 9781518505683 (kindle edition) | ISBN 9781518505690 (adobe pdf)
Subjects: LCSH: Poyo, Gerald Eugene, 1950- | Poyo, Gerald Eugene, 1950—Family. | Poyo family. | Poyo, Gerald Eugene, 1950—Travel—America. | Hispanic Americans--Biography. | Hispanic American families. | Transnationalism. | United States—Emigration and immigration—Social aspects. | Latin America—Emigration and immigration—Social aspects.
Classification: LCC CT275.P769 A3 2019 (print) | LCC CT275.P769 (ebook) | DDC 973/.0468092—dc23
LC record available at https://lccn.loc.gov/2019029044
LC ebook record available at https://lccn.loc.gov/2019029045

∞ The paper used in this publication meets the requirements of the American National Standard for Information Sciences—Permanence of Paper for Printed Library Materials, ANSI Z39.48-1984.

19 20 21 22 5 4 3 2 1

For Isabella, Gabriela and Alexandra

Table of Contents

Acknowledgements

A Latino Memoir: Exploring Family, Identity and the Common Good reflects a lifetime of personal and professional inquiry, my family and our history, and many who inspired me along the way. Some of these people are characters in the text, but are only a fraction of those who befriended, taught and otherwise influenced me. There are too many to name, but I do want to acknowledge those who had a special hand in helping move this manuscript along to publication. My father, Sergio, Uncle José and especially Uncle Jorge shared many stories. The youngest of the brothers, Uncle Ernesto, died very young but his passing affected me in existential ways that I understood only years later. My brother Sergio spent time helping me remember, as did siblings Cindy and Jeffrey. Four colleagues and friends took time from their busy lives to read early drafts and advised me in important ways. Dan Bjork read the earliest draft and judged it worth continuing. Later, Antonia Castañeda reminded me of the critical need to always keep gender in mind and urged me to keep the women in the forefront. Arturo Madrid, who wrote an extraordinarily moving memoir, insisted I reexamine the text with an eye to making the story explicitly my own. As a historian, I have always written in the third person, and the shift to first person memoir was hesitant and awkward at first. I needed some pushing. Chris Ruud, a medical doctor and diligent reader of what he refers to as "cracking good stories," gave me the confidence to believe that my story could be one of those. I also thank Miryam Bujanda, whose unending support for my work gives me time and inspiration to get it done. Interested in publishing with Arte Público Press, I sent the manuscript straight to Nicolás Kanellos, knowing he would give it a thorough and critical reading. After the press accepted the manuscript, Kanellos' skillful edits transformed a text with too much historical background and detail into a book more friendly to a general reading public. I also appreciate the work of Gabriela Baeza Ventura and the entire Arte Público editoral team.

Introduction

This is a Latino story, in the broadest sense. It narrates my family's migrations over five generations in the Western Hemisphere, in the Americas. It is a story of a family's loss—the loss of a much beloved Cuban homeland over several generations—but also a story of new places and a US Latino destination. It links individual lives with the impersonal historical forces at work in the world. My family moved and adapted and, more than once, integrated into unfamiliar economic, social and cultural worlds. Transnational experiences formed us.

The Poyos lived under Spanish colonialism, embraced Cuban nationalism as a central purpose in their lives, experienced the realities of United States expansionism into their homeland and attempted to make sense of ideological debates about nationalism, capitalism, socialism, communism and religion. Some lived with idealism, while others lived more pragmatically to survive. As exiles, but also as migrants, they experienced want and privilege. Family members crossed borders, traversed the seas and landed in alien places where they reinvented themselves and thought about their lives in different ways. They combined cultures and religious traditions, changed nationalities, became bilingual, defended diverse political perspectives and shifted class identities. In exploring the experiences of each generation, this story reveals a family's constant search for security, stability and existential comfort.

My father, Sergio Poyo y Álvarez, was from Havana, and my mother, Geraldine Sylvis Darnell, was from Flint, Michigan. They took my older brother, Sergio, Jr., and me to Bogotá when I was six months old. I celebrated my eighth birthday in Tenafly, New Jersey and my tenth birthday when we got off the ship in La Guaira, Caracas' port city. I was twelve when we landed in Buenos Aires. Born in 1950, for most of the years up to my eighteenth birthday I enjoyed a life steeped in Hispanic cosmopolitan sensibilities. As I encountered new places and ways, my perspective changed, and my thinking took on complexity. Language, religion, education, food, politics, work, recreation, marriage and so many other things influenced how I viewed and lived in the world. Parents and some extended family formed me along the way. I moved easily from place to place, but it required not looking back. It seemed not only normal to *just* move on, but emotionally necessary.

I lived my childhood in wealthy American suburban bubbles inhabited by corporate leaders, US government diplomats and military personnel, as well as local elite families hoping to send their children to universities in the United States. At the same time, I lived in countries where economic position was people's primary concern, where there was little talk of the kinds of nationalist and aspirational ideals articulated as an "American Dream." No one made declarations of their nation's greatness—it was a way of life mostly defined by social class, not by national identity.

Migration compels a person to negotiate their identity in order to establish or maintain a sense of belonging. Anchored in some immutable characteristics, personal identity is always on the move. The old-self remains in the recesses as you adapt to new ways of doing things and cultivate new perspectives. Identity transformations are not choices, but rather survival strategies. They are rarely linear, but first circular, then a meandering river, and always a complicated terrain. The one continuity for me was the expatriate American communities in which I grew up. Despite my parents' efforts to raise me as an American, the truth is I could not be the American my Cuban father envisioned. Anyone could see my American socialization in my attitudes and my dress, in the way I spoke English like an American instead of the British-accented pronunciation preferred in Buenos Aires. I even looked the part of a stereotypical American: white-skinned with blonde hair. But I became a different kind of American: a hemispheric American, a borderless American, who crossed national and cultural boundaries, but never imagined myself to be an integral part of the various countries I encountered.

This lack of rootedness eventually provoked in me a determination to learn about the history of my family. I looked back. To write this story I *had* to look back. History is what I know, so I began with a traditional third-person narrative. A disconnected first draft left me disappointed, and I sought strategies for tying together disparate generational stories. History, economic theory and political and social history had commanded my reading and writing over the years, but these alone would not suffice for this telling. I finally realized this narrative required my presence in the text as a unifying thread along with the memories of those who had shared their past. I combined history and memory, which are not the same and often compete for authority, but when brought together in judicious ways they can provide a way forward. Memoirs, novels and biography gave me inspiration.

The occasion of a 1997 family reunion in Atlanta inspired me. José Francisco Poyo y Álvarez, my father's seventy-seven-year older brother, had prepared a brief thirteen-page family narrative entitled "The American POYO Family." Of the four brothers, Uncle José was the traditionalist and most attached to his Cuban past and culture, but whenever I visited him as a boy, which was not often, he rarely spoke to me. One of his sons later confided that he was not much involved in their lives either until they were fully grown, married and with children when he suddenly changed and left behind his stern patriarchal ways. Uncle José took more interest in me when I began asking questions about our family history and gave him family genealogical material I had gathered. Excited, he said he would write something about the family.

Family histories begin, he wrote, with "an outstanding, an unusual ancestor," who in our family was José Dolores Poyo, his great-grandfather. History placed José Dolores in Key West during the early 1890s "next to José Martí, the Cuban patriot and father of Cuban Independence." These historical events, Uncle José noted, "Brought about the first migrations of the Poyos to the United States." José Dolores and his family fled to Key West in 1869, where they remained for thirty years until Cuba's independence from Spain and then they returned home. Later, in 1942, his story continued, as a result of the difficult circumstances sparked by his father's untimely death; his mother, Sergia Álvarez y Rodríguez—"Nana" as we called her—and her four sons, including he and my father, had moved to Atlanta from Havana. Uncle José wrote, "It had taken forty years for the descendants of José Dolores Poyo to return to the United States," almost as if that interregnum in Cuba was but a detour from the family's manifest destiny to be Americans. My father had proudly expressed similar views about the family's Americanness, even in relation to their life in Cuba before immigrating. We were always Americans; his father and grandfather had been born in Key West—that made us so!

My uncle's narration told the family story in a straightforward manner with a sense of chronology, but with little reference to contexts or questions. There was no discourse of loss or nostalgia for their Cuban past, only pride in returning to their homeland, the United States. If our ancestors were American, why did they return to Cuba in 1899? They could have remained in Key West and become Americans, but they chose not to stay. How did they reintegrate into Cuban society when they returned? What about the powerful nationalist ideals that sent them to Key West in the first place? What was it about Cuban society that forced the family to definitively leave in 1942 and become explicitly American citizens? Why was it so important for them to emphasize the Americanness of their family and their destiny in the United States and ignore Cuba so thoroughly? Why did I grow up outside the United States, the country which they so revered? My uncle's narrative left so many of my questions unanswered.

Ancestral narratives often lack meaning for the following generations without historical context and reflection. I found my uncle's interpretation intriguing. In some ways, I thought his narrative a cry for belonging, a demand for acceptance in the United States. I had heard it before from other Latinos—Mexican Americans and Puerto Ricans—who incessantly declared their loyalty as a way of proving their worthiness as Americans. Yet, something inside me resisted this emphasis on being American to the almost complete exclusion of our family's history in Cuba. As I continued my research, I came to believe that my father and uncle's embrace of Americanness was too emphatic, too pure. Indeed, overdone. Why? I eventually learned that despite my father's best efforts to become American, in many ways he never fully felt a confident sense of acceptance. Of this he never spoke. Ironically, on the other hand, when I arrived to live in the United States in 1968, I didn't really aspire to be American—although I was, more than I realized—and my certainty that I did not belong inspired me to look to his homeland for clues to my heritage.

Like my uncle, I too began with José Dolores Poyo, the earliest personality accessible in family memory, and I eventually wrote a book-length biography, *Exile and Revolution: José D. Poyo, Key West, and Cuban Independence*. Unlike Uncle José, I did not interpret his presence in Key West as a "first" migration to the United States, but rather as an exile experience in a thoroughly Cuban community sixty miles from Havana. From a psychological and cultural point of view, the Poyos had never really left Cuba, did not want to become American, and they returned home as soon as they could to build nation and nationality. But in reality, they had already fallen into the orbit of the United States. They did not come "back" to the United States after forty years, but they did bring with them signs of having been in the American orbit for many decades.

Relatives, living and deceased, helped me in this intimate work of uncovering the family's past. Family stories defined the central themes, and historical research followed the clues. This book considers the ways families cope with disruption and rupture, but remain connected across generations, whether they know it or not. Tracking the generations through various historical moments and contexts, I learned that we did what we did because of our heritage and personal quirks, but also because of the unpredictable, impersonal forces always at work in our lives. Our ways of thinking and actions reflected our times. The historical past was imprinted in our persons, a gift from the dead, expressed in our genes but also in other mysterious ways.

Even without at first realizing it, ancestors I never knew taught me about politics and economics; about culture and religion; about women and men; about the importance of place, circumstance and experience. The living told stories and gave me old documents and photographs, while the dead left behind forgotten evidence of their lives in archives, churches, cemeteries and even museums. Sometimes the ancestors even visited in the night—a legacy of spirit and faith, I suppose. Aspects of our past were also revealed in neighborhood spaces and tombs. Family aspirations, actions, sacrifices and even disappointments could be excavated and interpreted.

A meticulous man with a penchant for order, my father was fond of his garbage bin, but he kept more than I would have expected, including documents belonging to my mother. These documents allowed me to know about their lives as never before and included letters, grade-school report cards, military documents, old passports, business newsletters, newspaper clippings and an impressive photograph collection. I applied my historian's training to this obsession for recovering my family's hidden past, including complementing it with archival and library research of the rich body of documentary and oral history family members contributed. Archives, libraries and a new invention, databases, yielded access to a family history that may not have been expected to leave a paper trail that could be tracked over generations.

Activities of wives and mothers were less well documented than their husbands' careers and actions in the world, but their testimonials offered critical information and insights. Women obviously played a central role in each generation as actors in their own right, as partners in the enterprise of family and life, transmitting cultural values, promoting relationships, often maintaining stability in times of trouble and ensuring continuity. We know that women in our family shared many of the same experiences as their husbands, but how they interpreted these same events and what they meant to them was not always easy to determine. These women left only some correspondence, and even the oral tradition for some was sparse, but women especially appear in sections narrated as memoir. One of the great benefits of writing this family story as a memoir has been capturing the women who would otherwise have remained silent in a strictly historical and third-person narrative. While family patriarchs dominate the storyline, women are often the interpreters of our story and appear explicitly with voices intact. The text includes much about the Poyo women, but sadly a great deal about their lives is forever lost.

The first part of this book traces my parents' and ancestors' stories. They were everyday citizens, revolutionaries, housewives, baseball players, government officials, business and corporate leaders and wives, all trying to negotiate life in a complicated Cuba, Latin America and the United States. Often weighed down with difficult and painful historical baggage, they struggled to make things better for themselves and the people around them. The second half explores how family and historical forces set the contours of my own life. My experience included the Cold War; difficult relations between Latin America and United States; American business enterprise in Latin America; hemispheric discourses of sovereignty, nationalism and imperialism; politics and ideology; concerns about poverty and the common good; religion and spirituality; the inexorable trek of Latin Americans into the American orbit; and a search for belonging as US Latinos. Each generation examined here, including my own, inadvertently or intentionally made decisions that in a circuitous fashion transported the family across the Americas and eventually to the United States with Cuba in the foreground, or at least the background.

1
Bygone Generations

Stern-looking armed military personnel eyed us closely from the tarmac as we descended from the airplane at José Martí International Airport in Havana. Even more serious-faced officials dressed in Ministry of Interior military-style uniforms offered only a solemn greeting at customs. Just two and a half hours earlier, on a sunny March day in 1979, I had boarded the chartered flight in Tampa. My anxiety about Red Carpet Airlines didn't suppress the excitement, and neither did the World War II vintage DC-3 prop with two pilots who didn't look a day over twenty-one. Either my life would end that day, or it would change. After a moment of buyer's remorse, I settled in for a noisy and bumpy low-altitude flight along the Florida coast, across the Keys and the Straits of Florida. My life changed.

The customs agent's eyes seemingly endless rapid motion between my passport picture and face made me uncomfortable, but he finally concluded they matched, and he passed me through. Friendlier smiling hosts from the Instituto Cubano de Amistad de los Pueblos, the country's official hosting organizations for foreign visitors, whisked us to our accommodations. After dinner, I walked through the little beach town of Guanabo east of Havana, where our group stayed that first night. I came upon a CDR (Committee for the Defense of the Revolution) office, one of the revolution's most ubiquitous and controversial institutions in the lives of Cubans. Designed among other things to watch for potential counter-revolutionary activities, even spying on residents, CDR offices existed in every neighborhood and were staffed by local residents fully committed to the

Revolution. I entered the office, where a woman, perhaps sixty, sat at a desk just inside the door working her shift.

I introduced myself as from the United States, wanting to learn about the Revolution. After some time answering questions about CDRs, her curiosity got the better of her. "*¿Y tú, cómo hablas español tan bien*?" My father is Cuban I told her, and I introduced myself. "Poyo?" she said. She laughed. In high school, during the late 1930s, she had dated a young man named José Poyo, whom she had always remembered. Their first evening out, he dented his father's car, which he had proudly borrowed for the first time. He was so mortified that he dropped her back at her place early, sped home and confessed to his father. José is my uncle, I told her. We could hardly believe it. "Yes, I can see in you the same light skin and *ojos claros*," she said. After just a few hours in Cuba, I had already encountered a Poyo footprint.

In the final days of the ten-day visit, I attended a seminar on Cuban history and society. I immediately recognized Julio Le Riverend among the panelists. One of Cuba's most important historians and director of the Cuban national library, I had just recently read his economic history of Cuba for my dissertation proposal.

When I introduced myself, he paused. "Are you by chance a descendant of José Dolores Poyo?"

"I am," I said, somewhat startled that he knew about someone I thought was an obscure historical figure. I then explained my doctoral project on Cuba's nationalist movements in the United States during the nineteenth century and that I hoped to conduct research in the national library.

"Of course, you're welcome in Cuba anytime," he said. "Let the Cuban Interest Section in Washington know when you want to come, and we'll arrange everything."

The next morning, a longer conversation with Le Riverend and a tour of the Biblioteca Nacional José Martí told me he was serious. Completed in 1957, the fourteen-story national library building was relatively modern, in Cuban terms. It holds among other things the *Colección Cubana*, a treasure trove on all aspects of Cuba's history, including the extensive correspondence of Cubans who lived and worked in New York and Florida during the 1870s and collections of exile newspapers. LeRiveraend also arranged for me to meet with scholars at the Centro de Estudios Martianos, the official guardians of José Martí's historical legacy, which was housed at the time in the national library. Martí Center's director, poet and essayist Roberto Fernández Retamar; prominent Martí scholar, Cinto Vitier; a young researcher my own age, José Toledo Sande; and a few others asked about my research plans and repeated Le Riverend's praise of José Dolores. They too offered to host me in Cuba. I couldn't believe it!

On my return to the United States, I set to work finding travel funds for an extended research stay in Cuba as I completed doctoral course requirements and began writing what I could of the dissertation. On a hunch, I called the Department of State Fulbright Program and, not surprisingly, learned that no program existed for Cuba. No one had ever traveled there on a Fulbright Fellowship, but I learned that nothing in the Jimmy Carter administration's policies prohibited using Fulbright funds for research in Cuba. The representative on the phone encouraged me to apply. My persistence paid off with a fellowship, and the Cuban Interest Section in Washington, DC issued visas for me, my wife Betty Kay and sons Jeremy and Noel.

The election of Ronald Reagan did not immediately derail this opportunity, but dark clouds threatened United States-Cuban relations during 1981. Elected on the promise of heightening Cold War tensions with the Soviet Union, the Reagan administration became increasingly bellicose toward Cuba for its support of rebel groups in Central America and Africa. He blamed the Soviet Union and Cuba for the social unrest in Central America, conveniently ignoring the historic inequality and military brutality against the people, which had finally inspired them to organize, resist and launch guerrilla movements. As popular unrest and guerrilla movements spread across Central America, especially Guatemala and El Salvador, the US government under Reagan funded the military governments and blamed Cuba for the conflicts that ensued.

I watched the troubling news as I waited for travel permits from the Treasury Department and a green light from the Cuban Interest Section. Half expecting an invasion, Cuba allowed the international press to observe the mobilization of armed citizen militias and promised to fight American intrusions to the last person. My father-in-law asked me if it was smart to take his daughter and his grandchildren. Could I go alone, he wondered? The United States would not dare attack Cuba, I assured him, not totally convinced. Anyway, Betty Kay was game, and it would be a wonderful experience for Jeremy and Noel.

Until the very day we left, I expected a phone call from the Fulbright Program retracting the fellowship, but it never came. On January 6, 1982, we boarded a Continental flight to Cancún and connected with Aero Caribe for a six-month stay in Havana. A representative who would serve as our host met us as we cleared customs and drove us to our apartment. A very simply furnished and roomy two-bedroom apartment, with marble floors and a combined living-dining area, a bathroom and kitchen in the heart of Vedado greeted us. In the master bedroom, a piece of plywood covered a hole in the wall where an air conditioner had once cooled the room. Later, I noticed that at some point somebody had removed the air conditioners from all apartments in this once upscale neighborhood abandoned by those fleeing the country. Perhaps they ended up in the offices of revolutionary officials. Our fourth floor apartment at no. 14, apt. 8, calle 21, *entre N y O* had large plate glass windows in the living room and a wonderful porch open to the breeze and a breathtaking view of the city. Across the street from the Capri Hotel, owned by Tampa-based mobster Santo Traficante, Jr. in the 1950s and down the block from the historic and imposing Hotel Nacional, we could see the broad Malecón Boulevard that ran along the waterfront.

During the first week, we explored the downtown Habana Vieja neighborhoods to get the lay of the land. The great fortifications of La Fuerza, La Punta and Morro Castle built at the end of the sixteenth century and protecting Havana harbor were part of the legacy of the city's critical role in the Spanish empire's commercial system from the sixteenth to the eighteenth centuries. When Diego de Velázquez and Pánfilo Narvaez launched a major campaign from Santo Domingo to conquer and settle Cuba in 1511, they established seven settlements, with Santiago on the island's east end as the capital. Several hundreds of soldiers crossed the island, killing the Taíno natives, breaking all resistance to the invaders and enslaving the survivors. It was a virtual annihilation later recorded by a member of the army, Bartolomé de Las Casas.

From Cuba's southern coast, Spain dispatched expeditions to explore and conquer Central America, Mexico and Florida. Havana assumed its central commercial importance when Spain began shipping Mexico's wealth across the Atlantic. The port city's strategic location soon converted it into the Caribbean's most important city. From Havana, naval vessels protected merchant ships carrying gold, silver, tobacco and other products from marauding French, English and Dutch privateers and pirates. Gathered in Havana, the fleets caught the gulf currents through the Florida Straits, up the Florida coast and across the Atlantic to Cádiz.

We walked Havana Vieja exploring the fortresses and docks. I asked Jeremy and Noel to imagine the hustle and bustle of a colonial port city. I also noticed something that brought my thoughts back to the present. Anti-aircraft gun placements along the shore east of Havana provided an ominous sign of the heightened tensions between Cuba and the United States that I hoped would not interfere with our stay.

I quickly got into the swing of things. On my first research day a week after settling into our Havana apartment, I walked to the Biblioteca Nacional José Martí, a trek that became a daily ritual. From my apartment, I walked to calle 23 and L, where I purchased the morning newspaper and a cigar that I placed in my *guayabera* pocket for my evening smoke on the apartment porch with a drink of Habana Club rum. Then I headed down L to calle 27 de Noviembre at the University of Habana, where students filled the streets hurrying to work or classes. I turned right along the university, passing Calixto García hospital, named after an independence-era general José D. Poyo had worked with. I reached Avenida de los Presidentes, one of Havana's most elegant boulevards, and turned left. That street merged into Avenida Rancho Boyeros, the road to the airport. As I walked down

Rancho Boyeros, I could see the Plaza de la Revolución and the large statue of José Martí. I entered the plaza and saw the iconic image of Ernesto Che Guevara displayed on the Interior Ministry building. On the left was the library. Perhaps two miles, I could have taken a bus but preferred this round-trip walk each day. For exercise, but also to watch all the goings-on.

Le Riverend made the necessary inquiries to get me permission to research in the national archive, which for some reason took quite a while. Located on the eastern end of Compostela Street in Havana's colonial section near the harbor, the nineteenth-century stone National Archive building had been a military installation known as the Cuartel de Artillería. Before that, known as El Palenque, the building served as a barracks for government-owned slaves laboring in public works. Minutes after checking in at the front desk promptly at nine in the morning, a short stout woman in her late sixties approached me. She said that the *compañera* at the reception told her my surname was Poyo. I nodded affirmatively.

"Are you related to José Dolores Poyo?"

"Yes," I responded, "through his son Francisco Andrés."

She broke into a broad smile, shook both my hands vigorously and introduced herself as Nieves. "My husband is Luis Alpízar Leal, an archivist here," Nieves said excitedly. "He is your cousin and descends from Poyo through his daughter América, who married Francisco A. Alpízar."

In a few minutes, Luis arrived with an equally broad smile and held both my hands tightly for a long time. He was my father's age and short and soft spoken like everyone in that Poyo-family generation, he immediately wanted to show me around the building. Reminding me that José Dolores had been the third director after independence and had served for nine years; he led me to a staircase and pointed to the wall at the first landing. There staring back at me was a portrait of a distinguished-looking José Dolores, with spectacles, a large mustache covering his lips and a serious demeanor, the painting's dark background seemed to envelop him. Years later, I came across an article in *El Mundo* reporting on the ceremony at the National Archive unveiling portraits honoring José Dolores and his predecessors, Nestor Ponce de León and Vidal Morales y Morales, for their foundational work in the archive after Spain's departure.

After the tour, Luis whispered, "Can't talk comfortably here . . . Come to our home on Saturday."

They lived just a few blocks from the archive on Calle Habana between Paula and Merced. That Saturday, my family and I got off the bus at Paula Street by the José Martí birth house museum across the street from the Central Railway Station, where we saw the remains of the walls that had once enclosed the city. This, I later learned, was the neighborhood where my family lived when they had returned to Cuba in 1899. The Poyo family lived at 66 Cárdenas Street, which intersected with Arsenal Street at the central train station. The Martí house was a cherished place the family occasionally visited and a reminder of their history with the Cuban liberator in Key West.

We walked up Paula to Habana and turned left along narrow streets framed on each side with a continuous line of two-story colonial buildings set on the edge of the curbs. Voices of neighbors in conversation echoed off the walls as we moved along. They watched us with curiosity from their windows or standing in the large entrances to the buildings that periodically appeared as we passed. Not many foreigners wandered these streets. People also stood on their balconies talking to others below or shouting loudly across the narrow divide to neighbors on balconies across the way. Laughing kids played stickball, avoiding the accumulated, smelly garbage in bags waiting for collection, many ripped open by dogs. We found the entrance to Luis and Nieves' home, a four-plex at 923 Habana.

Reaching the top of the marble staircase, we turned to apartment C and knocked. Dogs barked and then Nieves' voice echoed from within, "*¡Ya llegaron!*" Nieves opened the door and greeted us warmly and excitedly with hugs for everyone, especially tight for the kids. Never having had children, she fell in love with Jeremy and Noel and eventually referred to them as her grandchildren. Behind her stood Luis, for whom I would become the son he never had. The dogs continued barking with even more enthusiasm. "*Cállense*," she yelled at the dogs, which I still didn't see. We entered a large sitting room with a high ceiling. Family portraits hung on the walls, large bookcases overflowed with books, magazines and newspapers, and several tables displayed a doll collection Nieves had accumulated over the years, before the Revolution.

At the front of the apartment, a balcony looked over the street, but we turned toward the interior.

"Come," she said, "see our home, such as it is."

To the left of the entrance hall was a study packed with more books and papers, and to the right a dining room with a long table and chairs. Before the Revolution, Nieves reminisced, she and Luis had hosted large dinner parties. We entered a dark corridor, and I saw three small skinny dogs of mixed pedigrees at the end of it behind a little wooden fence. A strong scent of urine filled the air, and the intensity of the barking increased. "*Cállense*," Nieves yelled again. Suddenly, the wall on the left gave way to a large open space and the sky above. I looked down over a railing and saw a patio belonging to the apartment below. Spanish-Moorish architecture, I thought. We walked past the bedrooms and the bathroom at the end of the corridor. To the left of the bathroom where the open space ended was the kitchen. Nieves let the three little mutts out to greet us, tails wagging and noses sniffing. "They are my babies," she said.

This had been a grand home before the Revolution, but now stained and water-marked walls with peeling paint spoke of difficult times. Due to a lack of supplies, the marble floors had not received a thorough cleaning in years, and the sound of water leaking in the toilet only stopped when the city cut off the water for the customary five or six hours each day. In the dining room, the ceiling sagged, and when I walked onto the balcony a little later, Nieves warned me not to lean on the banister. It could collapse. I handed Nieves several packages of coffee I had bought at the *diplotienda*, stores for foreigners not available to Cubans. She thanked me profusely and told Luis to take us back to the front sitting area while she prepared the coffee and brought some *galletas* for Jeremy and Noel.

Sipping coffee, Luis proudly told me that his father, Bolívar Alpízar Poyo, had also worked in the archive and had encouraged him to do the same. Named in honor of Simón Bolívar, a hero of the Poyo family, Luis' father began his career in 1902, inventorying the archive of the Junta Superior de Sanidad containing the city's public health records of the Spanish era that José Dolores had found hidden away somewhere in Havana and transferred to the National Archive. Luis felt an obligation to carry on the family legacy in the archive and developed a deep historical knowledge of the institution and its holdings. Along with Nieves, who also dedicated her entire working career to the archive, Luis helped me interpret the very complicated place that was revolutionary Cuba.

Like previous Poyo generations, Luis and Nieves idolized José Dolores Poyo. Nieves talked more about him than the history of her own people, who were tobacco growers in Cuba's westernmost province, Pinar del Río; their crops probably ended up in Key West cigar factories, generating money for the nineteenth-century independence movement. Both of Luis' parents were also born in Key West's legendary nationalist community.

"Surely, José Dolores must have left his papers in the National Archive," I commented.

"No, he didn't," Luis explained. "My father told me that Pancho had the bulk of his father's papers, so I went to see him in the late 1950s."

José Dolores' only son, Francisco Andrés Poyo, known as "Pancho," had agreed to let Luis see the collection. While examining the papers, Luis casually asked if he would consider donating them to the National Archive, with assurances that he would personally care for and process the documents. Pancho not only rejected the idea on the spot, but, Luis complained, Pancho even became suspicious and refused to leave him alone with the papers for a single minute. When Pancho died in 1961, the papers disappeared.

We usually visited Luis and Nieves on Saturdays, but spent most Sunday afternoons with Margo Valmaña, my grandmother's cousin. Nana had gleefully greeted the news of my impending trip to Cuba in March 1979 and gave me Margo's address. She would connect me to others, Nana said. My first awareness of Cuba came from Nana, who introduced me to her homeland with her stories when I was six years old. Cuba became a mythical place for me then. One day I awoke with painful bloated cheeks and fever: the mumps. My family had planned a vacation in the popular resort town of Girardot, a few hours from Bogotá where we were living. Disappointed that the trip may be cancelled, Nana immediately told my parents to leave as planned: "*Váyanse*." They did, and she and I stayed behind. She regaled me with stories of Cuba, especially of Caimito de Guayabal, where she had been born.

A petite woman in her seventies, slender and fragile looking, Margo wore her hair short and stylish. All I had was an address, 3611 1/2, *avenida 33, entre calles 36 y 42*, in Almendares. No telephone number, so I appeared at her home unannounced. A widow without children, she lived alone. Dressed in her well-preserved pre-revolutionary wardrobe that included a pearl necklace that she was never without, her lips glistened with carefully applied lipstick. She exuded an aristocratic manner and, when I introduced myself, she spoke very formally, enunciating every word deliberately and clearly (unlike most Cubans). Though she had a hard time containing her excitement, she was composed, smiled carefully and extended her hand to invite me in. Holding my arm and elbow, she escorted me to a couch in the living room and sat down beside me. She asked about Nana and then wondered who my father was.

"*Ay*, Sergio," she exclaimed when I told her, loosening up a bit. "He was so sweet," she remembered.

Margo lived just two blocks from my grandfather's and great-grandfather's homes.

"Let's take a walk," I said excitedly.

It seemed a fantasy not only to be in my father's childhood barrio but right outside his boyhood home. Communist *dirigentes* now lived in Nana's house, but I was more interested in great-grandfather Pancho's home.

"I wonder what happened to all of Pancho's belongings and papers after he died," I said.

Margo smiled, "Let's ask!"

We continued over to Pancho's house, now occupied by his former housekeeper, whom Margo knew through neighborhood meetings.

An Afro-Cuban woman maybe in her mid-60s answered the door. After a cordial greeting, Margo introduced me to Marta. Her eyes widened in disbelief, and she quickly asked us in. We sat in the living room while she prepared the obligatory *cafecito*, always part of such visits in Cuba, if they had any to serve. The conversation began awkwardly. Not wanting Marta to misinterpret my visit as somehow scoping out the home for eventual reclamation, I told her of my interest in family photographs and papers. What began awkwardly quickly became easy.

Marta spoke fondly of Pancho and especially remembered Nana, who visited from the United States in the summertime during the 1940s and 1950s with my uncles Jorge and Ernesto and stayed at the house. Nana had been warm to her, and they had enjoyed each other's conversation. Marta also said that she and Pancho's daughter María had tended to him during his last days in 1961 after which María officially turned the home over to her and left Cuba. In a hurry to get out, María left the furniture in the house but gave the bulk of the family's possessions, presumably including the archive, to her friend and hairdresser who lived in the neighborhood.

"When I go to church in the morning," Margo said, "I'll ask the priest if he knows the hairdresser."

The priest knew the woman, Margo told me later, but she had died a decade earlier and the family had left Cuba. The trail ended there.

~ ~ ~

I was learning more of the Poyo genealogy from Luis, Nieves and Margo and visiting family neighborhoods was giving me a sense of family connection to this geography. But an excursion to Havana's cemetery fused me to Cuba forever. I stepped off the packed bus and pushed through the crowd waiting to board. Like a small city, Cementerio Colón was reminiscent of the Recoleta cemetery in Buenos Aires, with chapels, monuments and mausoleums lining the paved paths and roads, it reminded me of how Latin American elites tried to take their worldliness with them. Actually, Colón could not measure up to Recoleta in pure economic investment, but the grandiose style of the marble family mausoleums that were designed to affirm a family's wealth and position was similar.

An old man greeted me as I entered the cemetary archive building just inside the front gate.

"I've come from the United States and am searching for my family burial plot," I said.

He smiled and said that many Cubans from Miami came for the same reason. With a cigarette hanging from his lips, he looked through old badly battered registers and surprisingly found the records of our family interments quite quickly. He scribbled on a small piece of paper: "Bóveda de Francisco Andrés Poyo, NE 24-c/c." Things in Cuba did not usually move that fast. He also drew me a rough map.

"Gracias," I said, and he just smiled again and waved as he took the cigarette from his lips.

I followed the directions carefully, winding along the various paths, peeking into several mausoleums and reading inscriptions. Perhaps my family had such a resting place, I thought. My father certainly never mentioned such a thing, but then he never said much about Cuba unless I asked. I finally came upon a modest marble vault with the inscription *Poyo 1913* at the foot, but only one tomb. Several granite stone carvings with inscriptions sat atop the tomb undisturbed through time. "*EPD* Carmen Poyo Skillin, 23 Mayo 1930" was my grandfather's sister Carmen who had died in childbirth. Just a few years earlier, I had met Carmen's daughter in Gainesville, where she and her husband had settled after the Revolution. Another stone had a dedication to my grandfather from his family: "José Rdo. Poyo, 3 Enero 1942: sus padres, esposa e hijos." A third memorial, to my great-grandmother, Louisa Skillin, read "A Mamá de María y Nelly, 5-29-54," from her daughters. Pancho, who died on March 7, 1961, had no dedicatory stone, since María had left Cuba as soon as she buried her father there. I finally realized that what remained of their bodies resided in the same vault. With each new interment, the bones of the previous loved one were gathered and placed in an ossuary at the head of the tomb.

Emotion got the better of me. Both my grandfathers died before I was even born, and I had not been present at either of my grandmother's funerals. The experience of these rituals, the younger generation burying the older, cements identity and instills connection. The intimacy of death in a lifeless corpse did not intrude into my life until later when my mother passed in 1996. These encounters with family, living and dead, during my visits in Cuba unexpectedly unleashed a new vision of self, rooted on this island, beginning with José Dolores.

Even before this, my first curiosities about the Poyo family origins began with Uncle Jorge. A genuine Hispanophile, he was the first in our family to travel to Spain. A bit of an eccentric, animated and with a quick wit, he possessed a prodigious knowledge of the Spanish language. A sophisticated reader of the Spanish classics, he recited endlessly from *Lazarillo de Tormes* and *Don Quijote* and could charm and win over most anyone. Besides Spanish and English, he spoke Portuguese, French, German and Italian. When he later married Marianne, a delightful young woman from Denmark, he picked up a bit of Danish as well. He took his love of language seriously and became a self-taught etymologist and quite knowledgeable of history. He even regularly studied dictionaries in the various languages to increase his vocabulary. When I once told him he had missed his calling as a scholar, perhaps as a linguist, he said he had no idea what the discipline was or entailed when he was a business major in the late 1940s.

On his occasional visits to Buenos Aires in the 1960s, we spent time together. For whatever reasons, Uncle Jorge always took an interest in me and shared stories of his many travels. I especially liked his story of a visit to the little village of Poyo in Galicia not far from Pontevedra and Santiago de Compostela. The innkeeper where my uncle stayed, delighted in hearing our surname, swore we must have originated in that Galician village. Uncle Jorge didn't disagree, and before it was all said and done, the friendly man refused payment for food and drink in homage to a returning son. We grew comfortable with the idea that we were *gallegos*, but my own later travels revealed that the village of Poyo had originated as a settlement attached to the nearby and quite famous Monasterio de Poyo, which derived its name from the fact that it sat at the top of a hill, a *poyo*. Nothing to do with us!

Eventually ending up at the Spanish national library in Madrid, Uncle Jorge consulted a heraldic encyclopedia that traced the Poyo (also rendered Poio) surname to Toulouse in the tenth century. Apparently, Poyos entered Spain as part of the Christian *reconquista*, participated in the taking of Valencia from the Moors and migrated along Spain's southeastern coast. Even today, the Poyo surname seems most common in that region. Uncle Jorge then decided we may have been French Basques originally and told me a story of visiting a Basque village in Spain. Impressed with the *boinas*, or berets, the men wore; he wanted to take one home.

He entered a small shop and the shopkeeper asked, "What color do you want? Black or red?"

"One of each, I should think," my uncle answered.

The shopkeeper brought a black one and carefully placed it on my uncle's head, securing it close over his eyes. Uncle Jorge adjusted the beret, pushing it back so his forehead would show. Like what "New York journalists in the 1940s movies did with their hats," he told me. The shopkeeper said nothing while my uncle inspected himself in the mirror. Then he asked to see the red beret. The shopkeeper retrieved the article, removed the black beret from my uncle's head and replaced it with the red one. Again, the shopkeeper placed it snugly on his head, again over his eyes. My uncle again pushed the beret back, revealing his forehead, and the shopkeeper could stand it no more.

"*Pero no me lo eches para atrás, ¡coño!*" he blurted out with impatience. "*¡Así no se usa!*"

Taken aback, my uncle quickly pushed the beret down over his eyes and responded, "*Me llevo los dos*." That day, he told me, he learned that *coño* was not a Cuban invention, and like Cubans, Spaniards used it with gusto.

"You see, that is where we are from!" he had noted with pride as he took another sip of wine while we waited for our *caldo gallego* at Los

Gallegos restaurant in Westchester, where he lived, just a couple of miles west of Miami. Whether we were Basques or Gallegos, did not matter—we were neither Uncle Jorge simply loved Spain.

Uncle Jorge's stories entertained, but they didn't shed light on Poyo origins in Cuba. Luis and Nieves helped when they gave me a transcribed copy of the last will and testament of Francisco del Poyo Vallejo y Camacho, perhaps the first person in Cuba with the Poyo surname. A native of Ysla la Palma (Canary Islands), Poyo de Vallejo arrived in Havana in 1580 as a royal notary (Escribano Mayor de Minas y Registro y Relaciones de la Isla de Cuba). He left a significant notarial archive, which Luis spent years transcribing. Lacking protection from the tropical climate over the centuries, the notarial documents were in their final stages of disintegration when Luis began the project. He transcribed each page and, when he lifted the completed pages off the stack to work on the following pages, they crumbled in his hands. Francisco's son, Lucas del Poyo Vallejo y Carrión, migrated to Mexico City in the seventeenth century, ending their one-generation residence in Havana.

Our family did not descend from this family, but Luis and Nieves helped me find a way forward again. They gave me an old *carpeta* of unknown origin that contained penciled transcriptions of baptismal, marriage and death entries from Havana's church records. Among the entries was Antonio Poyo, a Spanish immigrant from El Puerto de Santa María, a small port town across the bay from Cádiz, who had settled in Havana in the early eighteenth century. The other entries connected him to José Dolores; Antonio was our connection to Spain. Apparently for centuries a seafaring people, the Poyos had been engaged in trade with the Americas in Sevilla, Cádiz and the Canary Islands.

Uncle Jorge often said that today the family is unable to understand the depth of nationalist feeling of José Dolores Poyo, he and the other revolutionary activists in Key West were a people without a nation who struggled to gain one. Future generations of the family lost that nation and, once gone from Cuba, their feeling for the place faded. In my case, transnational sensibilities replaced a sense of being rooted. Once imprinted in this way, one touches ground as a transient expecting to move on, even if you never do. One avoids belonging;

community is avoided so as not to feel the pain of disruption when another moment of change arrives. Commitments are also avoided so one is not disappointed when they are not honored. José Dolores Poyo and his entire family had roots, community and commitments that so captured my imagination that I spent forty years excavating their legacy and perhaps seeking to discover how I might create connections like these in my own life.

2
Struggled in Radical Ways

Lacking an appreciation for nationalism in my own life, it took time for me to understand José Dolores Poyo. An earlier version of the many revolutionary leaders who had emerged in Latin America in my own era, José Dolores not only wanted a Cuban nation, but a country where every citizen had a stake regardless of their class or race, which I appreciated as a socially aware university student a century later.

My first encounter with José Dolores, when I stumbled across José Martí's letters to him, sent me scurrying to the card catalog. I found two works about him. One of his grandsons, Luis Alpízar Poyo, son of daughter América Poyo, and Fernando Figueredo, his best friend and revolutionary colleague, wrote brief biographical treatments that provided the basic facts of his life and work. Two books by former residents of Key West, who knew Poyo, contributed significant contextual information. In 1900, a Methodist reverend, Manuel Deleofeu, wrote *Héroes del destierro*, a history of the Cuban community that highlighted the career of José Marti and spoke of José Dolores and his family. Thirty-two years later, Gerardo Castellanos García published a more comprehensive history, *Motivos de Cayo Hueso,* and several other studies, which also highlighted José Dolores' life work. Later, Poyo received some attention in the works of two historians José Rivero Muñiz, "Los cubanos en Tampa," in 1958 and in the first general study of Cubans in the United States in the nineteenth century, written by Juan J.E. Casasús, *La emigración cubana y la independencia de la patria*, which appeared in 1953 on the centennial of José Martí's birth.

These writings inspired me to keep searching for primary sources, which slowly revealed a man with whom I felt a sort of affinity. However, he was a nationalist, not me; and a revolutionary zealot, not me either. I never possessed his confidence and determination to act as a leader and agent of change, but we shared radical instincts. At first, I thought the word zealot was derogatory, but it just means a person with a burning will to act with conviction in extraordinary ways. Zealotry is a kind of possession at the very heart of activism. He possessed nationalist passion, a feeling emanating from enduring attachments to a specific place and culture, and a sense of belonging, which my own international, cosmopolitan, middle-class experiences in South America did not instill. My life contrasted with the nationalist, neighborhood-oriented and working-class realities of that ancestral generation. Armed with revolutionary methods and ideals of social justice, José Dolores struggled in often radical ways most of his adult life to transform Cuba from a colonial possession into an independent republic.

In the tattered archival folder filled with genealogical information Luis and Nieves had given me, I found information on José Dolores Poyo y Remírez de Estenoz and his wife in Cuba before their exile. He was a third-generation Cuban born on March 24, 1836 within the jurisdiction of the Nuestra Señora de Guadalupe Parish, located just outside Havana's city walls. He married Clara Leonor Camús y de la Merced de Hoz on March 25, 1861, a woman of a modest family from the same parish born on September 13, 1837. From Santander in Spain's Basque country, her grandfather, José Camús, had married Clara de Sotolongo in 1804, a Cuban woman. We had some Basque in us after all, Uncle Jorge was happy to learn.

José Dolores came of age during the 1840s and 1850s at a time when many were increasingly questioning Spain's firm colonial grip. He lived the everyday existence of a Havana resident, earning a modest living as a newspaper copy editor at *La Gaceta de Cuba*. I imagined him walking the narrow cobble-stoned streets, standing near the harbor entrance looking across to the Castillo del Morro and feeling the winds coming off the Florida Straits while enjoying the palms dotting the urban landscape. I imagined this informed his sense of belonging and helped him draw a distinction between Cuba and Spain. I imagine him wondering why Spanish citizenship, rather than inspiring the island's inhabitants with a sense of comfort and pride, imposed hardships even as Spain claimed Cubans as subjects. He developed strong anti-Spanish attitudes, which were perhaps fueled by unresolved anger. In 1854, police had arrested his father, Francisco Antonio Poyo, in Havana for reading a clandestine political broadside opposing a new conservative captain general in public. What became of his father I don't know, but this may have made him determined to fight Spanish rule in Cuba.

Like mainland Latin Americans in the 1810s before him, José Dolores experienced the transformation of his sense of Cuban cultural distinctiveness into a force for the overthrow of colonial rule. This radicalization eventually sent him into exile after the insurrection broke out in October 1868. Cuba cannot be properly understood without a knowledge of the history of anti-colonialism and the nationalist movements it produced. Latin America's poverty and inequalities were the legacy of a Spanish and Portuguese colonial model designed during the sixteenth century to transfer as much wealth as possible mostly in the form of commodity exports from the Americas to Europe. These structures remained intact well into the twentieth century. Whether silver, gold, sugar, tobacco, coffee, cotton, indigo, tropical fruits, wheat or beef, products of this kind required control of vast acreages of land, cheap labor, capital and transportation networks designed for export purposes.

Spanish and Portuguese elites and their *criollo* descendants in the Americas subjected Africans to a system of race-based slavery and Native Americans to forced labor institutions known as *encomienda* and *repartimiento*. Ever since, Europeans and their white descendants have generally benefitted at the expense of Native Americans, African Americans and their mixed descendants. Latin American independence from Spain brought the abolition of formal forced labor institutions, but less formalized systems of debt-peonage maintained the colonial social structures intact and compatible with the continued reliance on export economies.

Anti-colonial movements challenging European rule began during the late eighteenth century and coincided with the European Enlightenment and the Age of Reason. Orthodox religion's grasp on western societies weakened as philosophers argued that men could think for themselves. This undermined the legitimacy of absolutist monarchical rule and inspired the rise of nationalist revolutionary movements that displaced direct European rule in North America, Haiti and Latin America in the fifty years following the 1776 Declaration of Independence in Philadelphia. Anti-colonialism gave birth to nationalist movements offering alternative visions of New World identities and temporarily unified people to oppose British, French, Spanish and Portuguese rule during the first quarter of the nineteenth century.

The independence era that brought political freedom to most of the Americas left only Cuba and Puerto Rico as traditional colonial territories. These tightly controlled Caribbean islands that were closely linked to the sugar and the slave trade produced elites with little taste for revolution. Only after the US Civil War did revolution begin to seem plausible to citizens of the two islands, in spite of Spain's vow never to allow Cuba or Puerto Rico to break away. Besides the allure of sugar wealth, the Spanish government maintained control as a matter of honor; the two islands were all that remained of Spain's American empire. Spain did not even trust its colonial subjects sufficiently to allow any significant measures of self-government or economic and political autonomy.

Beginning in the 1820s, Cubans began to demand an easing of Spanish rule, but those who did usually ended up deported to Spain or fleeing to France, England or the United States. Direct American investments in sugar increased as US-Cuban commercial relations strengthened throughout the century. Communities of Cubans in New York, New Orleans, Florida and numerous coastal cities along the Atlantic also grew. Many Cubans in the United States organized political movements designed to separate Cuba from Spanish rule, but few advocated for independence. Most elites preferred a reformist solution in which Spain granted Cuba autonomy within the Spanish nation, while others preferred annexation to the United States. They thought that independence would bring with it political instability, dictatorship, economic stagnation and social unrest, as it had across Latin America. But after a major insurrection on October 10, 1868, the time for debate had passed. Insurgents either joined the armed forces in the countryside or went into exile and fought for independence in other ways. José Dolores became an underground activist supporting the insurrection in Havana, but soon chose exile.

In January 1869, José Dolores Poyo, Clara and three daughters—Celia (1862), América (1864) and Blanca (1869), just weeks old—arrived in Key West on a fishing boat. His sense of obligation to family had determined his decision to leave Cuba rather than join the insurgent forces in the field. His underground political activism in Havana had placed his wife and three young daughters at risk, since they had no means of support other than him. As a political activist, he always considered the impact of his decisions on his family, and he sought to balance his support for the insurrection with his obligations to those closest to him; he created a seamless relationship that weaved together a tight-knit family life and the cause of independence. This included expecting his wife and children to support nationalist politics and share in the inevitable material sacrifices inherent to this kind of commitment.

In Key West in 1872, Clara had a son, Francisco Andrés (Pancho) and then at least three other sons, Juan Bautista and Carlos Manuel (1874) and Juan Luis (1876), who lived less than four years—this was not unusual in this era of high child mortality. They joined a growing Cuban community composed of political refugees seeking safety from Spanish persecution and cigar makers, tobacco leaf selectors, cigar sorters and leaf strippers (mostly women) employed in a newly founded cigar industry. Thousands of tobacco workers followed the jobs, and during the 1870s, Key West became one of the important cigar producing cities in the United States. Some workers established small *chinchales* (store front cigar-making shops), and a few grew into large factories employing hundreds of workers. Cubans also provided the services necessary in any community, including restaurants, health clinics, mutual aid societies, pharmacies, grocery stores, boarding houses, hotels. The result was fully self-sufficient Cuban neighborhoods capable of reproducing their culture.

One of the first things I learned about José Dolores was that he had worked as a lector, or reader in Key West. *Lectores* read aloud to workers while they labored. The practice first appeared in Havana's cigar factories during 1865 and was promoted by a worker-oriented weekly newspaper, *La Aurora,* as a way of educating workers. Several factories experimented with the idea, and despite resistance from colonial authorities, the practice of reading to the workers endured. *Lectores* had to be relatively educated men who could project their voices well across the factory floors and perform with an animated style and a flair for the dramatic. They usually possessed political and social consciousness and sufficient literary knowledge to recommend classic as well as contemporary literature from which workers would choose.

A light-skinned man with curly light hair and a mustache, Poyo stood about five-feet six inches tall and took great care in his personal appearance, dressing impeccably with a coat and tie. His friend and revolutionary colleague, Fernando Figueredo, described Poyo as a man of considerable education with a knowledge of many topics, especially Latin America. Erudite and reserved, he took much care in his personal relations and cultivated an ability to deal well with people, though he could be intractable and stubborn when it came to matters of importance to him. In the early years, Poyo would have stood or sat among the workers and read. In 1873, a *New York Times* correspondent visiting Key West described Cubans and the institution of reading, perhaps even seeing José Dolores himself: "Their excited discussion of home politics and affairs has led the proprietors of every considerable factory to employ a 'reader,' who sits in the midst of the workmen and engages their attention by reading in a loud voice all the news, rumors, and speculations of the day, as set forth in the newspapers, private correspondence, etc. This reader is a most valuable and well-stored personage. He reads rapidly and loudly and is so well supplied with reading matter, either in print or in manuscript that he goes on all day without exhausting his material."

Even in large factories, cigar workers heard the lectors across the workplace floor, disturbed only by the occasional bursts of approval produced by the cigar makers' *chavetas* (knives) in unison rapidly and repetitively hitting the tables in response to especially poignant passages in the readings. Besides educating and entertaining their working-class audience, good *lectores* also established a moral authority on the factory floors, earning the respect of foremen and manufacturers alike. Trusted readers often represented the workers on ceremonial occasions and even mediated between the foremen and workers. Interpreting the *lectura* as a labor efficiency strategy, the *New York Times* correspondent concluded that refugees listened and worked and did not waste time in animated debates. The article missed the literary and educational aspect of the *lectura*, but it did confirm the popularity of the institution in Key West within a short time after the founding of the cigar industry.

Not all workers arrived in Key West with nationalist orientations, but the *lectura* usually politicized them in short order and opened them to nationalist thought. As *lector,* José Dolores promoted revolutionary consciousness. Besides the literary works often requested by the workers themselves, he read newspapers and pamphlets with reports and correspondence about the war in Cuba. "Reading in the factories on the surface seems insignificant," José Dolores explained, "but it is actually a perennial service of instruction, as much for the readers themselves as those listening." He thought readers should entertain but also introduce ideas that illustrated the benefits of progress, which required leaving aside the idealized and symbolic approach of the Romantic school that emphasized distracting "fables." Instead, readers should select texts from the school of Naturalism, which he referred to as the Modern school, exemplified by Émile Zola in the 1880s. José Dolores argued that Naturalism described believable and unvarnished everyday reality, "the truth as it unfolds, embellishing with rich ostentatious and ponderous imagination that unending source of learning called existence." Reality offered readers a photograph of humanity's "crimes" and "goodness" and, when effectively presented, could motivate people to action. "It seems useful," José Dolores thought, to read what "maintains alive the memory of the atrocities committed in Cuba by the Spanish government." Exiles would not only return home as revolutionary advocates but well instructed in the history of Cuba and prepared to be propagandists. The *lectura* could serve as a revolutionary tool, and he undertook the job in that spirit.

On my second day at the archive, Nieves said, "That's José Luciano Franco." One of Cuba's most distinguished historians, among many things, Franco wrote a classic three-volume study of Cuban independence leader General Antonio Maceo, which was always at arm's reach as I studied my great-great-grandfather's career.

She saw my expression. "Want to meet him?"

"Yes!" I responded.

Nieves introduced me. "He is a descendant of José Dolores Poyo," she said.

He nodded and said, "Yes, he was a grand patriot, *un hombre muy valioso*. His life's greatest work was his newspaper, *El Yara, un periódico de combate*," he said and turned back to his work.

Over the years, as I studied José Dolores' nationalist career, I remembered José Luciano Franco's brief description of *El Yara.* The first copy of the newspaper I found was an 1889 issue at the Library of Congress microfilmed for the University of Florida Special Collections. Published for twenty years in Key West, I was surprised to find no other surviving issues anywhere in the United States. How could they have all disappeared? I later learned how United States libraries and archives rarely worried about collecting or saving what they considered insignificant Spanish-language publications.

In Cuba, I had more luck and found partial collections at the Biblioteca Nacional José Martí, the Instituto de Linguística e Historia (the former Sociedad Amigos del País) and the Archivo Nacional, but in very poor condition. Without the possibility of having them microfilmed in Cuba's resource-poor libraries and archives, I handled them very carefully, read them and took what notes I could in the limited time I had. They provided a partial picture of José Dolores' thinking and career, but only many years later did other collections fill in the story and make a full-length biography possible. These I tracked down in Spain.

Consistent with their responsibility to gather intelligence on anti-Spanish activities, Spanish consuls in Key West collected newspapers when they appeared on the streets and sent them with their correspondence to their embassy in Washington, DC or to the foreign ministry in Madrid. The various issues eventually ended up mostly well preserved, folded neatly in Spanish diplomatic correspondence held at the Archivo General de Administración in Alcalá de Henares, the Archivo del Ministerio de Asuntos Exteriores and the Archivo Histórico Nacional in Madrid. Over many months, I reviewed thirty years of correspondence and, with the magic of today's technology, had the newspapers digitized. Only in *El Yara* and his other newspapers did José Dolores reveal his nationalist and revolutionary thinking about Cuba, exile, revolution and many other topics. His thoughts appeared nowhere else.

On October 12, 1878, José Dolores published the first edition of *El Yara*, named after the town where the insurrection known as the Ten Years War began a decade earlier. He called it a radical nationalist newspaper dedicated to continuing the fight against Spanish colonialism. Earlier in the year, the Cuban insurgent government had capitulated after ten years of war and signed the Treaty of Zanjón. Most rebels quit the fight, but an important handful did not, including the mulatto general Antonio Maceo, who remained on the battlefield. José Dolores sent him a congratulatory letter for his courage and assured him Key West would continue raising money for much needed weapons. Before *El Yara*, José Dolores had edited *El Republicano*

(1869-1874), which he helped found with José María Reyes, a fairly well-known journalist from Havana who also fled to Key West, and two short-lived newspapers, *La Igualdad* (1876-1877) and *El Patriota* (1878). In his "*periódicos de combate*," as José Luciano Franco referred to them, José Dolores disseminated nationalist arguments and agitated for a new rebellion throughout the 1880s and early 1890s. Circumspect, meticulous and methodical, Poyo emerged as the most recognized revolutionary figure in Key West.

El Yara was a labor of love and nationalist commitment. Each family wage earner contributed resources from their work in the cigar factories to publish the newspaper. Initially produced in his home, José Dolores gathered news content, wrote and edited while Clara took care of the many logistical challenges. Drawn to the newspaper's nationalist vision, two young tobacco worker volunteers, Manuel Patricio Delgado and Francisco Alpízar, also helped, although initially they may have been attracted as much by Poyo's daughters, Celia and América, as his newspaper; they married the girls two days apart in 1886.

Delgado and Alpízar worked on the layout while Celia and América tracked down the ink and paper with Clara's help, and printed the newspaper on a hand-cranked press. Everyone volunteered their work, and Poyo reinvested whatever profits remained from the five cents charged per issue, which later rose to ten cents. The family received payment for newspapers sold in Key West, New York and other exile centers, but they distributed free a significant portion of their circulation to clandestine networks in Havana and throughout Cuba. *El Yara* represented an inordinate sacrifice for the family. They lived modestly and often went without, in part because of the insecurities of a volatile cigar industry, but also because the newspaper consumed whatever remained after paying rent, food and other necessities. Nevertheless, the family never questioned their commitment. *El Yara*, "like a luminous torch projected light on the conscience of Cuba and Free America," declared Raoul Alpízar Poyo.

José Dolores recounted in *El Yara* Cuba's struggles against colonialism and challenged his readers to question the status quo and take up the revolutionary cause. At heart, his ideological inspirations sprung from principles of Freemasonry, which José Dolores embraced throughout his adult life. I don't know whether he ever practiced his Roman Catholic baptismal faith, but once radicalized he firmly rejected the Church. He viewed it as a pillar of Spanish colonial power, the target of his revolutionary credo.

Masonic secret societies emerged in England during the early eighteenth century advocating "truth, morality, tolerance and charitable works," and spread throughout Europe and the Americas. With the rise of more liberal governments in Spain during the 1850s and 1860s, Masonic lodges reorganized in Cuba after colonial authorities had crushed an earlier flourishing. In 1862, the Gran Oriente de Cuba y las Antillas (GOCA) formed and promoted democratic and republican ideas and values, and an independent Cuba. GOCA stood for Cuban sovereignty, freedom to work, religious and individual freedom, right of association and social equality, which incited condemnations from Spanish authorities, the Catholic Church and high-class society. Its members sparked the uprising in Oriente province in 1868 and provoked a pro-Spanish violent repression, which especially targeted Masons. It is not known exactly when José Dolores became affiliated with Freemasonry, but he was about twenty-five when the GOCA formed, and his initiation likely occurred soon after.

José Dolores took his Masonic commitment to Key West, where in 1872 he and others founded the Dr. Félix Varela Lodge No. 64. The lodge's namesake reflected the clear political inclinations of Cuban Masons in Key West. Cuban priest Félix Varela had been an exile in Philadelphia, New York and Florida since the 1820s. Despite the strong anti-Catholic traditions of Freemasonry, the Cuban masons honored Father Varela for a number of reasons. He ministered among the poor Irish Catholic immigrant community in New York for many years, and his writings, as well as his newspaper, *El Habanero,* publicly advocated Cuba's independence from Spain. Complementing the political goal of independence, Freemasonry inspired José Dolores to exhort his readers to help build a virtuous society that benefitted all of its citizens.

El Yara routinely attacked all those who supported continued Spanish rule. It characterized Cuba as a despotic and corrupt colony administered for the benefit of Spaniards, who controlled trade, banking, finance, industry, manufacturing and property generally. Spaniards also dominated the middle-class economy as shopkeepers, merchants, artisans, government bureaucrats and office clerks. Even worse, they preferred to hire their compatriots and openly discriminated against Cubans in the cigar factories and other related jobs. High unemployment plagued Cuba during the 1880s, and thousands left the island while immigrants from Spain were entering the country simultaneously. José Dolores envisioned an inclusive Cuba governed with democratic values and a spirit of honesty and integrity informed by a sense of right and wrong that would avoid the pitfalls of authoritarianism or instability that had plagued newly independent Latin America nations for half a century.

In addition to his anti-colonial propaganda, José Dolores advanced a popular nationalist agenda that reflected the interests of Key West's multiracial working-class community. This most activist and radical exile constituency challenged traditional Cuban liberal nationalists, who sought political and social rights for themselves but dragged their feet on extending those rights to the majority of their compatriots. As José Dolores saw it, Spain governed in the interests of Spaniards and the collaborating Cuban elites, while most Cubans suffered second-class citizenship, slavery and poverty. In a future republic, all Cubans would participate equally, which required the abolition of slavery and the full integration of Cubans of color. Well into the Ten Years' War, the fear of slave insurrections remained alive among many nationalists, who still believed Cuba to be a white nation steeped in tropically influenced Hispanic traditions. They were suspicious of a broad-based multiracial popular movement that transformed slaves into free citizens, but this was precisely what José Dolores believed was necessary to break from Spanish control, resist United States annexation and create a unified nationality.

José Dolores also eagerly engaged the problem of class inequities and divisions in society, proposing that a successful republic should provide opportunities for Cuba's working classes. Not until the 1860s did a Cuban cigarmaking proletariat appear with a distinct identity. This coincided with a brief period of liberalization in Cuba that allowed greater freedom of association and of the press. Discussion of political, economic and social matters in the press encouraged factory owners to extend worker's rights, but the war in 1868 ended this liberalization. A decade later, *El Yara* began addressing articles directly to Cuba's tobacco workers. Spanish mismanagement, the newspaper argued, had reduced the country to exporting its best tobacco leaf to Cuban manufacturing centers like Key West and New York. In Cuba, the cigar industry preferred to hire Spanish and Chinese workers, who dominated trade and commerce in Havana, while Cuban cigarmakers were forced to find work abroad. The newspaper remained confident that in time workers would join the revolutionary effort: "that mass which represents an important segment of the Cuban nation cannot remain indifferent to the cause of their country's regeneration."

José Dolores founded his revolutionary career on the necessity of unwavering revolutionary action against Spain, but the depth and radical nature of his work surprised me. Secondary sources highlighted his constant call for renewed revolution after the end of the Ten Years War, but only his newspaper and the correspondence of Spanish consuls in Key West revealed the details of his political rationale and strategies.

Throughout the 1870s, middle-class professionals and even wealthy Cubans in New York provided leadership and guidance for the rebellion, but many lost confidence in further action and returned home after Cuba's pacification in 1880. José Dolores remained in exile with other ideas. "Before the cold and calculating Reason of State," he wrote in 1884, "the politics of sentiment is a dead letter." Originally introduced by Niccolo Michiavelli, the idea of Reason of State justified advancing state interests without reference to religious or moral constraints, which Poyo argued had always been Spain's *modus operendi* in Cuba. José Dolores believed that Cubans had to confront Spain with similar determination. Only force achieved rights in the modern age; there was nothing else. Only through a commitment to self-determination and resistance, without waiting for the intervention of foreigners, could the Cuban victims of oppression establish their rights. In the face of an unequal struggle, Cubans possessed the legitimate right to consider all tactics and strategies in their struggle to destroy Spanish colonialism.

El Yara maintained a constant drum beat for insurrection. Cuban insurrectionists had gained valuable experience raising money and organizing expeditions during the Ten Years' War. Whenever news spread in the neighborhoods and factories that revolutionary leaders seeking resources to carry on the fight in Cuba were about to arrive, welcoming contingents gathered at the docks to greet the visitors. They paraded them through the streets accompanied by the Cuban Libertad band to community centers for ceremonies. After speeches and meetings with local leaders, the visitors generally toured the factories and political clubs, where they exhorted people to contribute. Receptions in the large factories with two-to-five hundred workers could be breathtaking as workers welcomed visitors with the sound of their *chavetas* hitting the top of the wooden worktables. The best patriotic speeches opened pockets, and Cubans gave from their hard-earned wages, routinely contributing from a few thousand to tens of thousands of dollars. The visits generally lasted a few days but sometimes a couple of weeks, raising nationalist fervor in the community and strengthening the political reputations of the local leaders within the broader insurgent constituency.

Destroying Spanish colonialism, *El Yara* insisted, required immediate revolution—something the established classes would not be counted on to support. Only the humble would take disinterested action in support of independence, while the rich preferred to wait and act in their own interests. A nationalist, self-determining and fully Cuban initiative organized inside Cuba would reanimate the Cuban people for another insurgency. During the Ten Years' War, Cuba's army survived long and difficult periods without much support from the outside, fighting a powerful, well-supplied enemy. If Cubans could do that then, they could do much more in the future with tested, first-rate military leaders like Máximo Gómez, Antonio Maceo and Calixto García. José Dolores believed Cuba's unstable rural districts could be revolutionized—not an unrealistic assessment. After the Ten Years' War, a significant portion of Cuban sugar plantations lay ruined or bankrupt, but those that managed to produce faced lower-priced European beet-sugar production throughout the 1880s. The efficiencies needed to compete with European sugar required capital investments in new machinery that many Cuban producers simply could not afford. Cuba's share of the sugar market declined, businesses closed, banks failed and unemployment increased.

In 1886, Spain finally ended Cuban slavery, and hundreds of thousands of former slaves now lived as free citizens, but in a Cuba not prepared to absorb them socially or economically. The economic and social dislocations, poorly managed by the political system, produced many disaffected—blacks and whites alike—with limited opportunities and strong anti-Spanish attitudes. Many turned to banditry, including veterans of the war of independence, and with impunity operated in regions where they coexisted with their neighbors and focused their attentions on large landholders who benefitted from the colonial state. Some justified their activities in the name of "Cuba Libre," while others simply made a living. José Dolores believed that it was the common people in Cuba's rural areas and small towns who possessed the most revolutionary potential, and if properly encouraged and organized, they would serve as the insurrectionary spark. Even if military leaders did not inspire a large-scale revolution, Poyo remained confident they could conduct strategic guerrilla operations, especially if they were supplied with new technologies of warfare.

In February 1884, an inflammatory and controversial article publicly associated José Dolores with a new radical approach to fighting the Spanish. *El Yara* declared that in 1868 Cubans had launched a sustained war against Spain with thousands of men armed mostly with machetes. Now a kind of "scientific war" was possible. Just a few men with dynamite could destroy entire Spanish military contingents or naval vessels. Insurgent cells on the island with reliable supply lines abroad, capable of providing munitions and explosives, could spark the revolution. Tactics would include burning sugar fields and mills, raising money by kidnapping and holding for ransom prominent supporters of the colonial regime, and even destroying offices and public buildings associated with Spanish rule. These small groups of insurgents would create havoc, deepen general discontent and prepare the way for a general revolutionary uprising led by Generals Máximo Gómez and Antonio Maceo, who were waiting in Honduras for the right moment.

José Dolores practiced what he preached throughout the 1880s. He raised money, rented or purchased boats, secured weapons and launched numerous expeditions. None of these efforts sparked revolution, but they kept the Spanish government in a constant state of alarm and they kept the cause of independence firmly in the consciousness of Cubans. Authorities in Cuba considered Key West an existential threat because of its veteran leadership, tobacco wealth, radical working class and proximity to Cuba.

Many skeptics viewed renewed revolutionary action in the 1880s as an overwhelming and unrealistic task, requiring more resources than the communities could muster. Even more important, they did not believe Cubans on the island were in the mood for another bloody revolution. Among the most adamant and articulate opponents to revolution in the short-term was the young nationalist writer and orator José Martí, who arrived in New York just as the first insurrection ended. Martí also had little confidence in a new revolutionary push, but his reasons differed from those of his more conservative friends who feared revolution. Martí did not fear revolution but doubted Cuba could be liberated exclusively by the use of military force. The failures of the 1870s convinced him that only island-initiated and island-organized movements could inspire confidence and revolution. This would only happen when Cubans united behind a political program that offered a viable and clear alternative to Spanish rule. A revolution based solely on military leadership was dangerous to the nationalist movement's democratic goals and had to be avoided at all costs. Nationalists had to wait for the definitive failure of the autonomists and patiently rely on propaganda and persuasion to unify Cubans behind the idea of another independence war. This had a better chance of provoking rebellion than invasions.

Harshly rejecting such ideas, *El Yara* speculated that perhaps those unwilling to act suffered a paralyzing passivity that had been instilled in them by the Spanish colonial oppression. Centuries of Spanish tyranny and colonial control, the newspaper said, had cultivated a "lamentable heritage," a belief that liberty would somehow be freely given, a belief that there would be no need for Cubans themselves to take extraordinary action, a belief that they would not have to take responsibility for insurrection. But to achieve liberty, Cubans had to want, feel and think of it as a necessary good, a right for which one had to fight.

A life of tyranny, the newspaper feared, had created laziness among Cubans in this regard. Liberty was a right and laziness the enemy on which despots relied. Spain's commercial monopoly and the imposition of a slavery had given the Cuban people a lazy conscience, lazy reasoning and lazy hearts, which inhibited redemptive struggles for freedom. Overcoming obstacles represented a lot of work, and Cubans preferred to submit peacefully: "Today does not exist; it is substituted for tomorrow, which never arrives." That attitude, *El Yara* insisted, was the lamentable, wicked fruit of Spanish colonial domination. José Dolores did not criticize Martí's person, but certainly his opposition to immediate revolutionary action. In the midst of this, Spanish consuls in Key West warned their superiors in Washington, DC, Madrid and Havana to worry less about the more eloquent and socially influential Cuban propagandists in New York and instead combat the activist and radical insurrectionists in Key West.

Eventually in late 1891 and early 1892, Martí traveled to Florida, where he experienced a change of heart. In visits to Tampa and Key West, he spoke of the need to unify the exile communities and finally agreed that the time for revolutionary action had arrived; José Dolores supported his idea for a Cuban Revolutionary Party. The two men developed an effective working relationship based on the compatibility of their roles and goals. Martí saw in José Dolores a dedicated and talented grassroots leader who had played a leading role in creating the most cohesive and militant nationalist community in exile. José Dolores valued Martí's extraordinary intellectual and oratorical abilities and natural leadership skills and supported him as the obvious candidate to lead a united revolutionary movement from exile. They corresponded regularly, and Martí addressed official as well as personal letters that expressed admiration and affection for the Key West leader. In February 1895, the insurrection began and in short order Martí and Generals Máximo Gómez, Antonio Maceo and Calixto García arrived in Cuba, while José Dolores remained in Key West raising funds and sending expeditions to reinforce the insurgent army.

~ ~ ~

The great challenge in strategizing for the Cuban independence war was the danger of trading one colonial master for another: the United States. José Dolores was not anti-American; he expressed gratitude for Key West's reception of Cubans and respected its democratic traditions, but he also knew the history of US expansionism. José Dolores kept this in mind, as did José Martí, who wrote about the threat at the very time he died in battle at Dos Ríos, Cuba in May 1895. United States slave interests, José Dolores knew, had hoped to annex Cuba and, after the Civil War, he expected that northern capitalists would attempt to do the same. During the Ten Years' War, the United States refused to recognize the constituted Cuban republic-in-arms or grant belligerency status that would have allowed exiles to freely reinforce the liberation army and defeat the Spanish outright. During the second war in 1895, the United States maintained similar policies until 1898, when it intervened directly to end the war without acknowledging any Cuban authorities on or off the island.

Recognizing the American threat, José Dolores had always opposed any direct US involvement in Cuban insurrections and did what he could to assure a Cuban military victory over Spanish colonial rule. Unfortunately, the most that Spanish and rebel forces could accomplish was fighting each other to a stalemate. This made US intervention inevitable, and the sinking of the warship *USS Maine* in Havana harbor, sent to protect American citizens in February 1898, when anti-American riots broke out, provided the McKinley administration with an opportunity. After a quick and ultimately inaccurate investigation, American authorities concluded that Spain had destroyed the ship, and the United States declared war.

The United States had never intended to support Cuban insurgents and their aspirations for independence. Its goal was imperial expansion. As the United States commenced plans to invade, many Cubans distrusted American intentions, feared outright annexation and raised objections. Under pressure to mollify Cuban nationalists, the US Congress passed the Teller Amendment that acknowledged Cuba's right to independence but failed to recognize the authority and legitimacy of the Cuban government-in-arms or the liberation army. For José Dolores the situation was bittersweet. All he could do was hope the United States would honor its commitments under the Teller Amendment, but he remained skeptical.

In 1898, four centuries of Spanish colonial rule in Cuba ended, but foreign rule persisted with the United States ensconced on the island. Clues about American intentions became evident very soon after July 16, 1898, when Spanish military leaders formally surrendered Santiago de Cuba to US generals. Even before Cubans fully celebrated Spain's defeat, they learned to their amazement that US General Shafter had excluded Cuban General Calixto García from the surrender ceremony and that Spaniards remained in positions of authority in the city while Cubans stood sidelined. Ignoring the important fighting performed by García's forces, Shafter responded to Cuban complaints by saying that the war was between the United States and Spain, and Spain had surrendered Santiago to American forces. This disregard and disrespect for García and the Cuban liberation army that had fought with determination for three years prior to the United States landing angered José Dolores.

More insults followed. When Key West sent expeditions of clothing and provisions to Cuban troops, the US government prohibited resupplying Cuban troops in the field, foreshadowing American intentions to disarm the Cuban army. In September 1898, Cubans learned of their total exclusion from treaty negotiations in Paris, signed in December, finalizing the war and placing Cuba under direct and exclusive US control, which José Dolores characterized as a simple real estate transaction. At a noontime ceremony on January 1, 1899, again with no Cuban representatives present, General John R. Brooke, the US military governor of Cuba, received formal command of the island from Spain at the Captain General's Palace in Havana. A US officer at the Morro hauled down the Spanish flag while another raised the Stars and Stripes. Spain's rule ended, and formal US occupation began. No Cuban flag flew in any official capacity. Originally, the new authorities planned a day of festivities for the people of Havana, but the Cuban Commander-in-Chief, Máximo Gómez opposed any celebration, saying that Cuba was not yet free or independent.

José Dolores had never intended to stay in Key West longer than necessary and now felt an urgent need to return. In the United States, the family had rarely left the confines of the Cuban ex-pat community in Key West, except for revolutionary business, usually in Tampa or New York. Despite having become American citizens, their loyalty to Cuba never wavered, especially since obtaining citizenship was a political strategy designed to protect them from Spanish harassment. Now it was time to return home and help rebuild his devastated nation, but the affronts to Cuban nationalist sensibilities continued.

In late December, General Calixto García died in Washington, DC while serving with a Cuban Assembly (successor to the government-in-arms) delegation that met with President McKinley in an effort to gain some measure of recognition. Elected at the beginning of the insurrection in rebel territory, the Assembly claimed legitimacy as the voice of the Cuban people, but the United States begged to differ. Not only did McKinley refuse to recognize what he referred to as the "so-called Cuban government," he made clear his intention to rule Cuba directly until the establishment of a "proper" Cuban authority. José Dolores arrived home in January 1899, in time to witness the arrival of García's body on the *USS Nashville.*

While the body lay in state for public viewing, careful conversations between Americans and Cubans determined the protocol for the funeral procession. On February 11, the various dignitaries arrived and took their places behind the horse-pulled hearse, but as the procession commenced, the agreed-to plans changed. General Brooke's cavalry escort forced its way between the American general and the officials of the Cuban Assembly, to avoid any appearance of legitimizing the Assembly. The stunned Assembly members withdrew from the procession, as did General Freyre de Andrade, commander of the Cuban honor guard, who ordered Cuban troops to leave the formation. José Dolores, like most Cubans, felt the affront. One of Cuba's most beloved military leaders, who had already suffered several humiliating rebuffs at the hands of American authorities, was buried by occupying forces without the participation of his comrades-in-arms. This incident left no doubt that the US government had no intention of recognizing Cuba's revolutionary government.

Ironically, Cuba's fierce nationalist movement of the late nineteenth century foreshadowed similar movements across Latin America in the twentieth century, beginning with the Mexican Revolution in 1910, but nationalism in Cuba faded with the US occupation. It dissipated quickly as Cubans jockeyed to benefit from the new colonial power. Cuba's heroic but terribly destructive anti-colonialist and nationalist wars against Spain ironically launched the Poyo family's multi-generational journey into the economic, social and cultural realm of the United States. In exile, the family and thousands of others unwittingly opened themselves and Cuba to forces and influences that changed them, marked their descendants and transformed their homeland.

When José Dolores and Clara returned home after thirty years in exile, they knew Cuba had entered a new orbit around a new sun, the USA. For many Cubans who were radicalized in the hyper-nationalist independence era, the transformation of their homeland into a virtual American protectorate proved to be a challenge. José Dolores had never envisioned a Cuban republic politically and economically beholden to the United States, and his expectations were shattered by the cruel realities of a nation plagued by the chaotic aftermath of war. Raoul Alpízar Poyo wrote that his grandfather did not anticipate, "the great number of disagreeable surprises and painful obstacles that waited. He did not imagine that his entire life had been a glorious fantasy that would collide with a disconcerting reality very different from what people in exile had dreamed." Revolution reached its limits, and the family adapted. Cuba's independence now rested on the dispositions of the American government and the negotiating skills of an emergent Cuban political class.

3

A Sense of Ambiguity

"Abuelo passed away in Havana," I overheard my father telling my mother in March 1961, in Caracas. Family and friends called him Pancho, but my father and his brothers knew him as Abuelo, grandfather. His full name was Francisco Andrés Poyo y Skillin, son of José Dolores. My father announced his death, simply as a statement of fact. I heard no more about him until many years later when my father and uncles began speaking of him, always in affectionate tones. They had been close to him as children in Havana, having lived just around the corner, but life intervened and my father last saw him in 1949.

A humorous and talkative Abuelo who often took his grandsons to see their favorite baseball team, Almendares, at Estadio Tropical and regaled them with tales of his own career as a player and umpire. He showed them letters addressed to his father from José Martí and independence war generals Máximo Gómez, Antonio Maceo and Calixto García. He explained how together they had struggled for an independent Cuba. They also experienced a brooding Abuelo. The family retellings were never very detailed, but the anecdotes suggested an unhealthy dichotomy that pitted Pancho's love of Cuba, which he had acquired in Key West, against his disappointment in the aftermath of the family's return. Many times, Pancho said he could have gotten rich working at his job in Havana's municipal offices. Many did. Despite the independence wars' goal to rid Cuba of tyranny and corruption, he said that Cubans in the end acted just like Spaniards because "we carry their blood in our veins." Not at first, but eventually, ambivalence colored Pancho's attitude toward Cuba. If José

Dolores' generation cultivated nationalism, Pancho's generation were saddled with confusion in the face of US interference and Cubans' acquiescence to that reality.

Pancho watched former insurgents disagree among themselves when he arrived in Havana in 1899. It was clear the United States would not leave anytime soon. Only returning to the insurrectionary field could challenge the new reality, a difficult even foolhardy option in the face of overwhelming US military power and proximity. Few Cubans considered resisting occupation militarily and they were unable to present a united front on how to deal with the Americans. During the war, General Máximo Gómez on numerous occasions had strenuously disagreed with the governing insurgent Assembly. After the war, he cooperated with US authorities in undermining whatever little legitimacy it enjoyed. The Assembly tried to take the lead in raising money to disband the liberation army, but at the end of May 1999, Gómez acted on his own and accepted three million dollars from the US government to do just that. This miniscule sum provided seventy-five dollars for each of almost thirty-four thousand soldiers. Without access to an army, without formal political authority in the face of Gómez's actions and with little public standing even among Cubans, the Assembly dissolved.

Without independent civil or military authorities or structures to defend sovereignty, Cubans could only watch as the US military consolidated its occupation and used the US Congressional Teller Amendment's open-ended language, which guaranteed Cuba's independence but did not define its terms, to remain in Cuba as long as needed. American military officials formed a neo-colonial government with Cuban collaborators, who had mostly supported Cuban independence but now reluctantly accepted the protectorate arrangement. Most top-level civil servants had long established ties to the United States and spoke English fluently. Accountants, clerks, bookkeepers, managers, sales personnel and even servants, maids, housekeepers, cooks and laundresses gained an edge if they knew some English.

The occupation government facilitated and oversaw the rush of American investors and protected established Spaniards, who continued to prevail over Cubans in commerce, retail trade and industry. Spaniards also remained strongly represented in the professions, education, the press and publishing; they also maintained a strong influence in the Catholic Church. When necessary, Spaniards sold their lands and other assets mostly to Americans, not Cubans, who had little capital or access to credit after the devastating war. Most Cuban planters lost their productive capacity. Devastated by war and facing bankruptcy, they also sold to American interests that included land speculators and real estate companies. Flooding into Cuba, they bought up abandoned estates at deflated prices. In 1905, 13,000 Americans owned land in Cuba with investments of more than $50 million. As one observer in 1909 noted, "the Cubans, the real Cubans, do not own much." Foreigners also quickly dominated mining, banking, utilities and transportation. US interests bought the tobacco fields and Havana's cigar industry. English investors controlled the railway system, and Americans owned gas, electrical and telephone services. US contracting companies established offices in Havana and competed for government contracts. Initially, Spanish capital controlled the banking system with participating US, English and French interests, but later Americans came to dominate the industry.

Keeping its promise to grant Cuba independence, the United States withdrew its troops in 1902. Nevertheless, much was not well. During the previous two years, a Constituent Assembly wrote Cuba's constitution, but the US Congress forced an attachment to the document known as the Platt Amendment. The amendment gave the United States, at its own discretion, the right to intervene in Cuban affairs to protect American interests. Despite Cuban protests, the United States firmly warned that military occupation would not end until the Constitutional Assembly approved the amendment exactly as drafted. After a bitter debate, the delegates finally accepted the imposition by one vote. Cubans paid a heavy and humiliating price in exchange for the withdrawal of American troops.

Cubans made the best of a disappointing situation and celebrated on May 20, 1902 at the inauguration of Tomás Estrada Palma, the

Cuban republic's first president. Pancho, his mother Clara and sisters Celia and America, and their families, gathered with José Dolores and Clara that day. José Dolores received an invitation from the president-elect Estrada Palma to join him, General Máximo Gómez and the new governing authorities at the Captain General's Palace in Havana, but he preferred to stay with his family. He nervously paced the floor for the sounds of canons from the Morro fortress across the bay confirming the transfer of power. When the first one sounded, José Dolores looked at Clara, his body trembled and tears ran down his cheeks. As the canons continued to sound, his grandson Raoul Alpízar remembered, "nervous, [he] raised his hands to his head as if to grasp the thoughts that pounded in his brain on that historic occasion."

"'Clarita,' he declared, 'we are free! Viva Cuba Libre!' He then sobbed like a child."

If the family felt overjoyed at the symbolism of Cuban independence, they remained disillusioned with the United States and bitter about the humiliating limitations it had placed on their republic. Even worse, the pro-American Estrada Palma administration acted quickly to further consolidate Cuba's economic dependency on the United States. A Reciprocal Trade Agreement gave Cuban agricultural products, especially sugar and tobacco, preferential access to US markets and reduced tariffs on American imports. This further saturated the Cuban market with American goods with which small Cuban-owned enterprises could not easily compete. Most Cubans concluded that the nationalist project had done what it could and turned their attention to making a living, but anti-American sentiments already embedded in sectors of Cuban society did not disappear.

Pancho shared the family's nationalist ideals. Born in Key West in 1872, he fully imbibed the community's patriotism, political instincts and progressive social attitudes. What he knew of Cuba he learned from his elders, including the deeply engrained myth of the future paradise they would build on that island just across the Florida Straits. He and his three sisters learned much about Cuba at Key West's San Carlos Institute, a school founded in 1871, where teachers taught in Spanish about Cuban history, culture and society. The Poyo children grew up feeling fully Cuban.

Pancho always knew that Key West was only a temporary residence until the family could return safely to Havana. The young boy accompanied his father, mother and sisters to community patriotic events, including speeches, picnics and bazaars that supported revolutionary leaders seeking money and weapons for military expeditions to Cuba. Visits of such fierce and legendary independence fighters as Ramón Bonachea, Carlos Agüero, Flor Crombet, Antonio Maceo and Máximo Gómez, who at different times during the 1880s traveled to Key West seeking resources and political legitimacy, further inspired Pancho's nationalist ideals. All except Gómez eventually died fighting. Always a community spectacle, speeches at San Carlos and parades honoring the visitors drew large crowds.

Pancho's mother and older sisters were models of patriotic zeal. On December 6, 1878, Clara, Celia and América and forty other women formed the Club Hijas de la Libertad (Daughters of Liberty). Key West's women organized the club in solidarity with General Antonio Maceo's rejection of the Zanjón Peace treaty that the almost defeated insurrectionary government signed with Spanish authorities in February. Maceo declared the fight would go on, and Key West's women raised money. Although Spain finally pacified Cuba in 1880, the women did not desist.

Clara, Celia, América and the youngest Blanca remained stalwarts of the Hijas de la Libertad, often served as officers and took the lead in organizing the annual November 27 commemoration. One of Key West's most important patriotic events, November 27, memorialized the execution of eight Havana medical students in 1871 by Spanish loyalists. Historian Manuel Deloufeu knew the Poyo women and wrote that Celia was the club's last president before its dissolution in 1898. He remembered that when November arrived, "she put everything aside with selflessness, faith and perseverance, overcoming all obstacles of working with institutions, and always before us at the San Carlos Institute, accompanied by her noble sisters, presided over the commemorative celebrations of that mournful event."

Consistent with accepted norms of the time, women of Las Hijas de la Libertad and other women's clubs did not occupy community-wide leadership roles but acted to implement the political decisions of male leaders. Only some ten percent of women worked for wages outside the household in the 1870s, a proportion that increased to about twenty-five percent twenty years later. The three Poyo daughters married cigarmakers and appeared as housewives in the census, which gave them more time to work for the cause. They took the lead in organizing fundraising parades, banquets, raffles and picnics; they hosted visiting political leaders; they collected contributions door to door from households and businesses. The women also passed on their nationalist values and culture to the next generation.

In struggling for independence, most Cuban women in Florida accepted established gender roles, but toward the end of the century, after so much work, their thinking changed. Working in the factories, women engaged in the political and socioeconomic debates of the day, including anarchist and socialist discourse that questioned traditional ideas about gender relations. Each of the important exile communities had a local governing council of the Cuban Revolutionary Party, the *cuerpo de consejo*, run by the presidents of the constituent clubs. In Key West, the women's clubs participated in electing the president of the *consejos* only through proxy male representatives, since women did not enjoy the right to vote. Women eventually questioned this procedure. In October 1896, the Hijas de la Libertad requested that the *consejo* declare support for women's suffrage in the future republic. After considering the request, the *consejo*, headed by José Dolores, declared that as a local governing body it had no authority to take such stands. Nevertheless, after thirty years of activism in favor of Cuban independence, the Poyo women of that generation certainly thought they should have the right to be involved in public affairs and to vote.

It was women like them—politically conscious and animated to act—who promoted women's rights in Cuba later. I have no way of knowing whether Poyo women threw themselves into the political fray for gender equality when they moved to Cuba, but given their history in Key West, I imagine them supporting an emerging feminist movement and embracing the many changes in gender laws in subsequent years. After World War I, the Cuban congress passed laws that liberated women from the tutelage of their husbands, allowed divorce and safeguarded women's parental rights. They gained the vote in 1934 and voted for the first time two years later. The Constitution of 1940 recognized women's civil rights; they also gained the right to manage their property and carry out economic transactions without their husband's permission. Whatever their activism in Cuba, Poyo women in Key West made their modest contribution to the gender rights movement of the early twentieth century.

Pancho did what most Cubans in Key West did for a living: found a job rolling *puros* (pure Cuban leaf cigars) in factories. He learned the trade from master cigarmakers through a union-sponsored apprenticeship. After earning his own cigarmaking table at the Hidalgo Gato factory, he worked with mostly Cuban workers listening to the *lectores*, often his own father, promoting nationalism and socialism, and talking about a better Cuba organized around principles of freedom and dignity. Like most workers, he contributed to the revolutionary cause from his modest earnings. On January 1, 1892, Pancho joined in greeting José Martí during the nationalist orator's first visit to Key West at the Gato cigar factory. The factory's workers prepared an album containing *pensamientos* (thoughts) to honor the distinguished visitor. Pancho's notation reflected the general tone of the entries: "To be free, it is necessary to comprehend the rights and duties that liberty requires, and among the apostles that teach these [rights and duties], you, illustrious Martí, are one of the best." This and other comments demonstrated the workers' familiarity with Martí's writings and nationalist thought read to them in the factories for years.

Pancho made his living making cigars, but his real passion was baseball, which is what I first learned about him. My father loved baseball and he often told us about how his grandfather had been a *pelotero* of considerable renown, but he knew few details. Having left Cuba in 1942, he didn't even know that his grandfather had been inducted into the Cuban Baseball Hall of Fame in 1946. An active baseball community linked Cubans in Key West, Tampa, Havana, Matanzas and other places, which anticipated the much broader baseball exchange between the US and Cuban baseball during the twentieth century. The game began its march as Cuba's national sport in the mid-nineteenth century. Many young Cubans embraced the game while residing in the United States for work or education and took it home as early as the 1860s. The first professional baseball clubs formed in 1870s: Habana (1872), Matanzas (1873) and Almendares (1878). They formed the Liga General de Base Ball de la Isla de Cuba, and the next decade amateur teams formed across the island. Teams competed in local championships, especially in the summer months.

Baseball was more than a game for many Cubans. Ironically, baseball helped them express their nationalist vision. It represented modernity and progress as modeled in the United States and stood in stark contrast to the traditional and "barbaric" sport of bullfighting. As historian, Louis A. Pérez, Jr. noted, "Cubans subsumed baseball under notions of civilization and bullfighting under barbarism and drew a Manichean moral: between the Old World and the New, Spain and the United States, the past and the future." Cubans interpreted the sport as promoting values of individualism, discipline and patience as exemplified by individual athletic ability for the benefit of the team. Many Cubans generalized these values to the nation; baseball became a metaphor for the new nation, of Cuban nationalism itself.

My father's stories about Pancho's baseball career inspired me to learn more. At the Biblioteca Nacional José Martí, I found a few issues of a baseball magazine published in Tampa in the 1890s that included coverage of competitions between the Key West and Tampa clubs, including Pancho's team Cuba. I eventually came across a brief essay Pancho wrote about Key West baseball that showed how he and his friends made baseball their own. He first competed on teams composed mostly of Cuban tobacco workers who played friendly games on Sunday afternoons, but, in 1887, the sport took on heightened importance and a semi-professional character when local enthusiasts created the first organized baseball league. That year, Pancho's team Cuba formed, and he joined as a fifteen-year-old catcher. Other teams included Esperanza, Habana, Fe and Key West Gray's, a team composed of American players.

Cigar entrepreneur Eduardo Hidalgo Gato donated land on the south side of Key West, close to the beach, for a baseball field complete with stands for spectators and a fence. The first formal season in 1888/1889 played its games on Monday afternoons, since local religious codes prohibited professional contests on Sundays. Fe won the championship. The next season Habana emerged victorious and in the 1890/1891 season, Cuba triumphed. Key West teams also played against Cuban teams in Ybor City (Tampa), where the Niagara Baseball Club had formed in 1887. Cubano and Porvenir teams followed.

Key West clubs Habana and Fe took their names to honor well-known teams in Cuba, which they followed closely. The Spanish banned the sport during most of the 1870s, but at the end of the first war of independence, the game reappeared in Havana with the founding of the Almendares baseball club. Baseball in Cuba during the late nineteenth century was mostly a white, middle-class "gentlemen's" game associated with social clubs, but in Key West baseball emerged among a multiracial tobacco-worker population that organized their teams in the factories.

Players from Cuba competed in the Key West league, and vice versa. Pancho competed with and against many legendary ballplayers in Key West during the Cuban off-season, including Antonio María García, who played for Fe in Cuba and won various batting titles. Observers in the early twentieth century considered him the best Cuban player ever. Key West players, in turn, competed in Cuba. Pancho's Key West friends Agustín (Tinti) Molina, Florentino González and Alfredo Crespo played in Cuba for Matanzas, and Rafael (Felo) Rodríguez for Habana. Pancho would have accompanied his friends, but his father's high-profile anti-Spanish activism as editor of *El Yara* and close relationship with the martyred José Martí made this inadvisable. In any case, his father would have disapproved so long as Spanish rule persisted.

Players usually donated a portion of their earnings to the nationalist initiatives. On one of his visits to Key West, Martí accompanied José Dolores to a game that pitted the Cuba baseball club against a team of Americans. With Martí watching, Tinti Molina hit a homerun that won the game for the Cubans. Martí congratulated Tinti after the game, telling him that the victory represented a good omen for the war that was about to begin. Tinti later smuggled messages to activists on the island when he traveled there to play baseball for Matanzas. After the outbreak of war and Martí's death on a Cuban battlefield, a community group, Sociedad de Instrucción y Recreo José Martí, organized another formal "championship" to support the war effort.

Despite the close link between baseball and patriotic events, some nationalists expressed concern about what they considered Key West's exaggerated love affair with baseball. In an 1897 speech, socialist and nationalist activist, Diego Vicente Tejera, criticized Cubans' obsession with the sport. Unlike most local political leaders who welcomed baseball as a good fundraising activity, Tejera had his doubts. Tejera thought the sport a distraction. In his comments to the Sociedad de Trabajadores, Tejera said that rather than passing their time playing baseball, workers should prepare themselves for an independent Cuba, which was about to become a reality. Cubans would have to transform a country that had labored under colonial rule, which created indolence in the population that had to be changed. Cubans are energetic, he said, and capable of transforming their culture and way of life. Key West's commitment to the revolutionary movement for thirty years was ample evidence, he thought, but frivolity and lack of seriousness still distracted many. Baseball drained passions and energy better directed to serious tasks.

Despite Tejera's exaggerated scolding, Cubans, including Pancho, remained enthusiastic about baseball. The socialist leader underestimated Florida's Cuban ballplayers, thinking their activity frivolous and a sign of complacency. Many players joined the insurgent army after 1895 and lost their lives on Cuba's battlefields. Pancho remembered many players, including his good friend Chicho Frasquito, the great Key West pitcher who struck out fourteen players from Matanzas several years earlier and died on Cuba's battlefields. "In addition to playing in matches for the benefit of the homeland," he said, "they also gave their lives on the fields of the liberating revolution, resting today in unknown graves, without their families and friends having the consolation of giving them Christian burials and shedding tears on their tombs."

*

I imagined Pancho and his wife Louisa Skillin y Seguí's overnight steamer trip to Havana in January 1899, as a joyful journey. For him it was a first landing on Cuban soil, but for Louisa a return. She was born in Matanzas in 1872, the daughter of an American and a Cuban. From Portland, Maine, Nathaniel Louis Skillin, a cooper of Scot-Irish extraction, arrived in Matanzas in 1864, where he met and married María del Carmen Seguí y Jarchau. Many businessmen from the United States established commercial relations with Matanzas during the first half of the nineteenth century as the region became an important sugar and slave center. Besides investing in sugar, Matanzas provided other commercial opportunities. William Schweyer and Joseph Day of Portland, Maine, for example, supplied lumber for sugar boxes and hogsheads; perhaps Skillin arrived with businessmen like these.

Many Americans married Cuban women and assimilated into Cuban society, including Schweyer and Skillin, but by the mid-1880s Matanzas and Cuba faced a number of economic challenges. The Ten Years' War had left the sugar industry in shambles, and Cuba did little to prepare for the final abolition of slavery in 1886. A general economic malaise with high unemployment, rampant rural banditry and general insecurity caused many to leave, including Nathaniel Louis and María Carmen and their five children, who moved to Key West in 1886 to work in the cigar factories. There Luisa met Pancho.

The entire Poyo family returned to Cuba with high hopes, but it was also a leap of faith. The war had left Cuba devastated and the family not necessarily in touch with Cuban realities. They believed, Raoul Alpízar Poyo explained, that they "were going to have a free nation, independent, honest, worthy in every way of the efforts expended. Judging from the fantasies turning in the minds of the returning travelers, the desires of the old Cuban revolutionary émigrés was becoming a reality." Instead, they found a challenging transition.

Finding a job as a cigarmaker was the most logical choice for Pancho in Havana, but jobs were highly prized and not easy to get. US and English monopoly interests, La Havana Commercial Company and La Henry Clay Company, controlled over two-thirds of the cigar factories in Cuba, and Spaniards owned most of the small independent factories. Spaniards secured the best-paid jobs as foremen and cigarmakers in most factories, regardless of ownership, leaving the jobs that paid less for Cubans. This made it difficult for cigarmakers in Key West and Tampa factories to return after independence. Even Pancho's twelve years of experience did not secure him a cigarmaking table in Havana.

∽ ∽ ∽

If opportunities did not exist in the cigar factories, some did on the baseball fields, even if only tenuously. From 1895 to 1898, many players and leading baseball organizers in Cuba joined the rebellion or suffered imprisonment for their sympathies, but the sport continued. When Spanish authorities arrested and deported Emilio Sabourín, the most prominent baseball entrepreneur in Havana, who died in a Spanish prison in 1897, others stepped in to organize a championship in early 1898. Abel Linares and S.T. Solloso formed a team called Cuba in Havana and recruited Key West players Molina, Rodríguez and González, who had earlier played in Cuba. Though successful in winning six games, the team disbanded and the league suspended play when authorities learned they had secretly funneled funds to several insurgent generals fighting the Spanish. After Spain's defeat, Solloso regrouped Cuba with the Key West players and recruited Pancho as team captain and club director. Pancho and Tinti—both catchers—shared player-manager obligations and, from February through July 1899, they each played and managed six games. That first short and somewhat disorganized twelve-game season included only three teams, and Cuba fared the worst, winning only four of twelve games. Then, Pancho and Tinti became co-owners of the team with a new name, Cubano, and entered the 1900 season with a first-rate roster. Pancho mostly managed while Tinti played catcher, but the team ended up only in third place.

After that losing season, Pancho and Tinti could no longer sustain the team. Unlike Habana and Almendares with long histories and traditions in Cuban baseball and a significant following, the upstart Cubano club failed to compete adequately on the field and to raise the necessary capital to continue. Pancho retired as manager and player. At twenty-eight, he could no longer compete against a new generation of players entering an increasingly professional but still very small league. Managing slots were even fewer, but he remained in the game as an umpire during this formative period when the sport struggled to become an economically viable "favorite past-time." Pancho became one of the two most respected umpires in Havana baseball. One sports enthusiast of the period emphasized Pancho's "knowledge, rectitude and honesty," as an umpire, and his fluency in English gave him the opportunity to participate in a growing relationship between Cuban and United States baseball.

As the Cuban baseball leagues grew, the players became more proficient, and baseball in the United States took note. In November 1900, Cubano played against the visiting Brooklyn Superbs of the US National League. Cubano lost both games but helped initiate what became a *temporada americana* (American season) when US clubs traveled to Cuba to compete against local teams. Abel Linares organized the All-Cubans and toured the United States, which in 1900 included many of Pancho's former Cubano players. Within a few years, Cuban teams frequently beat visiting US clubs, which for Cuban players and fans took on meaning beyond the games themselves. Cuban victories elicited powerful nationalist feelings in the face of Cuba's subordinate status in the relationship with the United States.

Cubans recognized the attitudes of superiority among American players and relished chances to show Cuban prowess on the field against the best the north could offer. They had their chance when the American League champion Detroit Tigers traveled to Havana in 1910. Aware of the Tigers three consecutive titles, Cuban fans flocked to see a twelve-game series between Detroit and Cuba's best teams,

Habana and Almendares. My father and uncles with great pride often shared an anecdote at family gatherings of an encounter between Pancho and Ty Cobb, Detroit's star player. As I searched the sports pages of Havana newspapers *El Mundo* and *Havana Post* for more information, something made me smile and my heart quicken. Here it was, in the newspaper, confirmed!

Cuban fans especially wanted to see the legendary Ty Cobb, but they were disappointed. Already with a reputation as a racist, Cobb did not appear, saying he did not intend to play against blacks on integrated Cuban teams. The announcement did not depress the excitement; drama dominated from the beginning. Perhaps as a part of Detroit's strategy to rattle the Cuban promoters, the Tiger's manager complained publicly about the Cuban umpires after scouting the final game of a series between the visiting Negro league team Leland Giants and Almendares.

Once the series began, the manager routinely criticized the two umpires, Eustaquio Gutiérrez and Pancho. The Tigers protested many of Gutiérrez's calls behind the plate, prompting him to apologize and offer to resign, but they especially resented a call by Pancho in the field. He publicly admitted he had erred, although this was out of character for him. Fearing the loss of their investment, I imagine the Cuban promoters pressured the umpires to appease the Americans whom they feared would withdraw from the competition. The next day, the Tigers' manager threatened not to take the field again "until we are assured of a square deal." With that, Pancho had enough and resigned. The Cuban promoters replaced Pancho with an umpire from the United States but asked him to remain on the field until the American arrived. At this point, the series stood at 3-3, with one tie due to darkness. Concerned that they might lose the series, the Tigers finally persuaded Ty Cobb to join the team for an extra $1,000 and travel expenses.

Pancho umpired the Detroit star's first appearance in Cuba. In that game, Detroit faced Almendares and a melee began when Pancho called safe a Cuban stealing third base. This confirmed the family story about Cobb, who predictably rushed in from right field. Aware of Cobb's reputation as racist and bully, Pancho prepared for the confrontation. Cobb cursed in Pancho's face and placed a cleated shoe over his foot. Pancho told my father that as Cobb slowly pressed the cleats into his shoe, he stared him down without flinching or withdrawing his foot. Not successful in intimidating Pancho, Cobb thought better of his plan and backed away.

The American umpire arrived for the next and remaining games and worked with Gutiérrez while Pancho watched from the sidelines with his children. Cobb's presence made a difference, and the series ended with the Tigers winning seven, losing four and tying one. The Cuban fans were disappointed with the overall result, but they nevertheless cheered wildly in the last game when Habana pitcher, José Méndez, one of Cuba's many black stars, struck out the great Ty Cobb. For Cubans that was sufficient.

Pancho retired from baseball, but watched the sport take flight during the next decade. Baseball became an even greater obsession in Cuba, spreading to all realms of society. Men's amateur leagues sprouted up across the island. Secondary schools, social clubs, professional associations, businesses and other organizations had baseball teams. Provincial and municipal government teams formed as did teams connected to the armed forces. Elite social clubs competed against each other. Children's leagues formed in schools and neighborhoods, and corporations established their own leagues as a way of promoting company morale and solidarity. The Cuban Electric Company, the telephone company, railroads, cigar factories, mining enterprises and sugar mills had teams. Later, Pancho participated in old-timer games, and in 1946, he was voted into the Cuban Baseball Hall of Fame for his career as player, manager and umpire.

~ ~ ~

Baseball served as a convenient bridge from Key West to Havana for Pancho during a time when finding work in Cuba proved difficult. The game provided only a modest living not adequate for his large family and served as a certain distraction from larger Cuban realities. Pancho's struggle for economic security reflected the dilemma facing thousands of unemployed or underemployed Cubans in the American-dominated economy. With limited options in the private economy, they looked for government work, and Pancho landed a municipal job in Havana. Exactly when he started this work is not clear, but before 1906. Perhaps his friend General Alejandro Rodríguez, elected mayor of Havana in 1902, had found a place for him. Before joining the revolutionary forces and rising to prominence, Rodríguez had lived in Key West, where he and his wife had been active with the baseball league and knew Pancho well. With his baseball and working-class background, and lack of formal education beyond elementary school, Pancho probably did not initially qualify for a clerical job in city government, but the mayoral connection and his bilingualism must have opened the path. The rest he did himself and managed a long career. In 1913, Pancho became an administrative section chief in Havana's police department (*jefatura*) for a monthly salary of 2,800 pesos and later an office and section chief in the city's Office of the Secretariat.

Obtaining a government job was not easy and neither was keeping it, but Pancho hung on to his throughout the politically turbulent 1910s. Elections and political transitions were always delicate matters in a system where losing political power was equivalent to losing one's livelihood, not only for the officeholders but also for their surrogates and supporters. In 1921, the Cuban government faced imminent bankruptcy and the American and Cuban business sectors complained to the United States. An American envoy arrived in Havana to take charge of the economy and force dramatic budget cuts. Pancho's luck ran out. In April, he lost his job, along with dozens of others in massive layoffs. How he made a living after that is not clear. Perhaps he received a pension and his son, my grandfather José Francisco, provided as well.

By his own account, Pancho's awareness of the intricate world of Cuban corruption began with his work in Havana's government. At all levels, government officials accumulated power and wealth through political patronage and public corruption, but they could do little to promote the interests of the Cuban business class. Historian Louis A. Pérez, Jr. wrote that after withdrawing the occupation army in 1902, the United States used threats of reoccupation "to expand control over the course and content of state policy in Cuba to guarantee an open economy, reduce competition and preserve a cheap and plentiful supply of labor in a peaceful, orderly and prosperous environment." Policies helpful to Cuban business that constrained foreign investment did not go without complaint in Washington.

Pancho took Cuba's deficiencies to heart; not only had his father spent his life fighting to create a republic, but his own life had been defined by that nationalist world in which he was raised. It all seemed for naught. My father's stories suggested that Pancho's greatest disappointment was with Cubans themselves. Pancho knew well the consequences of the United States imposed Platt Amendment for Cuba, but blamed Cubans for most of the country's problems. It mattered that Americans pursued their own interests and structured economic and political matters for their advantage, but Cubans should have acted with honesty, integrity and concern for national dignity. Pancho remembered that his father had stood defiantly against those who preferred annexation to the United States, declaring that the Cuban people were perfectly competent and capable of ruling themselves. In his newspaper writings, José Dolores Poyo had also frequently pointed to corruption as one of the fatal flaws of Spanish colonialism, and now Pancho saw Cubans fall into a state of profound corruption in politics and civic life. They struggled for economic and political advantage over each other without concern for Martí's revolutionary ideals expressed in the phrase Cuba "for all, and for the good of all." These were the "bad Cubans," Pancho's nephew Raoul Alpízar Poyo later called them.

4

Better Forgotten

Abuelo often told his grandchildren that writers and historians distorted Cuba's past, they lied to promote their own agendas. Pancho and the entire family believed in José Martí's greatness, but thought that José Dolores had also been important in launching the war of independence. Pancho knew Martí personally. He didn't consider him very *simpático,* but said that he was eloquent and was able to mobilize the exile communities like no one before or after. Nevertheless, long before Martí appeared on the south Florida scene, José Dolores and his Key West colleagues had developed action strategies for launching the war. In fact, José Dolores, along with the entire Key West revolutionary leadership, became Martí's revolutionary mentors, a role that remained unrecognized and unappreciated by historians and was a source of disappointment for Pancho.

On arriving and settling in Havana in January 1899, Pancho, Louisa and the rest of the family watched José Dolores continue a brief but determined effort to carry on the nationalist struggle. In the first months, he considered Cuba's independence under threat from the United States. Using resources from the sale of his printing press in Key West and aided by the director of the *Gaceta de la Habana* newspaper (where he had worked before going into exile thirty years earlier), José Dolores published *El Yara*'s new incarnation in Havana. *El Yara* maintained its traditional support for labor rights and lamented the US occupation's repression of worker organizations. When dockworkers struck for higher wages, the American-appointed chief of Havana police, General Mario García Menocal, launched an assault and cleared the area. One of *El Yara*'s February issues expressed surprise that a decorated independence-war general, who had led courageous assaults on Spanish forts, could attack workers who had no more power than the value of their work. Occupation authorities opposed unions in order to maintain cheap labor for the flood of American investors entering the island.

José Dolores published *El Yara* in Havana for three months, but the effort to transplant his beloved nationalist newspaper soon faltered. In Havana *El Yara* had to operate as a profit-making enterprise in a competitive market. Poyo lacked working capital, probably possessed insufficient commercial acumen and certainly had few business connections. The complicated political environment and difficult economic situation together sealed *El Yara*'s fate. As historian Gerardo Castellanos García explained, "*El Yara* was as exotic and impotent in Havana as a *pitirre* [tropical bird] in the Sahara Desert. The emigres, like the majority of patriots on the Island, and even the liberators, had a misguided belief about the happiness emancipation would bring. We expected the emergence of a Utopia because Martí had proclaimed that Cuba would be for all and the good of all. Guided by that mirage, *El Yara* raised the patriotic banners." Few paid attention to this exotic nationalist voice, which after twenty years of continuous publication fell silent.

One would have thought that José Dolores' thirty-year revolutionary career would have garnered him a measure of recognition and respect, but his radical nationalism and work among the working classes in Key West did not translate into political prestige on the island. Educated middle- and upper-class Cubans who had found safety in New York during the war fared much better on their return home. Without military experience, a politically advantageous characteristic in post-Spanish Cuba, or the social standing necessary to catch the attention of Cuba's new elite powerbrokers, José Dolores exerted little political influence. For a time, sixty-three-year-old José Dolores worked as a night watchman at the customs house and walked the docks not far from his residence at Calle Inquisidor no. 31 in the old section of Havana. A better job as a clerk in the customs house improved his fortunes, but he still felt cast aside. Fortunately, unknown to him, his Key West friend and revolutionary colleague, Fernando Figueredo, and son-in-law Manuel Delgado, who worked together in the Department of Interior, watched out for opportunities for José Dolores. A cigar worker, Delgado had for years assisted José Dolores in editing *El Yara,* while Figueredo, ten years Poyo's junior, was among the leading revolutionary leaders in Florida. A military veteran of the Ten Years' War, Figueredo had arrived in Key West after the war and joined Poyo in reanimating the revolutionary cause. They eventually secured José Dolores a job as one of three under-secretaries to the director of the National Archive.

Thankful and excited, he began his daily trek from his home on Calle Arsenal, which ran parallel to the tracks at the central railway station, to the Castillo de la Fuerza, a former fortress that watched over Havana's harbor and housed the National Archive. José Dolores took the work seriously, as he did most things, and among his first assignments visited the country's major depositories to document their scope and condition. The dismal condition of Cuba's archives did not surprise him, and he recommended the transfer of certain critical documentary collections in imminent danger of deterioration to the National Archive for proper care and handling. In this way, on the job, he learned to be an archivist and experienced satisfactions as well as heartbreak.

On my first visit to his home, Luis Alpízar asked if I knew why one of the largest collections, or *fondos*, in the archive had the designation *miscelánea*. I had noticed but had not thought to ask. All the other *fondos* had precise headings, but not *miscelánea*. It included a little bit of everything, probably because of the great tragedies that befell the archive in July 1906, three years after José Dolores became the director. After organizing the archive those years, rumors of a rebellion prompted President Estrada Palma to install in the building a contingent of the Rural Guard to help protect the city. José Dolores complained and declared the situation untenable. The military's munitions and other flammable materials not only threatened the nation's documentary legacy, but no space existed for the rapidly growing collections.

As violence loomed, the government accepted José Dolores' recommendation to move the archive to the vacant and larger Cuartel de Artillería, the army's artillery barracks. Preparations began, but after a week, the president demanded the transfer be completed in forty-eight hours. Despite José Dolores' strenuous protests, public works officials took charge of the transfer, and the city's sanitation workers and their vehicles arrived to carry out the task. Workers constructed wooden slides from the windows on the second floor to the ground onto which they tossed the bundles of documents. "And as if throwing large quantities of trash from a building in demolition," noted the future archive director Joaquín Llaverías, they threw down tied bundles of archival documents, many whose cords snapped dispersing and damaging the papers and creating a terrible confusion. It left such a disaster, declared Llaverías, "that we hope never again to have to contemplate such a thing for the rest of our lives."

Workers loaded the bundles, as well as the loose papers strewn all over the ground, into horse-drawn garbage trucks and transported them to the new archive building, dropping documents along the way, some of which were salvaged by policemen accompanying the line of vehicles. At the destination, workers unharnessed the horses from the trucks and then raised the truck beds, dumping the documents in piles sometimes four meters high in the courtyard of the new archive building. A line of workers stretching from the courtyard to the interior of the building then passed bundles from one to the other while strong winds swirled the loose papers in the air. To make matters even worse, one night a torrential storm destroyed papers still outside as archive workers frantically tried to salvage what they could.

Even after the inauguration of the new archive on August 20, 1906, José Dolores could not be consoled. His official report to superiors at the Interior Department said that the transfer of the archive "had been carried out under the worst conditions with disastrous results" despite efforts by the archive staff to mitigate the damage during the days and nights that they watched the Department of Public Works ravage the nation's historical record. All the loose papers, Luis Alpízar explained, that never found their way back to their original collections became the *fondo miscelánea*, a constant reminder of those terrible days for the archive.

In protecting the nation's historical legacy, Poyo also contended with situations less dramatic than the wholesale transfer of the entire archive in forty-eight hours but that were nonetheless destructive to the integrity of the documentary holdings. In July 1907, some months after the disastrous move, Poyo denounced publicly the lack of sufficient authority to protect archival holdings to a reporter of *La Discusión*. He revealed the long-standing practice by previous archival and government officials of allowing prominent writers and scholars to extract original documents from the archive to consult them for their personal writing projects. Poyo cited the case in which the Secretary of the Interior ordered him to give a senator important historical documents for his personal use. Citing these threats to the integrity of the archive's historical documentation, *Discusión*'s article caused a public scandal. The senator and others quickly returned documents to the archive, but others never did. In publicizing the loss of important manuscripts, Poyo forced the government's hand, which then prohibited further extractions of documents from the National Archive. For José Dolores, this disorder was a microcosm of the chaos Cuba faced as a new nation. Luis said that these contentious struggles at the archive remained a sad memory, which even he still took to heart so many years later.

In 1911, already twelve years since the end of the independence war, José Dolores died without a single public recognition for his revolutionary work. The political and intellectual community's dismissal left Pancho and many family members puzzled and then embittered. José Dolores had been sick for a while, but only during the first week in October had he told the family of his cancer. He did not return to the archive. During the following weeks, he mostly remained in bed and reminisced with his wife Clara at his side, but stoic as ever, he refused morphine, preferring to remain lucid to the end. He prepared his burial suit and instructed his grandchildren to bury him in his old flexible shoes because his new ones would not fit his bloated feet.

José Dolores also requested that his body not leave home except to be taken to the cemetery, which indicated his disillusionment and distaste for how politicians and authorities used the passing of independence veterans to orchestrate emotional patriotic displays for political purposes. "You will see," he told the family around him, "as soon as I have died, the authorities, government officials, soldiers will come. . . . I am not interested in any of that . . . and neither should you. I complied with my duties. I was a good son, husband, good father, good grandfather and good Cuban." In the early hours of October 26, José Dolores announced the end. "Look, it has arrived. It is entering from below. My legs are already cold. Call the family." As they gathered, he spoke to each, giving his last blessings and advice. He passed at ten minutes to four in the morning and in his final breath called out to Clara, his wife of fifty-one years.

Pancho complied with his father's wishes for a simple burial. He placed the Orden del Sol (Order of the Sun) banner of the secret revolutionary organization his father had founded in Key West in 1878 under his father's head and covered his body with the Cuban flag that had been used by the Club Hijas de la Libertad (Daughters of Liberty Club) during their oaths of loyalty to Cuba. Without a priest, religious ceremony or ritual, a small group of government representatives, old comrades and ordinary people accompanied the family to the grave for a simple tribute. José Dolores' friend, José María González, a *lector* with whom he shared the *tribuna* at the Gato factory for many years, spoke warmly of him, as did General Enrique Loynaz del Castillo, a general José Dolores had helped to launch an invasion expedition to Cuba in July 1895. Later, Fernando Figueredo delivered a formal eulogy at memorial services in a Masonic lodge.

A simple burial was all the family could afford, but the dutiful son wanted more, despite his father's wishes. With Figueredo's indispensable help, Pancho came up with a plan to ensure that at least his father's remains rested in a more dignified grave. The following year, he published a manuscript from his father's personal archive entitled *Album del Estado Mayor del Cuartel General del Ejército Libertador Cubano (Album of the General Staff Headquarters of the Cuban Liberation Army)*. General Máximo Gómez created the document in 1898 as an homage to José Dolores' years of commitment to Cuba's freedom, especially highlighting *El Yara*'s enduring militant nationalism. The album included thirty-six *pensamientos* (reflections), including Gómez's dedication to that "ardent and loyal defender of the rights of the Cuban people, especially during the enslaved nation's most anguished times and moments when it seemed that all hope had died in the hearts of Cubans."

Figueredo wrote the introduction for the album stating, "Perhaps not many have heard of José Dolores Poyo, know nothing of *El Yara*, and maybe don't even know where Cayo Hueso is . . . Poyo grasped the torch of patriotism, which was *El Yara*." Figueredo told his readers that, Poyo died poor and probably forgotten, but happy. The reason for publishing and sale of the album was to raise enough money for his son Pancho to exhume his remains from an ordinary grave and reinter them in a modest but appropriate tomb. Pancho reached his financial goal after Havana's municipal council agreed unanimously to purchase three hundred copies of the book at one peso apiece and ordered them to be placed in the municipal government library and in schools across the city. In 1913, Pancho purchased a simple marble vault, where José Dolores' remains lied "tranquil and eternally."

Beyond a dignified grave, Pancho believed that his father deserved some official public recognition for his revolutionary career, despite his father's admonitions that having been a good Cuban was sufficient for him and his family. Figueredo did his part in November 1911, at the Masonic lodge's memorial service by presenting a twelve-page pamphlet, the first biographical account of José Dolores' revolutionary career. During the next several years on the anniversary of his death, the Association of Revolutionary Emigrés held public commemorations honoring his revolutionary career. On the fourth anniversary of his death, *El Mundo* newspaper published a lengthy front-page article highlighting his revolutionary leadership, and in 1918, the association honored José Dolores by transferring his remains to a newly erected pantheon in memory of exiled revolutionaries.

For Pancho and his cousins, this remained insufficient. In one of my last visits with Nieves, she gave me a worn book Pancho had published in 1923, titled *Acuerdos del Ayuntamiento de la Habana.* It compiled and indexed all the city ordinances, regulations and other measures passed since 1908, when the occupation government reorganized municipal governance. I noticed that municipal actions over the years included posthumous recognitions of independence war leaders in the form of books, plaques, statues, monuments, street designations and memorial galleries of various kinds. Honorees included generals, civilians and exiles who contributed in many ways. As Pancho compiled the documents, it must have pained him to see the honors given to people his father had worked closely with during the insurrections, but nary a word about him. The erasure was complete. Pancho could not forgive Cuba for sending his father into oblivion.

I didn't fully understand why recognition of his father was so important to Pancho, but it made me think about nations and their heroes. Who is chosen, and why? Why are some disposed of in the "dust bins" of history? Martí's singular rise to the status of national hero was rapid and well deserved. José Dolores had no doubt about where Martí should rank in the pantheon of the nation's independence leaders and martyrs. Martí had not only led the revolutionary party that launched the war but, more importantly, his extraordinary and much acclaimed body of writing expressed the very essence of what it meant to be Cuban; he had been the only one capable of such eloquence and insight. In 1896, José Dolores referred to him as the apostle of his generation and in 1903 served on a five-member committee that raised funds to replace the statue of Queen Isabella with one of Martí in the Parque Central, still the central commemorative statue in the country. At the statue unveiling in 1905, José Dolores offered words along with Estrada Palma, Máximo Gómez, Emilio Nuñez, Juan Gualberto Gómez, all who eventually received posthumous recognitions and honors in their own right. Only José Dolores remained unrecognized.

It is true that José Dolores did not make it easy for others to remember him. Figueredo acknowledged that his friend rarely spoke of himself and no one, not even his family members, knew much about his life before he arrived in Key West. He had little interest in promoting himself and he had no public life to speak of when he returned to Cuba. He never authored anything except articles in his newspapers and he rarely included autobiographical references. Furthermore, he did not donate his papers for public access and neither did Pancho, which suggested they had festering suspicions about the Cuban government. This may also help explain why José Dolores was not the subject of any of the dozens of biographies of revolutionary personalities written during the half century after independence. Only Figueredo's eulogy and the brief book by his nephew Raoul Alpízar told his story.

Trying to reconcile himself with this reality, Raoul Alpízar proposed in 1942 that "perhaps the best tribute to his memory is that he has been forgotten . . . oblivion is the most valuable tribute to his memory, for that is the prize that is usually given to those who serve well." Pancho did not agree and never let go of his disappointment about what he considered an affront to his father's patriotic career. This may have predisposed him to be ever critical of the Cuban republic. His dark view of Cuba extended a long shadow on his children and grandchildren, who fondly remembered his baseball stories, but also internalized his feeling that somehow Cuba had betrayed their family. In 1959, Fidel Castro's revolutionary victory reanimated Pancho, and perhaps he thought Cubans could finally redeem themselves. His daughter María pleaded with him to accompany her to the United States, but he refused. Besides being eighty-nine years old, which was reason enough to stay; Pancho insisted he would never leave Cuba, perhaps imagining what his father might have said. This revolution was a second chance; he may have thought redemption for a nationalist project gone wrong. He died right before Cuban exiles landed at the Bay of Pigs. María buried him and went to live with her sister in Louisville, Kentucky.

5

Aligning North

My father and his brothers fondly remembered their father, José Francisco Poyo y Skillin, or Papín as they called him, one of Pancho's sons. He sometimes took them on Saturdays to his job, where they helped stock shelves in a warehouse. In this way, Papín linked them to the American business world. They entered the complex entanglements of Cuban-United States relationships through their father's employment at an American automobile distributorship.

My grandmother, Nana, only occasionally mentioned her husband, saying that he was a good son, husband and father, and I lost the opportunity to delve further when she died shortly after my 1982 trip to Cuba. However, pieces of my grandfather's life emerged in the pages of *General Motors World* and *American Exporter* magazines and collections of *El Mundo* and *Diario de la Marina* newspapers. These sources had published his death announcement and scattered references to his work. Ancestry.com's digitized ship passenger lists included information on his travels, home addresses and other minutia. At an earlier time, collecting this material would have required years of searching in newspapers and federal government maritime sources, but now the research moved quickly. Contextualized in Cuban history and family stories, a portrait emerged.

Rather than feeling the need to seek political redemption in response to defrauded nationalist dreams, my grandfather set out in search of economic security. The family had lacked this for at least two generations. Working for American businesses offered better than average wages in Cuba and provided local employees a measure of security. Taking advantage of these possibilities required abandoning the previous era's strong nationalist loyalties, at least in public. I imagined my grandfather growing up listening to Pancho lamenting the shortcomings of the new Cuban republic, including the moral challenges of working in Cuba's public sector and politics. This condemned Cuban nationalism to irrelevance in his life, and my grandfather thus sought to benefit from Cuba's economic dependency on the United States.

To be sure, family traits were passed along. My grandfather possessed his father's and grandfather's moral sensibilities. He exuded integrity and honesty, "to a fault," according to my father. He worked hard to provide for his family in an economically tenuous and politically unstable country. While my grandfather took a more practical approach and sought economic security, he still internalized the moral values of freemasonry and revolutionary idealism that his father and grandfather had championed, but he applied them to the world of business. My father referred to this excessive moralism, or black-and-white thinking, as the "Poyo syndrome," which he presumed had begun with José Dolores. He warned against the dangers of this kind of thinking and with a knowing look at me claimed these traits lurked in the personalities of later generations too. That's not to say my father did not have a moral compass, but that business required a certain flexibility.

My grandfather pioneered the automobile business in Cuba and made possible a good life for his family, for as long as it lasted. No one in the family knew the circumstances in 1914 that led to his hire at a Ford agency in Marianao. He commuted there from his parents' home at 441 11th street in Vedado, but no longer lived with them when they later moved to 85 Calzada (7th Street), in the same neighborhood. The car agency in Marianao received automobiles from the Lawrence B. Ross Corporation, which represented Ford Motor Company in Cuba.

Working in white-collar jobs with foreign companies required Cubans to socialize and develop relationships with foreigners, who paid higher than average salaries in local currencies, which provided comfortable lifestyles. But these incomes were usually insufficient to build an independent capital base and independent livelihood. Cubans working for foreigners represented a dependent bourgeoisie, who were often without security within their own nation's economic systems. Although my grandfather's experience was of this kind, his three brothers were unable even to accomplish that in Cuba. Twenty-three-year old Laureano found his way to Mexico in 1926, where he worked in Guadalajara as an executive with Carta Blanca brewers. He married, had two children and became a naturalized Mexican citizen in 1937. His brother Luis received a degree in architecture from the University of Havana, but had difficulty establishing himself in Cuba. At first, he found work in the Cuban consulate in Miami in 1925, but then moved to Los Angeles where he worked for an architectural firm. There he met and married Ruth Price, and they moved to Seattle, where they had a daughter and son. They then followed Laureano to Mexico and settled in Mexico City, where he established a tourist newspaper called the *Mexico City Bulletin*. Ruth published tourist books and a directory of the city's Anglo-American residents. She published a similar directory in Havana in the 1950s out of Pancho's house.

Francisco, known as Panchito, the eldest of the four brothers, married Lourdes García in Havana and tried at various times to establish businesses in Cuba. In one such effort, Panchito had the idea of raising tropical fish for export to the United States and convinced his father to invest in building concrete tanks in the backyard of his house. The project failed, and Panchito left Havana, apparently leaving the empty tanks for his father to destroy, as Uncle Jorge said, "muttering curses with each crash of the mallet." He joined his brother Laureano in Guadalajara and in 1936 also became a naturalized Mexican citizen. In 1940, Panchito and Lourdes moved to New York City, where he enrolled in dentistry school, but apparently never practiced and returned to Guadalajara to enjoy a successful career as a businessman. None of these men found their place in Cuba during the 1930s with its depressed economy controlled by American interests. Mexico's larger and more diversified economy offered more possibilities.

∽ ∽ ∽

Automobiles secured my grandfather's living in Havana. Cars arrived with the US occupation, captured public enthusiasm in Cuba and symbolized the new era of American influence. Already in the 1920s, Cuban society fully embraced the automobile, and car companies did well. The car represented "modernity and progress" to a society increasingly tied to US economy and values. In 1921, the Cuban magazine *El Fígaro* noted, "Nowhere else like the beautiful city of Havana has the automobile acquired such a quick and natural quality." Despite a post-war economic downturn in the early 1920s and another crisis in sugar prices beginning in 1924 that dropped until the end of the decade, the total number of privately registered cars in Cuba grew significantly. Cuba ranked ninth in population in Latin America in 1929, but the island ranked fourth in the number of automobiles, behind Argentina, Brazil and Mexico, with a per capita car ownership of one for each 78.7 inhabitants.

My grandfather worked hard to rise in Cuba's automobile industry. On March 4, 1924, at twenty-eight, he placed an advertisement in *El Mundo* announcing that he had resigned from the Ford agency in Marianao "to dedicate our energies to the sale of Chevrolet and Oldsmobile automobiles." He saw General Motors' potential in Cuba and made plans to establish his own agency, called Poyo y Hermano, with his older brother Panchito. The advertisement assured readers that General Motors customers could conveniently purchase the cars through a favorable payment plan. Not wanting to alienate former Ford customers, the ad also promised to continue servicing and repairing Fords.

As it happened, plans changed. Instead of establishing a new car agency, later in the year my grandfather went to work directly as vice-president for Lawrence B. Ross Corporation, now representing General Motors Corporation. Serious, responsible and dedicated, my grandfather obviously impressed Ross, who likely needed a Cuban to oversee relations with local dealers. My grandfather's bilingual and bicultural background fit the bill, and they established a mutually beneficial relationship. Initially, the Ross Corporation's GM operation occupied offices at Padre Varela and Belascoain no. 17 in Havana and provided vehicles to agencies in Matanzas, Güines and Ciego de Avila. Later the offices moved to the corner of Calle 25 and Hospital in Vedado's central district, a prime commercial area. In my travels to Cuba, I saw the building, now a deteriorated state-owned garage needing much paint. Standing on the corner, I faced the empty automobile showroom and, down the block, the service department. I imagined a bustling street with pedestrians and cars, and the substantial building of a successful Ross Corporation, which also had a Chevrolet show room at Prado and Gerona in old Havana and a Cadillac agency at Marina no. 12.

The Ross Corporation maintained a strong advertising presence in Havana's press and it paid off handsomely. In April 1924, reports cited a rise in Chevrolet sales, despite the adverse political conditions, fluctuating prices and easier terms from competing dealers. "While six months ago," reported *General Motors World*, "practically no Chevrolets were seen on the streets, today approximately 500 are operating in Havana alone." During the first year, Ross Corporation sold 1,805 Chevrolets. In addition, the corporation in 1927 secured a contract with the Cuban Army Department to provide Chevrolet ambulances.

Running a distributorship required maintaining close personal relationships with GM officials in the United States, and Ross set the example with New York trips in 1924 and attendance at the First World Transport Congress in Detroit, an international gathering of the automobile industry, where he represented the American Chamber of Commerce of Cuba. The next year my grandfather attended the Congress in New York, probably his first visit to the United States, other than to Florida. At the Congress, he met with automobile dealers from across the world, including a strong contingent from Latin America, and attended the presentations of American automobile entrepreneurs. He heard about sales promotion, trends in highway development, traffic control issues, automobile servicing, including vehicle operation and maintenance, and problems of finance, among other topics. Conference organizers also arranged for international delegates to visit automobile factories. This must have been exhilarating for him as he broadened his knowledge and networks.

Trips to New York aside, my grandfather's primary responsibility was working with local dealers and building contacts within the automobile industry in Cuba. Having seen how industries in Cuba promoted themselves through social clubs, he helped establish the Auto Sport Club. The club sponsored automobile-related activities, but also included a baseball team and promoted gymnastics, among other things. The auto club enhanced connections and networking opportunities for those in the auto industry and helped my grandfather strengthen Ross distributorship links to local businesses.

In January 1928, the Ross Corporation invited ninety General Motors agents in Cuba to a convention at its Cadillac Company building in Havana to hear from New York-based General Motors officials, most prominently vice-president and GM Export Company general manager, L.M. Rumely. My grandfather not only organized the event but also served as translator during sessions that featured presentations on advertising, service, credit and lubrication. The conference presented new cars, including the 1928 Oakland that agencies were especially encouraged to promote that year. Presentations the next day featured the new model Pontiac and Chevrolet, emphasizing selling points and advertising techniques using "moving pictures and slides." The Ross Corporation's ability to attract top brass from the United States to the meeting testified to Cuba's attractiveness as an automobile market. Equally important perhaps was Havana's allure in the 1920s as an exotic place to visit.

In the 1920s, social divisions in Cuba and resurgent nationalist grievances about the continuing arrangements under the Platt Amendment sparked protests. Cuba's political parties were helpless. In 1907 and 1917, both political parties provoked US military intervention, and in 1920, they quietly accepted the arrival of American envoy General Enoch Crowder on a naval ship to take effective control of the Cuban government. Uninterested in another expensive direct military intervention, the US government simply coerced the sitting president to step aside while Crowder reorganized things. In flagrant, unapologetic and humiliating ways, Crowder imposed wholesale reform on a reluctant country. A blatant use of American power sparked public protests among resurgent nationalist sectors, including a new Cuban business class and organized labor.

These new sectors in Cuban society became established during World War I. A small national bourgeoisie independent of American capital seized opportunities when imports from the United States declined. They quickly gained footing. This sector included about a thousand factories and businesses across the island that produced a variety of consumer goods. New political groups representing Cuban businesses demanded better governance, less corruption and a merit system for public jobs, among other things. They also demanded trade laws that protected their products.

Recognizing the growing nationalist and reformist mood, Liberal Party politician Gerardo Machado appealed to this sentiment and was elected president in 1924, but he acted with caution knowing the United States watched his every move. In 1927, Machado responded to Cuba's nationalist business interests by passing a protective customs-tariff law. Duties on imports necessary for local production declined, while those on manufactured products competing with Cuban products increased. Over all, these policies encouraged a path toward light industrial development and some economic diversification that placed Machado in good stead with an important sector of the national business class. In an unanticipated way, the 1927 tariff law also encouraged foreigners with substantially more capital to establish subsidiary firms in competition with Cuban enterprises. Cubans could not easily fend off American determination to control the local market.

Machado's friendly attitude toward business did not extend to labor when it finally organized in the 1920s. The large presence of foreign workers was always at the top of Cuban labor's list of grievances. Almost 700,000 immigrants arrived between 1902 and 1909, and there seemed no end to foreign workers arriving. Spaniards especially provoked the anger of Cuban workers. Poor, illiterate and industrious, they competed with Cubans in all sectors of the economy. Americans liked the Spaniards. They kept wages low and labor organizations weak.

The United States had succeeded in undermining the left before, but in 1925, a National Labor Congress established a workers' confederation while another group founded Cuba's first Communist Party. In 1925, labor demanded that seventy-five percent of jobs nationally be reserved for Cuban citizens, who constantly competed with foreigners for employment. The American Chamber of Commerce in Havana denounced the proposal as harmful and called on the State Department to protest. Machado killed the legislation and launched repressive assaults against militant workers in order to gain US acquiescence for his middle-class reformist initiatives. The problem for Machado was that promoting Cuban business interests while at the same time crushing organized labor weakened his original nationalist coalition, but not before he changed the constitution to extend his time in office. When protestors proclaimed this to be a coup d'état, the president reacted with violence against them.

The economic crash in 1929 destabilized Cuba's already tenuous political situation, which worsened with the US government's passage of the protectionist Smoot-Hawley Tariff Act the following year. Cuba's share of the US sugar market fell by fifty percent, sugar prices fell by sixty percent and Cuban exports overall declined by eighty percent. Revolutionary middle-class groups, students and radical labor challenged the government at every turn, leading to major street warfare in 1931. The United States stood with Machado until August 1933, when it finally withdrew support and the Cuban military forced him out. Then noncommissioned officers led by Sergeant Fulgencio Batista overthrew the entire officer corps and took charge of the military. This led to the establishment of the first Cuban government that had been formed without the explicit blessing of United States, but the new government's nationalist policies quickly alarmed the United States, who persuaded Batista to replace the revolutionary he had installed with a more acceptable conservative politician under his influence. Throughout the 1930s, Batista governed Cuba as head of the military through a series of puppet governments until his election as president in 1940.

The political and economic chaos of the early 1930s made all businesses vulnerable, including car dealerships. Tumbling sugar prices and the Depression affected automobile imports and sales, and the industry was on the verge of collapse. But the Ross Corporation weathered this storm, and imports began to rebound as the Batista era brought a measure of political stability and better relations with Washington, DC. The United States accepted the abrogation of the Platt Amendment in May 1934, which took direct US military intervention in Cuban affairs off the table. This new relationship was in line with Roosevelt's Good Neighbor Policy. Instead, the United States relied on its soft power through diplomacy and economics. Short on capital during the 1930s, Cubans were no match for the mostly American foreign firms with abundant resources. New American businesses in Cuba produced processed foods, soaps, perfumes, textiles and other things. Among the new companies were Mennem, Armour, Proctor & Gamble, Colgate, Pabst and Fleischmann. Even the Swiss Nestle Company established a subsidiary to produce condensed milk and butter. All of this brought recovery to the Cuban economy, but increased dependence on sugar and damaged non-sugar entrepreneurial interests, which were unable to compete with US investments and imports. The Cuban economy fell even more firmly into the hands of American capital, and automobile sales were now again on a solid footing.

My grandfather's career in the 1920s and 1930s must have been difficult for him as well as ironic. Coming from a family with strong nationalist traditions, he found himself linked economically to interests decidedly opposed to nationalism. What did he think of Cuban nationalism? Did he find himself at odds with his father? What did it mean for him to align north? My father never spoke of this and probably had no idea what his less-than-talkative father thought about these things. Whatever my grandfather thought, his economic security depended on American automobiles and undoubtedly influenced his way of thinking. Those turbulent times must have been challenging for him.

Curiously, these complex political and economic crosscurrents of the Great Depression in Cuba that threatened our family's livelihood never surfaced in anecdotes and stories. I expected Uncle José, born in 1920, to have been aware of disturbances in Cuba in the early 1930s, and perhaps even my father, born in 1923, would have sensed problems, but they rarely spoke of that time. Only one story referred to those years of rampant danger. One evening, my father saw Nana helping his father with his coat before he returned to the dealership at night. An odd time to go to work, my father thought, but even odder and more alarming was the handgun he saw tucked in his father's belt. He saw the weapon for only a moment, as the coat was buttoned closed around his father's waistline, but he must have asked about it later. He learned that his father had gone to the dealership to help protect it from dissidents, who frequently "liberated" cars for their revolutionary activities. I imagined my grandfather doing this regularly during times of political turmoil in the early 1930s. Apparently, nothing of consequence ever happened to the dealership, but the anecdote highlighted the threats my grandfather experienced at that time.

During the final half of the 1930s, economic conditions improved, and this is what my father and his brothers mostly remembered. They all recalled a spectacle in Havana that in some ways symbolized the changing mood and provided the Ross Corporation with an extraordinary marketing opportunity. In January 1939, the distributorship sponsored a General Motors traveling exhibition in Havana derived from its pavilion at the 1933-1934 Chicago World's Fair, which highlighted General Motors' technological and scientific innovations in automobile design and engineering. The exhibition included eight buses and another eighteen support vehicles, known as the "Silver-Topped Streamliners," carrying sixty employees. Throughout 1936-1938, the caravan of vehicles toured 181 cities in the United States, Canada and Mexico and required a space equivalent to a city block. Displayed under a circus-"big top" tent that seated 1500 people, the exhibition received rave reviews and was much anticipated when the

Ross Corporation announced that it would sponsor its visit to Havana. Called the "Caravana del Progreso" (The Caravan of Progress), the Cuban Tourist Commission, the American Chamber of Commerce of Cuba and the Cuban Society of Engineers hosted the exhibition.

"We . . . are very happy to be able to present in Havana the internationally famous 'circus of science,'" declared the Ross Corporation's advertisement in the *Havana Post* welcoming the "Caravan of Progress." It "is a scientific exposition, conceived by General Motors for the education and enjoyment of the public" and "tries to show, with scientific experiments and exhibits, how industry, by means of its vast research laboratories, contributes to the progress and to the improvements in living conditions." The Caravan of Progress "is our expression of gratitude to the Cuban public for its decided support of General Motors products; and it enables us to give you a better comprehension of how General Motors unites science and industry in the service of human needs."

On Sunday, January 8, the vessel transporting the *caravana* arrived at the port of Havana. Ten thousand people lined the sidewalks as the busses drove off the ship and made their way to the capitol building. From there, they traveled to the coastal boulevard known as the Malecón. Then the convoy continued to the exposition site at the Castillo de la Punta overlooking the entrance to Havana harbor. My father's photograph collection includes an image of my grandfather, Lawrence Ross and the Cuban Tourist Commissioner greeting GM officials, including the caravan director, J.M. Jerpe, as they descended from their Pan American Clipper pontoon airplane at the harbor. They escorted the American visitors to the opening ceremony that evening. Other notables attending the ceremony included the US ambassador and his family, the Cuban secretary of commerce and all the members of the Cuban cabinet, foreign government representatives, president of the American Chamber of Commerce of Cuba and prominent businessmen and socialites. After the speeches and official fanfare, the gates opened to the public, and 22,000 people surged into the exhibition.

The "City of Progress" exhibit with more than 200 moving miniature automobiles, busses, trucks and trains on superhighways, illustrated the progress in US urban transportation networks, compound with another exhibit of Main Street in the 1890s with only four moving parts. Along the same line, another exhibit contrasted various rooms in the home of yesterday and of tomorrow. People saw the latest technological wonders, including an induction stove frying an egg through a newspaper without scorching the paper and light beams conducting a musical broadcast. Other exhibits included a strobescope, an oscillograph and a series of General Motors institutional and educational movies.

Lawrence Ross proclaimed the *caravana* a great success. "In spite of the fact that we had three days of bad weather, the total attendance count was above 188,000," he told a reporter. The "Caravana del Progreso" raised the community profile of both Ross and my grandfather. At the end of January, the Automobile Importers and Agencies Section of the Cuban Chamber of Commerce elected my grandfather vice-president, reaffirming his important role as the company's representative to the Cuban business community. Shortly after that, the American Chamber of Commerce in Havana elected Ross vice-president. Conditions for US automobile dealers improved in 1939, and car imports reached 2,000, mostly Chevrolets and Fords, which bode well for the Ross Corporation.

❧ ❧ ❧

The return to prosperity in the late 1930s surprised the Ross Corporation with unanticipated changes. Apparently, strains had developed between Lawrence Ross and General Motors executives in New York, resulting during late 1939 in Ross's sale of the distributorship to an Italian national named Amadeo Barletta. Originally, from Calabria, Italy, Barletta as a young man went with an uncle to work in Puerto Rico and in 1920 took a job with the first GM dealership in the Dominican Republic, called Santo Domingo Motors. In time, he bought the business, and Benito Mussolini named him Italian General Consul in Santo Domingo. Despite his success, in the mid-1930s, Barletta became embroiled in political intrigue against the Dominican dictator Rafael Leonides Trujillo. Barletta may have participated in a plot to assassinate Trujillo, who had him imprisoned, cancelled his credentials as Italian consul and confiscated the Italian's Dominican Tobacco Company. After forty-five days in prison, Mussolini came to his rescue, threatening to send two war ships to the Dominican Republic, and General Motors intervened on Barletta's behalf as well.

Released and no longer welcome in the Dominican Republic, Barletta went to New York, where he consulted with GM before moving to Havana, possibly to be brought up to speed on problems with the Ross distributorship. Lawrence Ross was vulnerable on a number of fronts, including less than hands-on management of the business in later years and, perhaps, a high-flying lifestyle. It seems that Ross enjoyed casinos and on one occasion in 1937 incurred a hefty IOU at the Casino Nacional, Havana's largest and most well-known gambling establishment. Enjoying his financial success, Ross gambled and drank excessively, spent much time traveling and relied on my grandfather to run the distributorship.

The little evidence available suggests that Ross sold the business to Barletta under duress. Barletta quickly cultivated a relationship with President Batista that in June 1941 resulted in the sale of fifty Buicks to the Cuban national police. The president himself attended the delivery ceremony. Barletta also curried favor with the American business community as an active member of the American Chamber of Commerce in Cuba.

Under Barletta, my grandfather remained with the company as vice-president, but most certainly with less authority. In September 1939, my grandfather faced new challenges with real potential threats to the business when Adolf Hitler sent his army into Poland, sparking World War II. Although the beginning of the war did not affect Cuba directly, it did bring attention to Barletta. Fearing growing fascist influence in Latin America, the Roosevelt administration monitored pro-Axis individuals and businesses in the region, including Barletta and his relationship with General Motors. In June 1941, the American ambassador wrote the Secretary of State with information on Italian investments in Cuba, citing Lawrence B. Ross Corporation, "controlled by Mr. Amadeo Barletta, the Italian General Consul at Havana." That same year, the State Department issued a "Proclaimed List of

Certain Blocked Nationals," to undermine suspected pro-Axis businesses. GM tried to protect Barletta as long as possible, but once blacklisted the corporation had little choice but to purchase the distributorship. On July 21, only a month after the profitable sale of the Buicks to the Cuban police, GM announced that it had acquired all the stock of Lawrence B. Ross Corporation. GM named E.G. Poxson, the truck manager for Foreign Distributors Division in New York, to run the distributorship. The *Diario de la Marina* reported, "The company's new directors retained workers, employees and department heads, providing a valuable example of the American politics of the Good Neighbor." Also responding to US pressure, the Cuban government closed all German and Italian consulates and ordered Barletta to leave the country by September 5. Barletta caught a flight for Buenos Aires.

My grandfather said nothing to his sons about these intrigues, but was happy to report on an opportunity to establish his own business. A troubled Chevrolet agency in Santiago de Cuba needed a new owner and GM offered it to him. During the previous twenty years, my grandfather had demonstrated his business capabilities repeatedly and gained the respect of the New York executive leadership. GM committed to finance the purchase through a dealer development program, so he took up the challenge of owning his own agency.

This new business opportunity in Santiago also opened a path for Uncle José and my father. At college in the United States, they fully intended to work with their father after completing their studies. They both told me that, besides the experience of going to the office with their father, the Caravan of Progress in 1939 had sparked their interest in the car industry. Uncle José even worked at one of the exhibits. In need of bilingual interpreters who could take instruction in English and translate it into Spanish, my uncle narrated to visitors the story of the 1908 Buick; he always dressed in an elegant uniform of white pants, a blue blazer and a white sailor-shaped cap.

In early summer 1941, my grandparents rented their home in Almendares and drove their Chevrolet across Cuba along the *carretera central* to Santiago to take charge of the agency and begin a new phase in their lives. Their initial excitement in taking over the dealership and moving to Santiago waned somewhat on hearing of the

December 7 Japanese air attack on the US naval station at Pearl Harbor. Having to divert resources to the war effort, General Motors suspended the dealership credit program, leaving my grandfather without any immediate way to purchase the business. Nevertheless, he had successfully managed the Ross Corporation through the Great Depression and remained confident things would improve after the war. In the meantime, the family's future seemed secure.

6

Americanization

My father and his brothers experienced Americanization in Cuba long before leaving for the United States in 1942. A person's identity develops over time, so slowly that we are only partially conscious of changes. Reluctantly, after much badgering over the years, my father explored these questions with me. American culture in Cuba presented Cubans with a set of values with which to consider their own condition. Economically dependent Cubans used American criteria to assess how they felt about their country, which inevitably left them feeling disappointed. A new form of colonialism was imposed on Cuba; it was steeped in American capitalism, a manipulated democracy and consumerism. My grandfather and father conformed to these values.

It is also true that American cultural ways had earlier influenced the family in Key West. Pancho, my great-grandfather, fully internalized that community's bilingual and bicultural reality. He spoke both languages fluently, learned the political values of the United States, had American friends and coexisted with American culture. My great-grandmother Louisa's familiarity with English and American ways came from her American father. At home, Pancho and Louisa spoke Spanish, but their seven children nevertheless grew up bilingual and bicultural in Havana. Three were born in Key West (Francisco-1892, José-1896, and Luis-1898) and four in Havana (Carmen-1900, Laureano-1903, María-1905 and Elena-1907) and although they never knew their American grandfather, they learned English at private American religious schools.

Ironically, in some ways, Poyo children imbibed American culture more thoroughly in Havana than in Key West. In Florida, Pancho lived in an insular working-class community, studied at a Spanish-language Cuban school and made his livelihood in majority-Cuban cigar factories, where even the few Anglo Americans working there spoke Spanish. On the other hand, in Havana, Pancho's two eldest sons, Francisco (Panchito) and my grandfather José Francisco attended Colegio San Agustín, a Catholic bilingual school for boys. An American Augustinian school founded in 1901 not far from the Poyo home, Luis Alpízar took me to see the building of the former school, where the order also had its convent.

My grandfather graduated from San Agustín in 1913 speaking fluent English, and then enrolled at Casado, a business school where he studied *comercio*, mastering typing, shorthand and accounting. At least two of his sisters, Carmen and María, attended Cathedral, an American English-language Episcopal school. My grandfather's English-language skills, general familiarity with American culture, fair skin and perhaps personal references from his Augustinian teachers made him an attractive candidate for US businessmen seeking local employees. Playing baseball at the school also contributed to his Americanization, to which his father had already introduced him. He followed American baseball news in *El Mundo* and the English-language *Havana Post* and after graduation, he remained active playing in Havana's amateur leagues.

Ongoing relationships with relatives in Key West also contributed to the family's bicultural character. The only Poyo who returned to live in Key West was author Raoul Alpízar Poyo, as Cuban vice-consul. He remained and later served as Cuba's honorary consul. Louisa's siblings all remained in Florida. Members of Louisa's family from Key West sometimes visited Havana and stayed with the Poyos while my grandfather reciprocated with trips to Key West. On one memorable trip during June 1920, Louisa traveled with four of her children—Carmen, Laureano, María and Elena (Nelly)—to visit her three sisters. At the family's old stomping grounds, they attended Raoul's birthday party. As the social columnist of Havana's *El Mundo* newspaper recounted, his house "was assaulted by a group of young ladies and men, intent on expressing their love and respect for our consular representative." Everyone feasted on candies, ice cream and a magnificent fruit punch, "since champagne is prohibited in those lands. . . . The beautiful señoritas Coralia and Lily González de Mendoza and señorita Carmen Poyo, who is enjoying a short stay in historic Key West, sang several beautiful songs." Afterwards everyone danced until two in the morning. Family visits between Florida and Havana during the first three decades of the century were a distant reminder of their nationalist past, but more importantly strengthened their bilingual and bicultural identity. This proved useful in a Cuba thoroughly under the economic and political influence of the United States.

It was in Marianao, my father and uncles knew, that their parents had met in 1914. From Caimito, Nana often visited her aunt and uncle, Joaquín and Concha, in Marianao. She and her cousin Margo enjoyed tennis together at the Marianao Tennis Club, and Nana met my grandfather there. Margo described the two as a very handsome couple and insisted that they fell in love immediately. They married on May 17, 1917; she was twenty-one and he was twenty.

Visits with Margo in Havana on Sunday afternoons during our time in Cuba turned into family history seminars about Nana's family. Besides describing personalities in the genealogy, Margo narrated a combination of history, gossip and scandal. Various tables in her living room proudly exhibited framed photographs. She gave them to me when we returned home, insisting that no one left in Cuba would appreciate them as I did. Unlike the Poyos, Nana's family descended from Spanish loyalists. Her grandfather, the family patriarch, was a military officer named Ricardo Álvarez y Fernández de Córdoba—the second surname is an important name in Spain, Margo claimed with pride. His photograph on her living room table standing in a military uniform was a spitting image of Uncle José.

Years later while researching in Spain, I was able to locate Ricardo Álvarez' records. In 1899, as Spain withdrew from Cuba, departing colonial officials loaded many of the colonial archives aboard ships and took them home. They ended up in dispersed locations, but the military *hojas de servicio*, or personnel records, made their way to the military archive in Segovia, housed at the famous Alcázar, a UNESCO World Heritage Site. While waiting for the documents, I told the archivist, a captain, that I was amazed these papers had arrived intact from across the Atlantic Ocean, then overland originally to Madrid and finally to Segovia. Just then a squeaking door announced the arrival of a clerk in a grey smock with an archival bundle at least eight inches high containing Álvarez's entire service record. I couldn't believe it.

Margo had assumed Álvarez was born in Spain. He was actually born in Cuba on June 7, 1835 (just a year before José D. Poyo) in Guayabal, district of Guanajay, Province of Havana. Of his parents, Marcelino Álvarez and Antonia Fernández de Cordoba, I learned only their names, but Álvarez enjoyed a long military career in the Cuban militias known as *voluntarios*. He entered service in cavalry regiments as a private and rose to rank of colonel. During peacetime, he served in and around his community, but often posted away from home during periods of conflict. In 1859, Álvarez shipped off to fight in the Spanish-Morocco War with the Regimiento Caballería de Lanceros de Lusitania and participated in the Battle of Tetuán on March 23, 1860, where the Spanish army defeated Moroccan forces.

During the first Cuban insurrection known as the Ten Years' War (1868-1878), he deployed to Las Villas, east of Havana. Álvarez fought the Cuban insurgents in Las Villas at the same time that José Dolores organized tobacco workers in Key West to provide resources for the rebel army. In 1894, some years after retirement, Álvarez received an honor, La Cruz Sencilla de la Real y Militar Orden de San Hermenegildo, in recognition of his loyal service to Spain.

Ricardo Álvarez and his family lived on a *finca* between Guayabal and the little village of Caimito, some thirty kilometers west of Havana along a road later known as the *carretera central*. One day browsing in a Havana used bookstore I found a rare and somewhat battered history of Caimito del Guayabal. This source recounts that after the Ten Years' War, the Spanish governor increased the number of official municipalities in Cuba, hoping to connect and control the island's small towns more effectively through direct Spanish governance. The largest village in the area and its convenient location as an overnight stopover for travelers between Havana and Pinar del Río, Caimito became the seat of the official municipality of Caimito del Guayabal in 1879 and gained legal jurisdiction over the smaller villages of Guayabal and Banes. In 1880, Caimito included about 500 inhabitants, with 41 stone adobe houses with tile roofs, 8 houses made of wood and tile roofs and 7 houses made of palm material and leaves. The town had two schools, six general stores, a barbershop, a shoemaker, a fruit vendor, a veterinarian, a carpenter, a slaughter house, an oven for producing lime and, of course, a billiards hall and bar. Colonel Álvarez served on the first municipal council and during 1887-1889 served as *alcalde* (mayor).

I learned little about Colonel Álvarez's wife, María de la Concepción González Mojena, but photographs Margo gave me that were dedicated to María from cousins and friends in Palma, Pinar del Río, suggest she may have been from there. These posed photos from the 1860s and 1870s, commonly taken and distributed to relatives and friends as an easy way to remain in touch, reveal formally dressed and seemingly well-heeled people, some taken in Havana's S.A. Cohner photography studio at 62 Calle de O'Reilly, entre Habana y Compostela, not far from where Luis and Nieves lived. Concepción had three children, Ricardo, Nana's father, and Joaquín and Concha, who Nana visited in Marianao. While the sons apparently sympathized with Cuban independence and the insurgents, according to Margo they did not join the rebels in deference to their father.

After the war, Ricardo, the coronel's son and my great-grandfather, remained in Caimito and took charge of the finca, but, lacking capital, he usually rented the land to nearby sugar estates that provided a modest but adequate income for the family. He spent most of his time on other matters, including politics. In 1910, Ricardo ran successfully for the council of the newly reorganized town government and subsequently served as council president. He married Tomasa

Rodríguez y Quintero (known to her grandchildren as Mamá Chocha) and they had six children: Sara, Sergia (Nana), Concepción, María Antonia, Ricardo and Tomás.

Tomasa eventually suffered the indignity of having Ricardo's mistress, with whom he had two children, living in a house on the far side of their finca. Margo even blamed Tomasa for the situation, saying everyone knew that she was distant and "*fría*." Somehow, it was the wife's job to ensure her husband did not stray. The story got even better. Ricardo died on a visit to see his mistress, leaving the family with the delicate task of recovering the body. The family persuaded the mistress to leave the house in exchange for their offer to pay for her two childrens' education in a boarding school. When I asked my father about this, he gave me a surprised look and asked how I knew.

"Margo," I said.

"Oh yes, Margo," as if it made perfect sense to him. He had not seen her since 1942 but remembered her well.

⁂

"*¡Soy guajira!*" (I'm a country girl), Nana always proudly proclaimed with a twinkle in her eye whenever she did something clever. She believed in living frugally and practically. In that sense, she was like my grandfather, who was also honest and practical. Even after her marriage and move to Havana, Nana visited Caimito frequently. She also spent time at the beach, not far from her home near the port of Mariel, where her mother Tomasa was born. Long after leaving Cuba, Nana reminisced about the *playas* of her youth, comparing them favorably to beaches in Miami, Key Biscayne or elsewhere. Nana's more traditional Hispanic and Catholic values and sensibilities had promised to balance somewhat the bicultural and masonic Poyo background from Key West, but American influence in Havana remained strong, and she found herself adapting to that reality. She learned that foreigners had a determining influence over many things, including the culture and language.

Nana gave birth to Uncle José (1920) and my father (1923) when they lived in Marianao. They moved to Vedado in 1924, no.10, Calle

K, where Uncle Jorge was born two years later, not far from the home of Pancho and Louisa and the distributorship. It was a beautiful setting just a block from the Malecón where the sea wall held back the Gulf of Mexico, but the area sometimes proved dangerous during hurricane season. On October 20, 1926, the most ferocious hurricane to hit Cuba in eighty years threatened the family. "As the sky turned purple-black," noted one newspaper report, "the hurricane's unusual voice was a deep and steady growl that sometimes changed to a terrifying shriek." Destructive winds reaching 130 miles an hour lashed Havana, breaking glass window in the downtown area, sweeping roofs off many houses and throwing cars and trolleys into the air as if they were toys.

On the Malecón, just a block from the Poyo home, waves twenty-five feet high sent walls of water over the seawall and across the broad boulevard. The howling winds sliced through the towering historic marble-columned monument on the boulevard commemorating the *USS Maine* (also not far from the Poyos), leaving it in two parts. The water crashed across the Malecón and into the Poyo house on Calle K. The waters rose quickly, and the family struggled to evacuate, but Nana, still recovering from giving birth to Jorge twenty days earlier, had trouble walking. Clutching her infant to her chest, the men carried her on a chair across the flooding street to a neighbor's house on slightly higher ground. Our family emerged unscathed, but more than 600 people died that day, mostly in Havana. The event remained imprinted, retold often at family gatherings.

Perhaps because of this experience, the following year my grandparents purchased a home away from the shoreline, but not in Vedado, which was too expensive and increasingly commercial. They bought one in Almendares, just west of the river of the same name within the municipal jurisdiction of Marianao. In a development called Nicanor del Campo, my grandfather built his new home at Avenida 8, between 11 and 13 (today Calle 34, between Avenidas 33 and 35). Pancho and Luisa also built a home just a block and a half away, which my grandfather probably funded. There, Nana gave birth to their fourth son, Ernesto, in 1931.

When the time came, the boys entered into a thoroughly American educational environment at Phillips School in Havana. In the 1920s and 1930s, Cuba's deepening economic dependence on the United States placed an even stronger premium on US-style education and English-language acquisition. Not surprisingly, Nana's mother-in-law, Louisa, counseled her to send the children to an English-language school, as she had done with her own. "Learn English," one school advertised, "the language of Progress. Increase your prestige and popularity—and earn more money. Never before have there been as many opportunities for men and women with knowledge of the English language." Nana did not speak English and knew nothing about the United States. Nevertheless, she saw the advantages of an American-style education and followed her mother-in-law's advice.

At the Phillips School, the four boys learned English fluently; the curriculum was modeled after North American schools, even avoiding the inflections of a Spanish-language accent. They also practiced English in the Almendares neighborhood. A district full of Americans who worked with companies Coca Cola, Swift, Trust Company of Cuba, First National City Bank, Chase Manhattan Bank and the Royal Bank of Canada, among others, the Poyo boys played with their children. They usually spoke English with their neighbors, because the Americans spoke very little or poor Spanish. Uncle Jorge's group of friends included Bob Tippett, Junior Todaro, Carlie Coleman and Chino and Gonzalo Godoy. Tippet's father had arrived in Havana in 1918 with Harris Brothers, an American import-export company. He lived in a boarding house where he met two young bachelors who worked for National City Bank and the Royal Bank of Canada. They recommended him to City Bank, and there he remained for the next thirty-five years.

Uncle Jorge's friend, Bob Tippett, studied at the German school in Havana until World War II began and then enrolled at Chandler Methodist School. Todaro's father worked for Coca Cola and Coleman's worked for Swift Company. After school, the kids gathered in a neighborhood vacant lot to play baseball; they built two fortresses from where they engaged in battle, lobbing stones at each other. The neighborhood fronted on an estuary where the water from the Almendares River ran through stands of royal palms and poincianas into the blue Straits of Florida. The children often hiked upriver into a wood thick with palms and dotted with ceibas and fruit trees from where they gathered mangos, mameys, papayas and guavas. With their air rifles, they shot mongoose, rabbit, *tocororo* and *toti* birds. They also punctured the bark of rubber trees and harvested sap that when dried could be rolled into little bouncy balls.

Other experiences contributed to the boys' Americanization. Of the Poyo brothers, only Uncle Jorge traveled to the United States before 1940. Each year the Havana chapter of the Propeller Club, an organization with numerous international branches dedicated to promoting the US Merchant Marine, held an essay contest. In 1939, Uncle Jorge won and earned a weeklong visit to New Orleans aboard a Merchant Marine vessel. He didn't remember much about the trip, only that New Orleans was not his idea of what the United States looked like. US customs also influenced household celebrations. The Poyo family did not commemorate Thanksgiving, but they certainly incorporated Santa Claus and the Christmas tree into their traditional Christmas celebrations of Noche Buena (Christmas Eve) and Día de los Reyes (January 6).

Nana had agreed to Phillips School through seventh grade, but then insisted that the boys' study at a Cuban high school. Uncle José and my father enrolled at Colegio Jesuita Nuestra Señora de Belén in the eighth grade, where they completed their secondary education. Their mother must have noticed their deteriorating sense of Cubanness, which my father confirmed when he told me that when he began his studies at Belén his vocabulary and composition skills were actually stronger in English than in Spanish. Nana, no doubt, also wanted to strengthen her children's Catholicism, which was only skin-deep. Her husband had little interest in religion, and she felt little need to go to regular Mass but wanted her children exposed to it. At Belén, the boys attended chapel every day and received a formal religious education. Although my father completed his secondary school education with a Catholic, Spanish-language, Cuban curriculum, the English language and American influences remained strong.

Uncle José graduated from Belén in 1939 and enrolled at the University of Havana, where much to his father's distress he became embroiled in student politics. His father's distrust of politicians and distaste for Cuba's turbulent political history convinced him to send his son to Georgia Institute of Technology in Atlanta for the fall 1940 term. It was common for Cuban families to send their children to the United States for university, or even secondary school; this had been their tradition since the nineteenth century, especially those involved in business and commerce. They often attended such elite schools as Harvard and Yale, but also educational institutions of all kinds. In the early twentieth century, this practice increased. Cubans knew that studying in the north gave them an advantage in a US-dominated Cuba.

In his last semester at Belén, my father knew that he too would go to the United States for college. One day, his father suggested General Motors Institute (GMI) in Flint, Michigan. What better education for a young man intending to help manage the family automobile business? As a graduate of Belén, my father could have attended any number of universities, but, like his father, he was a practical man not attracted to intellectual pursuits. He preferred a technical education and happily enrolled in GMI's unique Dealer Cooperative Program, which according to the school's yearbook provided students with "training that enabled dealerships to obtain men qualified in automotive operation, construction and repair. . . . Men thus trained accepted responsible jobs in sales promotion and automotive servicing."

The Poyo brothers grew up aligned with American economic and cultural forms that in many ways cut them off from mainstream Cuban society. In their comfortable middle-class neighborhood, they did not see the socioeconomic divisions that wracked the country, and they had only vague knowledge of the dramatic poverty that was rampant in sections of Havana and in the country's rural districts. On their occasional visits to Caimito, they saw the traditional *campesino* bamboo, reed and palm houses known as *bohíos* along the highway, but didn't fully understand the cultures and socioeconomic realities they represented. Because my father grew up around so many Americans, his self-esteem as a Cuban never evolved properly. This made it easier to let go of Cuba when the time came.

7

Of Economic Necessity

On July 25, 1941, my father boarded a ferry for Miami where Cuban-American relatives he had never met put him on a bus to Atlanta. He stayed with his brother José, who attended Georgia Tech University, and took a job for a month. After that, he continued on to Flint, Michigan and enrolled at General Motors Institute (GMI). Flint in August 1941 was both a daunting and exciting new place to be. He immersed himself in this alien working-class industrial city dotted with automobile and parts factories. When winter arrived, his excitement at seeing snowfall for the first time gave way to the stark reality of months of freezing temperatures. My father completed his first semester at GMI uneventfully, except for Japan's shocking attack. Since he lacked the funds necessary to return to Cuba for Christmas break, he worked at GMI and spent time with a friend who invited him to his family's home in Detroit.

He was uncertain what the war would mean for his studies, but this quickly became irrelevant when a Western Union cable from his mother told him that his father had fallen gravely ill and that he should get home as quickly as possible. My father and his brother set out on their respective journeys. He arranged a flight to Miami while Uncle José spent a restless night at the bus station in Atlanta waiting for his winter-weather delayed coach. Just the week before, their parents had driven from Santiago to Havana to celebrate the Christmas and New Year's season with Pancho and Luisa, their sons Jorge and Ernesto, and Nana's family from Caimito. They enjoyed Noche Buena together, no doubt talking about the business in Santiago, the war, their childrens' schools and their sons in the United States. Later in the evening, my grandfather felt ill and developed a fever. The next day things took a turn for the worst and my grandmother called the family physician.

Dr. Enrique Tasis Varona diagnosed malaria. A common ailment in Cuba, especially in Santiago where they had been living since the summer, the disease initially did not cause much alarm, but symptoms worsened. The doctor realized my grandfather had contracted a particularly virulent form of the disease and, during the next several days, complications affected his liver. Uncle Jorge remembered that his father looked jaundiced. "He called me to his bedside . . . and did recognize me, spoke my name and tried to talk, but was very agitated and incoherent, possibly somewhat delirious." Uncle Jorge also remembered Dr. Tasis' concerned manner. Nana sat with her husband through New Year's Day and watched helplessly as he came in and out of consciousness. He died on Saturday, January 3.

Even though my father and Uncle José had not yet arrived, the family made plans for the funeral immediately, which according to custom and law would take place within twenty-four hours. Employees of the José C. Vior Mortuary arrived at Pancho's house, where my grandparents had been staying, and supervised the preparation of the body and home for the evening vigil. Nana, Jorge and Ernesto, accompanied by Pancho and Luisa, sat with relatives and friends who visited the home, including the family from Caimito. Reverend P. Quevedo, a Jesuit priest, offered a service, while Nana prayed the rosary. Only the brothers who lived in Mexico—Panchito, Luis and Laureano—did not attend.

At 10 am Sunday morning, mourners arrived at Pancho's home and accompanied the casket a couple of miles to the family plot in Cementerio Colón, on the east side of the Almendares River in Vedado, which I would visit so many years later. It was a great tragedy for the Poyo family, but life went on as usual, an obvious but sometimes surprisingly difficult realization for those left behind. On that terrible Sunday, the headline of the *Diario de la Marina*, Havana's oldest and largest newspaper, reported that the Japanese had been bombarding Corregidor Island in the Philippines, where General Douglas

McArthur was holding out against advancing enemy forces. Advertisers announced their specials for the upcoming celebration of Día de los Reyes, with the famous El Encanto department store announcing, "The Kings have at El Encanto the books that children most like."

The sports page reported Almendares baseball club had defeated Habana the previous day. With the outstanding play of Jimmy Bell, Almendares remained at the top of the baseball standings. The Gran Casino Nacional reminded customers that it was open from three in the afternoon to three in morning, except on Mondays, and El Gato Negro announced the first lottery of the year for the 10th with a prize of 50,000 pesos. While Cuba read about momentous international events and local goings on, friends and acquaintances saw the death announcement on the bottom right hand corner of page seventeen and not only mourned for José Francisco but also for a family that would be seriously tested by his premature passing.

Uncle José reached Miami on Sunday morning and boarded an early afternoon Pan American flight to Havana. He learned the tragic news from his girlfriend, who met him at the airport and drove him to his grandparents' home, where the family gathered after the interment that morning. My father reached Miami the next morning and caught a flight to Havana. He learned the news from his mother and older brother, who met him at the airport. Neither son had the chance to see their father's body or grieve his death at a funeral. This they did alone in the privacy of their thoughts, in their own ways.

As breath faded from my grandfather on January 3, 1942, the life the Poyo family knew also slipped away, and things changed rapidly. Just forty-six years old, he had died in his prime. His career had just entered a new stage, and he was on a path to establishing an independent family business that he hoped would guarantee a future for his wife and four sons. He had worked hard to create the opportunity, but it was not to be. An early English-language education and connections to American businessmen had made possible a successful career. His honesty, dedication and persistence also contributed. He balanced a reserved, somewhat stern and perhaps even authoritarian manner with a strong and loving commitment to his family and an ability to engage people comfortably.

The family faced an immediate economic crisis. After a little over fifteen years working as vice-president of Ross Corporation, my grandfather died without savings or investments and left only a $5,000 General Motors life insurance policy. While he certainly earned a salary well above the Cuban average, the resources went out as fast as they came. He bought a house for himself and one for his parents. Pancho may have had a small pension from his employment in city government but could not have purchased a house in Almendares without my grandfather's help. Along with the rest of Cuba's middle class, the children attended private schools. My grandfather's salary as vice-president supported a Cuban middle-class lifestyle, but nothing more.

The family's sudden economic crisis in early 1942 reflected Cuba's economic dependency on the United States. Cuba never developed a strong, diversified economy capable of creating a secure national bourgeoisie. The economy was set up to entice foreign investors and allow them to export their profits, local entrepreneurs were an afterthought, this created a situation where often there were more incentives for Cubans to leave the country than to stay. My family now faced circumstances that forced a northward gaze.

Happily married and living a comfortable life, Nana now faced a frightening challenge. Her changing fortunes forced her to make decisions she could never have imagined, but her origins in Caimito and the Cuban countryside gave her the strength and practical down-to-earth perspective that allowed her to transition with grace from comfortable to struggling. Never having worked outside the home, she knew that few job prospects existed for her in Havana. Her two oldest sons would also have difficulty finding decent-paying work in Cuba. They needed to complete their educations, and she could no longer afford the private schools fifteen-year-old Jorge and ten-year-old Ernesto attended. She was not about to enroll them in the deficient public school system.

A woman of strong character not prone to falling into fatalistic passivity, after the funeral she immediately huddled with her two oldest sons to chart a future. Uncle José, as the eldest, took on the role of family head, a time-honored tradition in Hispanic cultures. He suggested moving the family to the United States, and the three agreed. The family would establish their home base in Atlanta while José continued university studies at Georgia Tech. My father returned to GMI in February. During March, Uncle José and Nana settled the family's business affairs in Santiago, left their Havana house leased for Pancho and Louisa to oversee and embarked on a new life.

~ ~ ~

My father's Cuban passport shows that he departed for Flint on February 18, 1942 with a seven-month student visa. He never used it again. Soon after Pearl Harbor, my father and Uncle José, both in the United States, had received letters from their father saying he planned to register the entire family at the US embassy. Even though he was born in Key West, my grandfather had never taken an American passport or even registered as a US citizen. When the war broke out, my grandfather's bosses in New York suggested he take out a US passport to ensure unrestricted business travel. He pointed out the advantages of American citizenship to his sons, but also reminded them they would be subject to the draft. He registered the family at the US consulate in Havana on December 23, 1941 just before he fell ill. When the US Department of State confirmed the family's citizenship registration on March 9, 1942, my father applied for an American passport, as did the entire family.

Raising children had kept Nana busy, and she had only occasionally traveled outside Cuba. In 1935 and 1936, she had accompanied my grandfather on business trips to New York and, in 1939, they had taken a vacation to visit his three brothers in Mexico. They drove their car onto a ferry, the *SS Cuba,* to Key West on January 31, 1939 and took the just completed highway that connected Key West to the mainland south of Miami. From there they drove all the way to Laredo, quite an adventure at that time, when superhighways did not crisscross the United States. They continued to Mexico City and visited with Luis. Then on to Guadalajara, where they stayed with Laureano and Panchito. In March, they crossed back into the United States and returned to Havana the same way they had come.

With only this limited experience of travel, Nana immigrated with her sons to the United States. In Miami, they caught a bus to New Brunswick, Georgia and stayed with friends while Uncle José made their living arrangements in Atlanta. Jorge and Ernesto began school in that Georgia coastal town. In the summer, the family rented a three-bedroom duplex at 691 Juniper in Atlanta not far from Georgia Tech, where José resumed his studies. Jorge started his second year of high school at Boys High (Henry Grady today) and Ernesto enrolled in a nearby elementary school. Despite not speaking English, Nana found a job at Woolworth's department store in downtown Atlanta, attaching price tags to merchandise heading for the sales floor. She also received income from her rental home in Havana and supplemented her income by sub-leasing one of her bedrooms to two Cuban students attending Georgia Tech. Jorge and Ernesto slept in bunk beds in the other bedroom.

Once installed in her home, Nana found friends. She had not attended church regularly in Cuba, but discovered a Latino community at nearby Sacred Heart Catholic Church, where a small group of Cubans, Peruvians, Mexicans and others, including students from Georgia Tech, gathered for Mass and social events. This became an important community for her as she adapted to her new environment. Almost thirty years later when I arrived in the United States for college, Nana still lived in that same neighborhood, and we walked daily down the street to a small Cuban bodega for groceries.

During the month and a half my father remained in Havana after his father's funeral, he pondered the fragility of life and how one's destiny could change so unexpectedly. Not only had he lost his father at a young age, but his plan to return to Cuba and work in the family-owned automobile dealership was no more, and with it, the family's entire sense of security was gone.

My father's frame-of-reference changed. No longer an international student, he became an immigrant and refocused his attention on GMI. The school began in 1919 as the School of Automobile Trades and in the early 1920s developed a "cooperative approach" to technical education that combined alternating periods of full-time classroom instruction with related work in automotive plants. The two-year program's slogan stated, "Earn While you Learn—the Trained Man Wins." The school's cooperative program appealed to General Motors, which in 1926 took over the school, extended its services to all GM units and renamed it General Motors Institute.

My father had a reserved manner and congenial personality, like his own father, which allowed him to negotiate social situations easily. He fit in easily at GMI and even joined the Alpha Delta fraternity. He was the only Latino in the fraternity and participated fully in its activities, including playing on the softball team. My father inherited his father's and grandfather's baseball talents and at Belén school in Havana was among the team's best hitters. He had also played on the Belén basketball team, but always acknowledged the limitations of his 5'7" stature for the game. Anyway, he preferred baseball. These athletic skills helped him gain acceptance in his new world.

In 1943, my father had not seen his girlfriend in Havana for a year; she seemed to him a distant memory when my parents met at a fraternity party. They were an unlikely couple. He was from a middle-class Cuban family and she was from a working-class Midwestern family. Her friendship and company gave him comfort during this difficult period in his life, and he adapted to her world of friends and family.

My mother had spent her first ten years in a poor farming community in southeast Missouri but grew up in working-class Flint. Born in the tiny village of Painton, Stoddard County, on February 17, 1923, my mother's family struggled to make a living as "dirt farmers," according to my father's disparaging description. Her mother's Patterson family and father's Darnell family had lived in southeast Missouri for at least two generations. Earl Vanoy Darnell, her father, was born in Puxico in 1891, some fifty miles to the west of Painton and her mother in Whitewater, Missouri in 1904. He seemed to go from job to job, but one such job was foreman at a planing mill in Sikeston that processed lumber. Originally from Illinois, his father James B. Darnell kept a restaurant in Dexter City, and his mother Iva was a housewife, originally from Indiana. Earl married and had a son, Elton, in 1915, and in 1919 married a second time. Just two years after that, in 1921, he married my grandmother, Edna Patterson, who was eighteen at the time. She embraced Elton as her own and had Geraldine in 1923 and Robert in 1926.

My mother refused to speak about her parents' troubled marriage that ended in divorce. She volunteered only that in 1933 her mother took Robert, Elton and herself from where they lived in Morehouse, Stoddard County, Missouri to Flint. My grandmother Edna's parents, William Patterson and Mary Irvin, in 1920 had joined the ongoing migration of impoverished people from the rural areas of the South looking for work in the industrial north. They found work in Flint's automobile plants. As a child, my mother and her brothers occasionally visited their father in Missouri but otherwise they had little contact with the Darnell side of the family. When her father died in St. Louis of a heart attack in 1946, my mother drove there with a friend and her brother Robert for the funeral, but never talked about the experience or about her father. I pressed her, but she said she just could not speak, that the painful memories made her sad.

She had a much fonder relationship with family on her maternal side. I remember her grandfather William Patterson, a tall and quite thin man, when we visited from Bogotá sometime in the mid-1950s. A stepfather named George Strong and his mother Betheny Strong had raised him. William had a brother James and half-sister, my mother's great-aunt Opal Strong, whom she saw occasionally when visiting her father in Missouri. According to my mother, William Patterson's father (my great-great grandfather) was half Native American. William's wife, Mary Irvin, also hailed from Missouri.

Like her father, Grandmother Edna was tall, with a strong character. I don't remember ever having any long conversations with her, but she could be kind one moment and stern another: hot and cold. I especially remember her crackling laugh. On arriving in Flint with her three children, she found work at the AC Spark Plug plant during an era of great labor activism. The same year she arrived in Flint, a series of strikes shook the auto industry, including at AC with its heavily female workforce. In the 1920s and 1930s, men dominated the auto industry; women represented 5% in motor vehicle plants, 10% in body plants and 20% in auto parts factories. Some parts plants employed thousands of women, sometimes constituting a majority of the work force. The AC plant in Flint employed the largest number of women in the city. Women tended to be concentrated in jobs that required meticulous handwork, such as assembling parts, sewing and preparing upholstery for automobile seats, finishing and polishing metal, small press operation and inspection. The auto industry considered women attractive employees in some jobs because they received less pay then men. In 1925, women earned on average 47 cents an hour compared to the 73 cents earned by men. In Flint's AC Spark Plug operation, women received the lowest pay of all autoworkers. Despite modest wages, my grandmother provided for her children and kept a close-knit family.

My mother kept an old newspaper clipping with a photograph of herself in her teenage years preparing Christmas Seals mailings as a volunteer with the Genesee County Tuberculosis Association. My grandmother had contracted tuberculosis in Flint and spent about ten months at a sanatorium in Pontiac when my mother was perhaps ten. She lived with her grandparents during that frightening period, which became especially scary when her doctors collapsed one of her mother's badly damaged lungs. My grandmother eventually recovered and she cared for her remaining lung quite diligently. Whenever my parents and my mother's two brothers, who smoked incessantly, gathered for a visit in Michigan, everyone stayed outside, which I thought strange, since my parents always smoked even in cars with the windows rolled up. That's how I learned my grandmother had only one lung, which at eight years old left an impression on me. For a number of years, she remained at work but then retired to Clio, a nearby town. In 1940, she married Russell Root, who worked as a store clerk; they divorced nine years later. A final, lasting marriage began in 1950 to a Canadian immigrant to Flint: Oscar Gorsaliz.

My mother remembered fondly Flint Central High School, where she enrolled in 1937. Her Commercial I curriculum diploma says she learned business and secretarial skills, including bookkeeping and typing. During her final semester in high school, she took a job as secretary at a retail store in Flint owned by H.W. Schaeffer on 134 W. First Street. After graduation, she remained there, avoiding the more grueling work in the auto and parts plants. She grew close to the Schaeffer family and enjoyed her work, about which she often reminisced as her only experience with paid work.

Photographs in my mother's photo collection show my parents spending much time together undisturbed by their significant class and cultural differences, but in the summer of 1943, my father moved to Indianapolis for the cooperative or hands-on aspects of his education at Allison Division of General Motors. GMI had discontinued the dealership program due to the war, so my father learned to be an air mechanic and instructor. During this time, he also expected his draft notice. Certainly, his fathers' death, the loss of family income, his mother's resettlement in Atlanta and accompanying disruptions during the previous year and a half weighed heavily on him, but his decision to become a US citizen also brought him face to face with decisions regarding wartime obligations to his new country.

In love and feeling alone and naturally anxious about what the war might bring, my father proposed marriage. My mother-to-be agreed, traveled to Indianapolis, and they married on August 7, 1943 in a civil ceremony solemnized by a Marion County Justice of the Peace. In a letter to her mother several days later, written on Hotel Lincoln letterhead, where they spent their honeymoon, my mother said, "I'm so happy, and I love my husband very, very much. He is so sweet." She also gave her mother the address of the apartment they moved to later that day: Mrs. Sergio Poyo, 1327 Park Ave., Indianapolis. "Sounds peculiar doesn't it?" she noted, referring to her new name. They had known each other for about eight months, but they were not the only ones during wartime who accelerated relationships and marriage.

A month later, on September 11, 1943 my father enlisted in the Reserve Corps of the Army of the United States as an Aviation Cadet. Earlier in the year, Uncle José had done the same, and in 1944, after completing high school, Uncle Jorge joined the Navy, leaving only Uncle Ernesto with Nana in Atlanta. Like my father, José joined the Air Corps for pilot training but ended up working instead with the Counter Intelligence Corps. The military took advantage of his Spanish-speaking abilities and stationed him in Mexico. Just seventeen, Jorge signed up with the Navy and went to Great Lakes, Michigan for boot camp. Assigned to the hospital corps, Jorge trained at the San Diego Naval Base, where he graduated as a hospital corpsman. From there he stationed at Pensacola, which was a center for naval aviation in the southeast. At first, he worked in a clinical laboratory on the base and then as an assistant in a medical research laboratory on aviation altitude studies. Uncle Jorge recalled returning home to Atlanta on leave to find his mother had displayed a military pennant with three stars indicating the family's contributions to the war effort in the large bay window facing the street. Although fearful of what might happen to her sons, Nana expressed pride and commented to Jorge about what an unexpected journey they had taken. Still too young to join the military during World War II, Ernesto joined the Air Force reserve in 1953.

In less than two years, my father's status changed dramatically from a Cuban student training abroad and learning how to help his father run a distributorship to a newly married US citizen preparing to go to war. Military training introduced my parents to the full flavor of US culture and geography, from the Midwest, to the South, to the West. My mother had rarely traveled outside Flint in her youth except to southeast Missouri to visit her father. After my father's induction in Indianapolis, he proceeded to Jefferson Barracks, Missouri for boot camp with the 35th Training Group. In December 1943, he began Army Air Corp cadet training at Middle Georgia College in Cochran.

In the middle of January, my mother joined him in Cochran, where she rented a room in the house of the A.A. Holcombe family.

My father lived in the college dormitories that now served as military barracks and trained while my mother kept busy doing a variety of things, including making friends with other wives of cadet trainees, planning dinners for my father on his days off and even helping Mrs. Holcombe with her dress shop. She also kept up a constant correspondence with her family and friends, especially her mother. Besides describing what she and my father were doing, her letters inquired about how her brothers Bob and Elton were doing in the military and why she did not get more letters.

She also struggled to convince her mother, who had relied on her a great deal, that they would both be fine in spite of all the changes in their lives. My mother soon became pregnant and in a letter to her mother in the middle of March, she said that she and one of the other wives took walks by the college. "I have to do something, as I'm getting so fat I can't walk. . . . Sergio, said he would have to send me home in a cattle car." They may have been exaggerating somewhat, since she was probably only about two months along, but she returned to Flint to live with her very pleased mother sometime before October 20 to give birth to a son, Sergio, Jr.

Second Lt. Sergio Poyo, in the meantime, moved on to Maxwell Field, in Montgomery, Alabama before beginning navigator training in San Marcos, Texas on November 16. My mother and Sergio, Jr. joined him soon after, and they all remained in San Marcos until he received his navigator degree on April 7, 1945 and entered active duty. Sergio then went to Fort Bragg, North Carolina to undergo advanced navigational training at Pope Field before spending time at Shaw Field, Sumter, South Carolina. Finally, he arrived at his active duty assignment at George Field in Lawrenceville, Illinois, with the 805th AAF Base Unit with the I Troop Carrier Unit, headed for the Pacific theatre.

As my father underwent final training, my mother expressed her fears to her mother. "I'm certainly gonna miss my honey when he goes overseas," she said. "And I'm sure gonna make these last few weeks or months count so if he doesn't come back to Sergie & I. . . . Don't worry, Mom, I'm just getting hardened to what may happen, after all, we have to face that chance, and although I have no doubts [that he will] be back, you still have to live in the present, and that is just what I'm doing." She concluded saying, "I'm so thankful that I have my baby boy, and I think he is what gives me so much faith. . . . He gets sweeter & sweeter every day, and he is sure another Sergio."

Fate intervened. As his unit prepared for deployment, my father fell ill with appendicitis, which kept him off active service during the summer of 1945. While still recovering, on August 7 my parents and the country learned of the devastating atomic bomb dropped on Hiroshima, and a second several days later on Nagasaki. The Japanese government surrendered unconditionally; the war came to a rapid and unexpected end. My father nevertheless still expected deployment, perhaps to Japan when he returned to duty on September 21. "His days of leisure are over," my mother commented to her mother. "I guess," she continued, "Sergio will be overseas by x-mas, but I still keep hoping for a miracle." A miracle indeed, it came in the form of demobilization. After completing navigation school in Texas, Sergio had been appointed and commissioned as a "temporary" 2nd Lieutenant in the US Army, who would serve "at the pleasure of the President of the United States for the time being, and for the duration of the war and six months thereafter unless sooner terminated." Much to my mother's delight, his separation came earlier than expected, on November 9, 1945.

My father never faced combat, nor even went overseas, but his experience in the military nevertheless left an enduring imprint. The certainty of heading to the Pacific theater sometime in the final third of 1945 provoked meditations on his mortality, and the unexpected close to the war brought great relief. "If it wasn't for the atomic bomb, you probably wouldn't be here," he declared years later in a conversation with me when I questioned the morality of using atomic weaponry to end the war against Japan. We had been discussing a national controversy generated by an exhibition at the Smithsonian Institution's Air and Space Museum in 1994. The exhibit, built around the Enola Gay, the aircraft that had delivered the bomb over Hiroshima, had disturbed veterans' groups around the country, with whom my father agreed. They took the museum to task for including in the exhibit the viewpoints of some who considered the bombs unnecessary to end the war. The controversy caused the Smithsonian to substantially revise the exhibit. Though my father rarely spoke about the war years, he did feel strongly about his time in the military and the rationale for using the bomb. He thought that without the bomb, he would certainly have participated in the inevitable assault on Japan and perhaps lost his life, which gave him little sympathy for those, including me, who questioned whether the use of atomic weapons was ethical.

With wartime demobilization, my parents returned to Indianapolis, where my father completed the cooperative aspects of the now reinstated GMI automotive dealer program. In August 1946, he received his GMI degree with a specialty in automobile engineering and dealership service and maintenance. My father immediately put to use his father's superb reputation among the executives of the General Motors Overseas Operations in New York and contacted Morris Clark, the General Manager of the Foreign Distributorship Division (FDD). It was Clark who five years earlier had encouraged my grandfather to take charge of the General Motors dealership in Santiago and suggested that Sergio attend GMI. Clark now offered Sergio his first professional job.

My parents and little Sergio moved to Fair Lawn, New Jersey and found a house on Sycamore Street. The war had challenged established notions of gender relations as women had gone to work in industries during the war, but returning soldiers expected things to go back to normal, and at least for a while they mostly did. Women returned to traditional domestic settings, and post-war economic growth and affluence made this focus on domesticity possible. Families bought homes often with the aid of the GI Bill, purchased the latest appliances, television sets and cars. New forms of advertising promoted the country's growing consumerism and materialistic appetites. All of this was contained within an ideological Cold War worldview that demanded conformity to American myths, including the critical role of the traditional family in sustaining the social order.

Whatever growing up in a working-class, labor-union family in Flint may have meant to my mother, she entered a solid middle-class lifestyle and accepted my father's corporate, political and patriarchal values. While he took the bus to his job in New York City each day, she settled into life as an American housewife with little Sergio and developed her network of friends in Fair Lawn, New Jersey.

My father worked at the FDD offices across the Hudson River in Manhattan on the second floor of the Argonaut building on the corner of Broadway and 57th Street, opposite the General Motors Building. The job paid $250 per month and involved providing automotive technical training and support for the service departments of foreign distributors in Latin America, which put his GMI training to good use and required extensive travel throughout the region. In 1948, Uncle José left the military, joined my parents in Fair Lawn, and also found a job with FDD in "single car sales" for Latin American customers who ordered vehicles directly from New York.

Shortly thereafter, Uncle Jorge moved in with them for several months. After his stint in the Navy, he enrolled at Emory University and became the first in our family line to achieve a university degree. During his training in the Business Administration program, Uncle Jorge took a course with a retired general who had overseen tank production in England during World War II. He spoke to the general about his father's automobile career in Cuba and, when the time arrived, the general contacted his friend, the president of General Motors Acceptance Corporation (GMAC), the corporation's credit branch, to recommend my uncle for a job. Uncle Jorge got the job, and his first assignment in 1949 was at the New York office for orientation. The three brothers commuted together each day across the George Washington Bridge to Manhattan.

My father always said that his Americanized life in Cuba and his father's untimely death defined his destiny. Born into an already bicultural family in Havana and socialized to believe that economic links with the United States provided security, he never questioned the path that opened before him. Once in the United States, his citizenship, marriage to an American, service in the Army Air Corps and post-war employment solidified his patriotism and sense of belonging to a country he had just recently adopted as his own.

8

An Unexpected Turn

"ARRIVED OKAY KIDS ARE FINE WILL WRITE SOON LOVE." My mother sent this Western Union cable to her mother in Flint on April 6, 1951 after a harrowing and seemingly endless Avianca flight on a four-engine DC-4 propeller aircraft from New York, via Miami and Panama, to Bogotá. My parents would not have chosen the life this move represented, but later, in hindsight, they said they would not have traded it for anything. I'm thankful for that.

Only in the 1990s did I learn why we had ended up living outside the United States. My father, I assumed, had always made affirmative choices in his life. He had never indicated otherwise. One evening I told him about some of my troubling experiences when I arrived in the United States to attend university, but more about that later. He listened and understood, and for the first time told me about his own early years in the United States. Settling in and working in New Jersey, he expected to live the "American Dream"—he was now an American, after all, but matters took an unexpected turn and instead of New Jersey, we ended up in Bogotá.

⁂

My father remembered a particularly distasteful experience during a stay with his brother in Atlanta in July 1941 before entering General Motors Institute. He worked in a warehouse for a month, with an African American work partner. White supervisors routinely demeaned and humiliated him, which my father could not understand.

My father didn't know that US history had always been deeply marked by race and ethnic discrimination and exclusion, and confusing, competing territorial and racial definitions of nationhood. He didn't know that the United States made distinctions between European-descended citizens and non-white inhabitants that became the litmus test for full acceptance into American society nor did he know that many southern and eastern European immigrants had also faced discrimination, but eventually assimilated and became part of the so-called "white" world this reality also marginalized people of Hispanic backgrounds. Mexican Americans since colonial times, and Cubans and Puerto Ricans since the late nineteenth century faced discrimination. Even white Latin Americans, who sometimes received a certain dispensation for their lighter complexion if they agreed to identify as Americans, could not avoid the condescending views of white Americans. Negative attitudes toward Latin Americans based on race and culture, or more generally, Hispanic civilization, had a long tradition in the United States.

Family members had earlier recognized these kinds of prejudices in the United States. In working-class Key West, José Dolores and Pancho saw first-hand the racial hatred of the Reconstruction and Jim Crow eras. They championed the need for Cuba to integrate fully its people of color. My ancestors knew that many white Cubans possessed similar racist attitudes toward Afro Cubans, which they observed in Cuba when they returned after independence. Nevertheless, in time this family awareness and sensitivity about racism had slipped away. As our family joined American circles in Havana, they were increasingly isolated from the Cuban working classes and people of color. My father and his brothers lived protected and isolated childhoods and adolescences in white neighborhoods, this was the rarified world inhabited by Cuban elites and their American employers who had unapologetically racist attitudes. My father never heard his parents or other family members speak positively or negatively about Afro Cubans. Cubans of color were simply out of sight and mind, and so it shocked him when he saw the humiliation his work partner suffered in Atlanta.

෴ ෴ ෴

It did not occur to my father that what African Americans in Atlanta had been made to suffer in 1941 people of Hispanic background might also suffer. As he strategized his own assimilation into American culture, he only slowly learned that acceptance had as much to do with the values and attitudes of the host society as with the immigrant's willingness to adapt. Just because he was willing to assimilate did not mean he was welcome.

My father first perceived negative attitudes towards Latinos while in the US military. During World War II, it has been estimated that 350,000 to perhaps 750,000 Latinos served in the US armed forces. My father overheard negative comments about Latinos from service men who had no idea he was Cuban. After the war, he saw, first hand, the fierce anti-Puerto Rican attitudes in New York and other cities of the Northeast. At some point, he realized that Latinos of all classes and races struggled for respect and equal opportunities in the United States. He even detected anti-Latino attitudes among my mother's friends and often heard them use the word "spic" when speaking of Puerto Ricans. They claimed not to consider him to be in that category, since they were friends, but they had no compunction about using such terms, even in his presence.

What my father saw and heard made him uncomfortable but inspired him to work harder to become part of the American mainstream. His full immersion experience, light skin, fluent English and lack of an accent helped him fit in. No one ever questioned his military service in white units, and he later spoke fondly of his experience. He could usually "pass" as an Anglo American. As an immigrant trying to carve out a life for himself and his family as a businessman in New York City, my father spent little time pondering life's inequities, except how to avoid them. If he could avoid discrimination, he would. With a wife and child to worry about, he didn't want unnecessary, and for him, avoidable, handicaps. Certainly, the practical means for achieving assimilation outweighed any thought of challenging societal attitudes. How different his life would have been with dark skin.

Because he was on his way to being fully accepted as an American, my father did not seek out other Cubans in the New York area. In 1940, 7,410 Cubans lived in New York, overwhelmingly of working-class background, a number that doubled by 1950. Although a predominantly white community, the significant black and mulatto component in some ways defined Cuban identity through their contributions to the city's Latin music scene. My father knew of the Latin community in New York, but did not engage with it. As a white, aspiring middle-class Cuban living in suburban New Jersey and trying to find work as a professional in the automobile industry, he rarely encountered and, perhaps, actively avoided the multiracial working-class communities across the Hudson, in the South Bronx, Washington Heights, East Harlem and other ethnic enclaves in the city. Had he engaged with Cuban communities in some way, his attitudes about assimilation may have taken a different form, but, as it was, he encountered few Cubans. He spent most of his time with his brothers, José, Jorge and my mother in Fair Lawn, a suburb with few Latinos. Outside the family, my mother's English-speaking white American friends constituted their social network.

One day, my father and his brother José got into an argument on their bus ride into Manhattan. They normally conversed in Spanish, but more and more Uncle José realized that when he spoke to his brother in Spanish on the bus, my father replied in English.

"Why do you speak to me in English?" José asked accusingly. "Are you ashamed of being Cuban and speaking your language?" My father angrily replied, "I'm not ashamed of being Cuban, but American society certainly holds it against me."

He went on to tell his brother that he did not want to be mistaken for Puerto Rican, not because he had anything against Puerto Ricans, but because of the ways white New Yorkers treated them. This was his strategy for coping with anti-Latino prejudice.

Assimilation strategies even extended to naming children. Naming often speaks to parents' aspirations for their children's identity. My mother had named their first son Sergio, Jr. At military training, my father learned of this only after the birth. He would have preferred an American name for his son, but this was resolved by calling him

Serge, which was the way my father introduced himself within a few years of arriving in the United States. My parents had hoped that I, their second child, would be a daughter, who they intended to call Geraldine, after my mother. Instead, I appeared, so I became Gerald, a name that remains strange and foreign to me even after sixty-eight years. It has never spoken to my sense of self. I just made do and adopted the nickname Jerry that an American ninth-grade science teacher in Argentina gave me. It caught on with classmates. She said it sounded less formal, and shortly everyone called me Jerry at school, except my Argentine coach and math teacher, who simply referred to me as Poyo or Poyito. At home, I remained Gerald, or Gerito, a nickname from Colombia that also stuck.

Much later, when I began traveling to Cuba, everyone wanted to call me Gerardo or simply Poyo. They did not understand why I had an English name in the first place and, like me, thought my given name was somehow inauthentic. The next two children born in Bogotá also received American names: Cynthia and Jeffrey. My parents, especially my father, determined that we would be Americans, not Latinos. Over the next few years, my father and his brothers became Serge, Joe, George and Ernie. In fact, Uncle Jorge once said that he had always counseled Latin Americans who settled in the United States to Anglicize their names as a way of announcing their willingness to assimilate, but he acknowledged it didn't necessarily change attitudes toward them.

Assimilation, my father reasoned, would pay off with a good job and life in a New Jersey suburban community, where they would buy a home, live happily and raise their children. His first professional job traveling in Latin America, especially to the Andean countries, he found interesting and even exhilarating, but he saw it as a first step toward securing a managerial job at a car dealership in New Jersey or New York. Perhaps one day he would fulfill his father's dream of owning such a business, but things did not work out. He was unable to find work consistent with his automobile dealership education and training. Puzzled, he could not figure it out at first, but then noticed that when the subject of his surname surfaced in interviews, more questions about his background followed. Potential employers, it seemed to him, lost interest in his application when they learned he was Cuban.

My father recognized prejudice, but he resisted this knowledge at first. Frustrated and disappointed, he finally acknowledged the reality to himself, and perhaps to my mother, that his Spanish name, which he would not hide or deny, trumped his willingness to conform to American ways. He never dared articulate it aloud until one of my visits to Savannah after my mother's death. As a proud American, it pained him to openly acknowledge the nation's warts, which I had always been so fond of pointing out to him. What I impatiently judged to be the country's long-established and seemingly, insurmountable racist character, he attributed to the difficulty if not impossibility of overcoming human flaws. They simply had to be recognized and negotiated as best possible. His reluctance to speak fell away, and he told me more.

Not having access to the work opportunities his training had prepared him for in the United States, he improvised. He heard one day in 1948 from his boss, Morris K. Clark, about the inauguration of a new building for Ambar Motors, General Motor's dealership in Havana. After the war, Amadeo Barletta had returned to Havana from Argentina, established Ambar Motors and was looking for good employees. My father inquired and with Clark's full endorsement accepted an invitation to interview in Havana.

He toured the state-of-the-art Ambar Motors facility, particularly focusing on his specialty, the service component. The shop had a comfortable waiting room and a courtesy car service to take clients home or to their offices while they waited for their cars to be serviced or repaired. The shop operated twenty-four hours and included a towing service that could dispatch repairmen or tow trucks at any time. My father appreciated Ambar Motor's motto: "Service always, and constantly improving."

Barletta also flew my mother and Sergio, Jr. to Havana so she could see the city for herself and meet the Poyo extended family, especially grandparents Pancho and Louisa, whom my father had not seen since he had left Cuba in 1942. My mother also visited the neighborhood where my father grew up, as well as Belén school and other places important to his formative years. In reading the English-language *The Havana Post*, my mother learned about the very American social environment in the city, including an active Woman's Club, an American Club and a Country Club with a Sunday supper dance. My mother immediately liked what she saw. After a few days, my father accepted the job, but negotiated for a higher salary. The Italian told my father not to worry about the money, because he took care of his employees. When my father persisted, Barletta became impatient and suggested that if he did not like the offer, perhaps he should spend a few more years in New York and contact him when he was ready.

Years later, my father reflected on this critical juncture, which determined the direction of his career. Despite a willingness to return to Havana and work in a thoroughly modern distributorship, he felt uncomfortable with Barletta, who he felt represented a traditional Latin American (or perhaps Mediterranean) business model based on a *patrón* relationship. The *patrón* model insisted on a strong and dependent personal tie between the employee and his employer, with no room for negotiation or questioning on the part of the employee. In this model, a contract salary did not define the employment relationship. The personal commitment of the employer to the employee and his family did. This included awarding end-of-year bonuses, celebrating birthdays and enjoying holidays with the "company family." In return for these benefits, the employer expected absolute loyalty and commitment to his interests. My father had seen some of this in his father's relationship with his employer Ross.

Having developed an independent streak and been trained in American capitalist methods, my father declined the job in Havana in favor of "modern" corporate business values. He and my mother returned to New York and never again entertained the idea of working for Barletta. In later years, my uncles José and Jorge both considered working with Barletta but came to the same conclusion as their brother. My father's fateful decision tore him, once and forever, from what was left of his Cuban identity and probably saved the family from the traumas of exile and displacement that would befall Cubans aligned with American interests during the Revolution a decade later.

During the summer of 1950, my father set out on a several month journey to Colombia, Ecuador, Bolivia, Peru and Chile, leaving my six-month pregnant mother alone to care for five-year-old "Sergie," as he was called. He felt guilty and, although he returned in time for my birth on September 15, he was now more determined than ever to find a job that did not require travel for months at a time. Just then, Morris Clark learned of another possibility with William A. McCarthy, a long-time FDD sales representative who had worked in Mexico and Colombia and had recently purchased a Chevrolet, Buick and GM Truck distributorship in Bogotá: Compañía General Automotriz. McCarthy needed a sales and a service manager, and Clark recommended my father and Uncle José. Ready for a change, my uncle stepped up first and accepted the position of sales manager, departing for Colombia in late 1950. Shortly thereafter Uncle Jorge left for Puerto Rico, where he began training as a "finance man" with General Motors Acceptance Corporation. After his training in San Juan, Uncle Jorge worked in Caracas for five years and then Brazil for ten before heading to Europe, where he completed his career. My father followed his brother José's lead and also accepted the job in Bogotá as service manager with a more satisfactory salary than Barletta had offered. At the same time, he launched the family into a transnational life that would affect us all to the very core. My father believed the job provided good possibilities for upward mobility, perhaps leading, eventually, to managing and even owning the dealership.

Uncle José greeted us at El Techo airport. Sitting on a plateau in the Andes Mountains in the middle of two ranges at 8,600 feet above sea level, Bogotá had only 700,000 people when we arrived. Today, it has a population of eight million. He took us to an apartment owned by the Compañía General Automotriz, where we lived for some months before moving into a roomy house that was striking for its modern look and numerous windows, which led my brother Sergio to dub it the "glass house." It was located in the newer, upscale northeast part of town. Within a couple of years, Uncle José married Colombian Consuelo "Connie" Leongómez and they had four sons. Our families socialized and remained close. My brother Sergio attended the American school, and so did I when I turned six, while my mother cared for my younger siblings, Cindy and Jeffrey, both born in Bogotá. She also oversaw the housekeepers who cleaned, ironed and cooked, and she pitched in with social obligations at the dealership, including organizing and hosting the annual Christmas Party for the children of the service department employees.

My memories of Bogotá are a series of disconnected episodes, not a narrative story line. I was still young. At the dealership service area, I inserted a coin and I pulled out an ice-cold Coca Cola bottle from the red dispenser. I rollicked in the swimming pools at the San Andrés and Los Lagartos golf clubs while my parents learned the game. Riding down a steep street in front of our house on wooden go-carts mounted on roller skates was always fun. For some reason my friend and I snuck eggs and a handful of matches from his mother's kitchen and in a vacant lot we built a small fire and fried the eggs in an empty can—just to see, not eat. A tall wall with broken bottle chards cemented on top enclosed and protected one of several residences we rented while in Bogotá. I climbed on large round boulders along a beautiful creek in a wooded area; a salty rock stimulated my tongue at the "salt cathedral," a beautiful church carved deep into a Colombian salt mine. And I laughed heartily at the dwarfs offering humorous interludes between the main events at the bullring, *la plaza de toros*.

∽ ∽ ∽

In the 1950s, my father and his two brothers were among General Motors' pioneers who promoted vehicle sales in the Andean countries and Venezuela.

In his travels through the Andean region in the late 1940s, my father observed firsthand the difficulties of developing automobile markets in countries mired in poverty, lacking dynamic consumer demand and without adequate transportation infrastructure. Another problem was the inadequate service support for vehicle owners. His arrival in Bogotá coincided with a heightened consciousness in the Latin American automotive industry about the important role of service operations in marketing and sales. Service operations in South America often faced obstacles, including irregular steamer connections for necessary replacement parts, ineffective ordering strategies by dealers and shortages of the parts themselves.

My father's decision to specialize in service and maintenance at GMI in part reflected the corporation's growing concern with this sector in the 1940s, but his father probably had urged him in that direction. Once employed with FDD, my father remained in this, recognizing its importance especially as technology made cars more complicated to fix. The Andean region was FDD's largest single market for trucks in the 1950s. Automobile agencies increasingly sought more cost-effective ways to deliver service; Automotríz in 1948 became the first dealership in Colombia to use air transport to deliver parts. In January, a Douglas DC-4 Pan American Airways plane delivered 250,000 pounds of parts and accessories to the coastal city of Barranquilla. From there, Colombian airline Avianca delivered the parts to warehouses in Bogotá (the headquarters) and to local dealers in Bucaramanga, Cúcuta, Tunja, Girardot and Villavicencio. Working as service manager at Automotríz, my father expanded his expertise directly to retail and provided the dealership with valuable experience and the latest innovations. He also for the first time had the opportunity of applying management skills to modernizing and improving service operations at the dealership.

Automotríz provided him with excellent experience and a decent salary, but he faced serious career obstacles nonetheless. McCarthy owned the business, but my father and uncle actually worked directly for Carlos Montoya, the Colombian vice-president of Automotríz who they thought had been hired less for his knowledge of the business than his good political and social connections in the country. They would run the business as sales and service managers while Montoya focused on cultivating the necessary business relationships. It did not quite work out that way. With McCarthy residing in New York, Montoya had a free hand and turned out to be fully in charge. Uncle José quickly crossed swords with Montoya and quit. In the next years, he worked with other dealerships in Bogotá and Cali. More tactful and accommodating, my father settled into his job and all was well until Montoya hired his two sons-in-law at the firm. Despite McCarthy's assurances about a good future there, my father suspected that the Colombian would eventually purchase the company and his sons-in-law would certainly prevail over him. My parents agonized about whether or not to remain in Bogotá and weighed the security of the job against the reality of their previous experience in the United States. They also had to consider unpredictable political conflict and guerrilla violence threatening Colombia's economic stability, which could leave the family's savings worth little.

Finally, in 1958, they took the risk and gave New York another shot. For me, leaving Bogotá meant leaving the only home I had ever known. My older brother and I shared a sad memory of our departure. I watched out of the car's back window as Uncle José held our black Labrador Mikey's leash. The dog had been with us since shortly after we arrived in Bogotá. Unable to take the dog, my uncle agreed to keep Mikey, but as we waved goodbye, suddenly the dog broke loose and bounded after the departing car. Sergio and I shouted for the vehicle to stop, and with tears streaming down his face my brother walked Mikey back and said his goodbye. My final memory of Colombia coincided with my first memory of flying. Shortly after taking off, the airplane bounced violently in the turbulence. Frightened, I wondered if it might crash.

My father found a job with Phillips Corporation in New York City, and we settled down into what my parents' hoped, after our Colombian detour, would be a prosperous middle-class existence in Tenafly, New Jersey. But once again, their American Dream quickly ran into difficulty. What at first seemed like a trouble-free move turned frightening. For no obvious reason, in early 1959 Phillips fired my father, or laid him off, as they called it. He had suspicions that his Cuban background had precipitated his firing; these suspicions haunted him and reminded him of why he had gone to Colombia a decade earlier. He anxiously questioned his decision to leave Bogotá. This most unstable moment in his life reminded him of the disruption and insecurity his family had experienced in Havana after his father's death, but even more acutely because he was now responsible for a wife, four children, car and house payments and other debts associated with the move. Nevertheless, he held tight to his claim of American identity.

Reengaging Barletta in Havana was no longer possible. On January 1, 1959, Dictator Fulgencio Batista fled Cuba. Fidel Castro and his army rode into Havana, and the next years saw the total communization of the island. Working in Cuba was out of the question. In a panic, my father went to General Motors' FDD offices in New York that he had left for his adventure in Colombia. Despite his mentor Morris Clark having passed away several years earlier, FDD rehired him. He worked at a lower salary than he had in Colombia, but at least he could support his family. While this was a huge step backward for him, he trudged on. He attended General Motors training workshops in Indiana and updated his knowledge on the latest automobile technologies and innovations in engines, transmissions and brake systems. And then he set out on familiar assignments and well-worn paths to the Caribbean, Central America and the Andean region to train service personnel. In March 1959, he traveled to Panama to hold workshops on care and repair of the Dynaflow automatic transmission system developed and built by the Buick division and used from the late 1940s through mid-1960s models.

In October, he returned to Panama to teach a class on the engine of the newly minted Chevrolet Corvair. GM produced the Corvair from 1960 through 1969, one of a new class of compact cars marketed in response to the small, sporty and fuel-efficient European automobiles manufactured by Volkswagen and Renault as well as their American competitors, the Ford Falcon and Plymouth Valiant. He repeated the training in El Salvador in November and in Bolivia during April 1960. In February 1960, he participated as an instructor at a "Commercial Vehicle Maintenance Course" sponsored by the Hawaii Employers Council in Honolulu and Hilo. His presentation, "The Electrical System—Practical Tips for Uninterrupted Service," was one of eighteen training lectures he presented. What I remember most about these absences were the postcards he sent, especially the one of an erupting Hawaiian volcano with an attached small plastic bag containing lava rocks. I imagined these exotic rocks blown from the volcano and thought them so extraordinary that I took them to school for show-and-tell. I kept them for years.

Like before, my father grew tired of the pace of travel. He had no option except to continue until he found an adequate opportunity in New York or in New Jersey, where the family now happily lived. Eventually, the south called again. Although my parents were not interested in another international move, General Motors hired its International Service Personnel, or its overseas employees, almost exclusively from among its existing employees. It was in this way that in late 1960, my father learned of the need for a Service Manager in the Caracas branch of the GM Interamericana Corporation, a GM affiliated corporate entity organized under the laws of Delaware to take advantage of certain tax benefits and good warehousing to improve product availability in Latin American markets. In addition to Caracas, Interamerican a Corporation oversaw GM branch offices in Lima, Santiago (Chile) and Montevideo. After some soul-searching, he concluded that his chances in the United States remained limited, and with my mother's acquiescence he applied and got the job.

We left New Jersey for a second time as expats, and like many expats found a comfortable and satisfying future in other places. "*Sin querer, queriendo*," legendary Mexican sitcom character Chavo del Ocho often said. This is what my parents would have said about having headed south despite hoping to stay in the north: "Without desiring it, wanting it."

A member of Spain's Cuban militias, my great-great-grandfather Col. Ricardo Álvarez y Fernández de Cordoba during his Cuban Ten Years War deployment in Las Villas, 1873.

My great-grandparents, Ricardo Álvarez and Tomasa Rodríguez, Cuba, c. 1890.

Baseball card of Francisco Andrés Poyo, drawn in 1932.

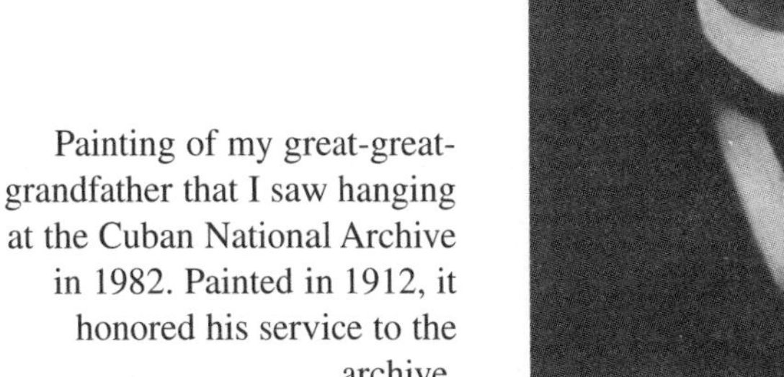

Painting of my great-great-grandfather that I saw hanging at the Cuban National Archive in 1982. Painted in 1912, it honored his service to the archive.

My great-grandparents, Louisa Skillin and Francisco A. Poyo (Pancho), met and married in Key West. He worked as a cigar-maker in Key West, played baseball in Key West and Havana, worked in Havana city government. c. 1940.

Formal photograph of my grandfather, José F. Poyo in Havana, taken shortly before he died. c. 1940.

My grandfather, José F. Poyo (on the far right), greeting a delegation of General Motors executives arriving in Havana from New York for the Caravana del Progreso exhibition. This photograph includes his boss Lawrence Ross (third from left), January 1939.

José F. Poyo and Sergia Álvarez, my grandparents, with their children, left to right, Jorge, Ernesto, Sergio (my father), José, Havana. c. 1935.

Joining a fraternity helped my father, Sergio Poyo, integrate into life at General Motors Institute in Flint, Michigan. He is at the top of the pile. c. 1942.

Enjoying a day in Indianapolis, Indiana, my parents, Sergio Poyo and Geraldine Darnell, just two months before they married, 1943.

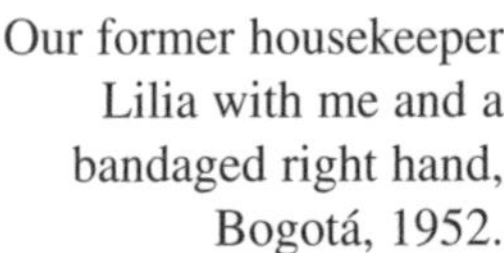

Our former housekeeper Lilia with me and a bandaged right hand, Bogotá, 1952.

Sergio Poyo's career with General Motors took him on many trips to Latin America. Here he enjoys a flight in the Andean region to train automobile dealer service personnel, c. 1948.

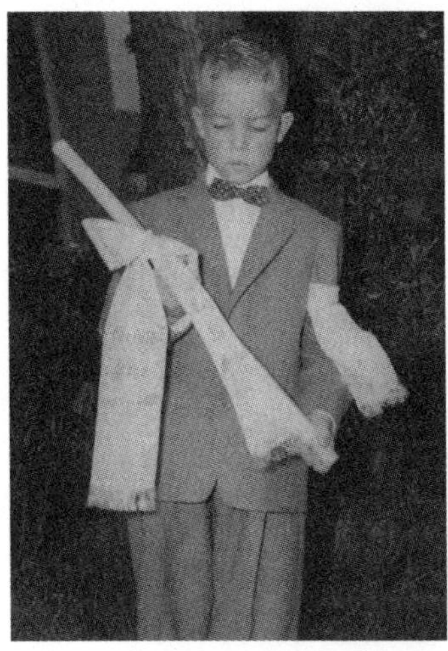

My First Communion in Bogotá, Colombia, 1956.

During travels mostly in Central America in the 1959, my father, Sergio Poyo, trained mechanics to repair GM engines. In this case Panama.

Sergio Poyo at business gathering in Buenos Aires, c. 1970.

Automobile executives in Buenos Aires received considerable press coverage. Sergio Poyo on cover of the Argentine business magazine, *Competencia,* December 1974.

Luis Alpízar and his wife Nieves Arencibia, both archivists at the Cuban National Archive who shared much family history and stories, at their home in Havana, 1982.

With my sons, Noel (6) and Jeremy (12), on the Malecón in Havana, 1982.

9

Corporate Foot Soldiers

"Selling cars in Argentina wasn't easy," my father told me one evening as we sat on his back porch in Savannah, Georgia. "The government regulated everything, and policies changed constantly, the labor unions disrupted production, local parts companies did not deliver quality parts on time, and constant inflation made pricing an impossible task. . . . I learned to work in that environment. And it made me indispensable, a safe position," he added tongue in cheek. My father knew Argentina well, and the corporation came to view him as their most knowledgeable executive in the country.

When I visited my parents in Montevideo in 1974, my father gave me an issue of the Argentine business magazine *Competencia.* There on the cover was his photograph. Later, after his death, I came across a collection of newspaper clippings among his papers about his business activities going back to the late 1960s. It had never occurred to me that a sales manager of an automobile corporation would have warranted such press coverage, but it made sense. Argentina's strategy for economic development required a growing automobile industry, which attracted press attention. At the Benson Library in Austin, I not only tracked down *Competencia,* but other important business magazines, such as *The Review of the River Plate*, *El Economista* and *Mercado.* Together they revealed a detailed story of the Argentine automobile industry during the 1960s and 1970s, including an accounting of my father's activities. Hearing the story from him would have been ideal, but these magazines provided a second best, but still valuable narrative.

∽ ∽ ∽

An observer of General Motors in the 1980s described its culture as requiring conformity above all else. "Once an executive reaches a level of prestige at General Motors," wrote Maryann Keller, "he hangs on for dear life . . . Gradually he stops seeing the company's flaws and begins to develop a defensive posture toward critics and skeptics. His place in the corporation becomes central to his personal identity and sense of worth." It was through General Motors that my father ultimately cemented his identification with the United States. His social circles, his belief in American economic prowess, of which he took part, and his evolving political ideas all stemmed from his experience with General Motors.

My father's loyalty to GM even endured into retirement. One evening he phoned and asked if I was ready for a new car. As part of his retirement benefits, he received a ten percent discount annually on any new GM vehicle. He only used it once every three years and passed the benefit on to family members the other years. His discount for the year was about to expire, so he offered it to me.

"I just bought a car last month," I told him.

"Oh, Gerald, why didn't you check with me for the discount?" he responded.

After an awkward silence, I sheepishly said, "I bought a Honda."

After an even longer silence and with considerable irritation, he said, "Now, why would you do such a thing? You've always bought Chevrolets."

"Dad, GM cars have left me in the lurch too many times over the years . . . too many mechanical problems."

He acknowledged this, but insisted, "They've worked through them."

He seemed hurt. As we finished the conversation, I was struck by just how deeply loyal he remained to General Motors and how much he wanted his children to feel the same. Thank God, my father did not live to see the debacle that was the US automobile industry during the Great Recession of 2008; that surely would have killed him!

Corporations hired executives to reside in foreign lands and introduce the benefits of American business culture. In 1960, General Motors' entire international workforce included only 200 employees, while some 900 to 1000 worked in the New York offices. It was not always easy to find employees willing to work overseas, which many considered a hardship or simply a disadvantage to rising through the corporation's ranks. Once out of the country, keeping up with opportunities in the United States was not easy, and there was a built-in prejudice against international employees when they later returned home. Managers in US-based corporate units considered international workers not sufficiently familiar with domestic operations to take a chance on them, making it likely they would remain in the international arena. Another drawback for many was that career internationalists moved jobs frequently and had little choice in assignments. Those employees who accepted assignments without complaint usually rose through the international ranks over time. An international career could be a hardship for those uncomfortable with cultural diversity and learning foreign languages, but it could be fulfilling for adaptable people full of curiosity for the world. For the most part, the GM international community of employees comprised a homogeneous cadre of Euro-Americans who crisscrossed the world, frequently crossing paths in different countries, providing GM with employees able to work in diverse cultural settings.

Unlike his father in Cuba, my father was not a "local man," but a representative of the largest multinational corporation in the world. As a foot soldier of US capitalism in Latin American for forty years, he believed the American corporate agenda was transparent and straightforward. Latin America needed foreign investment, technology and business savvy. People in Latin America needed jobs, and American corporations provided them in abundance. This would eventually transform and modernize the region.

My father became a GM executive at the very time when Latin American governments deepened their policies of state capitalism and promoted industrialization and economic diversification. General

Motors' investments in Latin American automobile assembly plants began in the 1920s, consistent with the hosts' nationalist aspirations to diversify their economies and labor forces. By 1961, when the job in Venezuela was offered to my father, he had developed the perfect resumé for a service manager. He knew the nitty-gritty of hands-on automobile repair, and his travels throughout Central America and the Andean region providing car distributors training and support on the latest automotive innovations gave him invaluable experience. He was well prepared to handle the state-of-the-art service department designed to orient and advise local dealerships in the repair and maintenance of vehicles at the Antímano plant near Caracas. His primary objective involved training and advising GM dealers and authorized garages on how to manage effective and efficient service operations. He understood the importance of service in the automobile industry as well as the need to establish strong relationships with dealerships, which turned out to be one of his greatest strengths.

During most of her almost thirty years in South America, my mother adapted and carried out her responsibilities in support of my father's career. She also engaged the local communities with enthusiasm and good cheer. Also a corporate foot soldier, she accompanied him every step of the way, but this was not a natural world for her. Endowed with an artists' temperament, she was introspective, emotional, sensitive, and was often lost in thought. Not naturally talkative, it was often hard to know what she was thinking. She watched people closely; she liked to see what was going on around her. She enjoyed a good party with plenty of drink, music and dance and, after a cocktail or two, loosened up and spoke more freely.

After leaving Flint, my mother never again worked for wages. She became devoted to her role of housewife and full-time mother. If we had remained in New Jersey, at some point, my mother might have reentered the workforce, but life in South America made working for wages outside the home impossible. Local labor laws prohibited foreigners from working without a permit; anyway, her "job" was GM wife. She may not have fully understood the implications of agreeing to move south but, as it had for my father, the corporation became her life. It set the rules on what was acceptable or not for wives. Corporate patriarchy was even more intense than in US society; it was patriarchy on steroids. Corporate wives remained by their husbands' sides at business events and participated actively in the American communities—not doing so would affect their husbands' careers.

American corporate wives abroad made difficult adjustments. Some women encountered extraordinary challenges in countries with radically different non-western cultures, low living standards, cities with poor infrastructures and high population densities, poor sanitation, inadequate schools for children and dangerous traffic conditions. Fortunately, for my mother, while Bogotá, Caracas and Buenos Aires faced some of these problems, they were eminently livable cities, where she found the charms far outweighed the drawbacks. My father always said that for a young untraveled woman from Flint, my mother took to Latin America "like a duck takes to water."

My mother conformed to corporate expectations, what one observer of women's corporate roles in 1960 called the "social whirl." Corporations encouraged socializing as a way of keeping women occupied while their husbands worked, but socializing was also one of few ways women sought status and self-affirmation in a society where they could not work. This included bragging about their husbands and creating pecking orders of sorts based on the importance of their husbands' job. Perhaps the most disturbing aspect was that most women did not engage much with the local population; it was simply easier to socialize with other Americans, and many never even bothered to learn the local language. Other factors also encouraged the "social whirl." Women with servants enjoyed an unusual amount of leisure and they did not have many other options to socialize, unless they sought out local culture, which some did. Even when they might have wanted to engage with the locals, they were often misunderstood or not well received.

Observers frequently lampooned life in the *American* communities as a "daily drudgery of bridge parties in the mornings, cocktails in the afternoons, dinners in the evening, with philandering thrown in occasionally to break the monotony." This stereotype was not far from the truth. My mother's General Motors job included accompanying my father on many of his business-related dinners and social events, as well as her own never-ending social obligations in the community. This included attending lunches, bridge clubs, coffees and teas, and even late afternoon happy hours with corporate and embassy wives before my father arrived home and they dressed for an evening function. At first, this was an exciting new world, and she had a lot of fun. In time, it became routine and eventually burdensome.

During the last days of December 1960, after two and a half years living in New Jersey, we boarded the passenger ship, *SS Santa Paula,* at the New York wharves for a leisurely trip to La Guaira, Venezuela's main port city. We excitedly waved to friends from the ship's deck as it moved away from the dock, sailed down the Hudson River and passed the Statue of Liberty. I stood on the deck and looked with awe at the iconic landmark, which I had learned about but had never seen. As we entered the Caribbean, on January 2, 1961, my mother wrote to her mother about the beautiful sailing weather, the shining sun and 80-degree day. "This is the most relaxing thing you can imagine," she said. "I'm sorry it's just for such a few days. The kids are wonderful and having a great time." The *SS Santa Paula* docked at La Guaira in the very early morning of January 4 after brief stops in Aruba and Curacao. From there we headed overland to Caracas.

Nestled in a valley in the Cordillera de la Costa Central, a spur of the Andean Mountains coming out of Colombia, most of Caracas sits at an altitude of 2,500 to 3,000 feet above sea level. Some 1,282,000 people lived in Caracas when we arrived. Today about 5,250,000 inhabit the metropolitan area. A tropical climate allowed for swimming all year round—a particular advantage for a ten-year-old.

At La Guaira, a GM representative met us at customs. Over the years, I learned that these representatives were paid to facilitate the customs experience, even paying bribes to officials when necessary to ensure no one opened suitcases with contraband kitchen and other household items prohibited under the tariff laws. A chauffeur drove us on a four-lane modern highway through mountain tunnels, over bridges and across deep gullies, but that only took one hour. As our vehicle entered the valley, the city came into full view. We went directly to the luxurious Tamanaco Hotel, named in ironic honor of a rebellious indigenous chieftain. On the mountainside overlooking Caracas, the Tamanaco's grounds were dotted with tropical palms, plants and bright flowers of all kinds. Guests sunbathed around an alluring, large swimming pool, where we too spent a couple of hours each day after school, before dinner. "I'm beginning to get a lovely tan sitting by the pool," my mother wrote her mother. "The children are as brown as berries already."

While we were at school, and with my father at work, my mother searched for a home to lease. Few, if any, executives purchased homes, since transfers happened all the time, often without much notice. In mid-March, after two-and-a-half months in the hotel, my father signed a contract for a house on Calle California in the exclusive Las Mercedes neighborhood, not far from the hotel. Called Quinta Villa Sol, the newly built Mediterranean-style two-story structure had four bedrooms. A second-floor porch at the rear ran the length of the house and became the gathering place for the family. In the evenings, we watched the sun set behind the beautiful mountainous landscape surrounding Caracas, especially Pico Naiguatá, the highest point of the range.

As in Bogotá, my parents joined a golf club, Club Valle Arriba. Their appetite for golf grew, while we children spent hours at the swimming pool. In time, with my mother's encouragement, I even attempted to play golf, an idea my father opposed. Not a children's game, he insisted, but my mother persisted and eventually enrolled me in golf lessons. While fun, my brain never successfully orchestrated the necessary coordination between legs, hips, head and arms to keep the little white ball on the fairway. A radical slice meant that my golf balls more often than not splashed into ponds and creeks, settled in deep rough and bounced off the rooftops of people's homes.

We sometimes went to Puerto Azul, a beach resort northeast of Caracas, which had a beautiful swimming pool that wound around the grounds like a river. Better than the beach itself, I thought, but my parents preferred the beautiful pristine sands. While they sunbathed, fishermen carefully maneuvered their boats to the shore and walked up and down the beach with pails full of oysters and bottled beer. When requested, they sat down on the sands next to the bathers, opened the shells and beer bottles and served them. There I tasted my first raw oyster and grimaced at my father's instruction that I let the creature slide down my throat. Usually, I returned home sunburned and spent the following weeks peeling the dead skin off my arms, shoulders and nose.

The natural world in Venezuela fascinated me. One time, we spent hours driving to Maracaibo, west toward the Colombian border. I don't know why but, along with my parents' friends and their children, we spent several days in cottages at a fenced-in oil camp. On our first night, hundreds of the largest frogs I had ever seen appeared on the grounds, making it difficult to walk without stepping on them. The squashing sounds and their cries really freaked me out. After that, I watched them from the window, but didn't venture out after dark. Near our home in Caracas, exploring nearby creek beds kept me busy and I occasionally came upon large fearsome-looking iguanas that always sent me stumbling backwards as they also retreated. One summer, I spent about ten days at a camp high in the Venezuelan mountains, hours from Caracas by bus. We bunked in small cabins each with its private outhouse and six kids to a structure. Most mornings we hiked, and my favorite route followed a creek up the mountain until we came upon a glistening pool of crystal-clear water. We dared each other to jump into the freezing cold water from a rocky ledge about ten feet above. I learned to paddle a canoe across a small lake we accessed from a dock; otherwise, we carried the canoe through thick mud that submerged our legs half way up the calves. In the evenings, we sang camp songs around a large bonfire. After two years at Calle California, my parents rented another larger house in a still sparsely built development in Prados del Este, in the hills east of where we had lived. I enjoyed exploring the hills around the house, looking for lizards and snakes, collecting stones and climbing through the sites of other houses still under construction.

One day, just weeks after this move, my mother received a call from my father while she was still unpacking. He asked her to sit down, which frightened her. He had been transferred to Buenos Aires!

"Why didn't they tell you this before we went through all the trouble of moving?" she complained.

"That's corporate life. It's like the military: you move when they tell you," he said.

The need to move again certainly unsettled the family but without major disturbances. Still young, Cynthia (8 yrs.) and Jeffrey (6 yrs.) accepted it easily enough, but I was now twelve and felt the stresses of having to leave school and friends once again after just two and a half years. Nevertheless, I was excited and curious about our new destination.

"Argentina?" I remember asking. "Is it like Venezuela?"

"I don't think so," my mother said.

"We'll see!" I told her.

In that spirit, we moved on.

~ ~ ~

My father's two-and-a-half year stint in Venezuela prepared him for an even bigger challenge in Argentina, where President Arturo Frondizi, the first civilian president since the military had deposed Juan Perón, announced in March 1959 that an automobile manufacturing industry would be established within five years. For starters, the government imposed prohibitive tariffs on fully assembled automobiles and parts, along with duties and surcharges. This raised the price of an imported standard Chevrolet passenger car from less than $2,500 in the United States to over $20,000 in the Argentine market. The government also required automobile investors within five years to manufacture at least 40 percent of the vehicle parts locally, including engines. In return, the government allowed duty-free entry of new machinery, tools and equipment; protected foreign subsidiaries against imported competition; and allowed the transfer of annual net profits earned on investment through a free exchange rate. Government policies increased the foreign share of industrial production in

Argentina to twenty-five percent by 1962, with automobiles constituting about a fifth of all foreign investment, placing that sector at the heart of the country's industrial policy.

GM calculated that local operations could cover the investment costs without any significant outlays from US operations and that Argentina was capable of rapidly developing a local parts and supply industry. In mid-1959, GM's Executive Vice-President and General Manager of its overseas division visited Argentina with a proposal to establish a twenty-million-dollar truck manufacturing facility in Buenos Aires. A refitted assembly operation in Barracas produced its first units in February 1961. Another twenty-million-dollar investment followed to manufacture a six-cylinder, four-door Chevrolet sedan at a second San Martín facility, which produced its first vehicles at the end of 1962.

General Motors representatives greeted us at Ezeiza International Airport, and so did the oncoming cold and dampness of autumn in Buenos Aires, which felt especially odd in April. Even stranger, I would find, was Christmas in the middle of summer, especially when my mother listened to Bing Crosby sing "White Christmas." The trip on Pan American flights had been long from New York to Miami, then to Panama, Lima, Santiago, Chile and Buenos Aires. My mother referred to this route as the milk run. In those days, flying was a formal event. My father and I both wore jackets and ties, and we received very personal treatment in the first-class cabin.

In Buenos Aires, we followed the same routine as in Venezuela. We stayed at the Claridge Hotel in downtown Buenos Aires. It reminded me of the hotels in New York rather than the tropical ambience of the Tamanaco in Caracas. The Claridge competed with the Plaza and Alvear as the most exclusive hotels in the city. We enjoyed a roomy, two-bedroom suite with a television and usually had dinners in the room. In the mornings, we dressed for school and had breakfast in the restaurant, usually hot chocolate and *medialunas*, a delicious croissant-like pastry. We had to be in front of the hotel at six-thirty to wait for our school bus. It would still be dark and cold when the bus arrived, and we'd settle down for the just over an hour ride as the bus picked up additional children at various downtown hotels and apartments and made its way to the school in the northern suburbs, known as the Zona Norte. We eventually would reside there along with the majority of the American community.

Buenos Aires' American community was long-standing. European immigration to the city during the late nineteenth and early twentieth centuries, especially of Spaniards, Italians, Germans, English and Irish, marked the city's culture. Although in much fewer numbers, Americans had also arrived, first as diplomats and missionaries, then as business people. As the number of American citizens in Buenos Aires grew, civic and social organizations of various kinds joined the diplomatic, religious and business groups. The community gathered at The American Club for social events, lectures and meetings. The American Chamber of Commerce of Buenos Aires kept an eye on economic matters, and a baseball league attracted teams from different American companies and associations.

My parents found a home in Acasusso, on Calle Guido y Spano, in the heart of the American residential area between the suburban train line and Avenida Libertador. Both crossed Zona Norte in parallel fashion toward downtown Buenos Aires. Just a block from our house was a roundabout street that encircled a small park with a giant Ombú tree that I enjoyed climbing. In due time my parents joined the San Isidro Golf Club, where, as in Bogotá and Caracas, I enjoyed swimming and had little success improving my golf. A network of inexpensive and efficient *colectivos* (buses) and trains moved people usually comfortably across Buenos Aires, and I rode them alone from the time I was twelve. I usually rode the school bus but sometimes took the *colectivos*, especially if I had overslept. Our new home was just a fifteen-minute *colectivo* ride on Avenida Libertador to the school located on the banks of the Río de La Plata in La Lucila.

After a year, we moved to a larger house on Calle Roma in Olivos, just two blocks from Avenida Maipú and across the street from the Northlands School for girls, originally an English school. To secure us as tenants, the landlords promised a swimming pool, which they built soon after we moved in. My parents moved again in 1969 to an even larger home on Calle Paraná in La Lucila just a block from the school. It too had a swimming pool, but with larger grounds, because as my father's career advanced so did his need to entertain at home. In 1972, another move just down the block, and finally, a move again around the block the next year concluded the game of musical homes.

Young, experienced and proven with fifteen years of experience, my father was a strong choice for Service Manager in Buenos Aires in 1963, but within two years, he was asked to move into sales, no doubt recognized for ease with which he interacted with Argentine automobile dealers. Following a month-long "Wholesale Sales Management Training Program" in 1965 at the General Motors Institute in Flint, my father became assistant sales manager, and then in 1968 he became sales manager. All told, my father served GM Argentina for fourteen years, a longevity at one post uncommon in the world of overseas executives.

My mother in the meantime also adapted. Within days of our arrival in Buenos Aires, her obligations began. We attended an afternoon welcome gathering at the home of one of the executives, where we became acquainted with the families of the General Motors leadership team. Over the years, GM wives often hosted mid-afternoon Saturday or Sunday family gatherings for dinner, socializing and considerable drinking that often went into the night. My mother took her turn hosting dinners, which in the end were as much about business obligations as friendship and connection. She also went to events at The American Club downtown and volunteered at the Big Switch, an annual fundraiser for the American school, which she chaired a couple of times and contributed to every year. She did this for years with enthusiasm.

My mother did carve out some time for herself. She painted with acrylics and oil, but it always remained a hobby. From my earliest days in Colombia, I remember her painting. A portrait of a clown she made for my sister Cindy when she was tiny still hangs in her home, and another deep blue image of the Nativity hangs in my home today. In Caracas, she painted a colorful mural of a tree inhabited by colorful birds of various species on the wall of our second-floor back porch. She worked on it for months and, when we left, it pained me to think that the next tenants would likely paint it over. My father's practical right-brain thinking had little appreciation for her artistic talents; it was a nice pastime for her, he thought. Like many businessmen, he evaluated things according to their commercial potential, and it probably never occurred to him that her painting might hold that potential. I'm afraid she never received much encouragement. Besides golf, theatre was the only other hobby I recall my mother engaging in purely for personal fulfillment. A group of American women ran a theatre group called the Suburban Players, and she contributed with stage designs consistent with her artistic gifts.

The role of corporate wife kept my mother away from home a lot, but mostly she was present. She asked about school and made sure I did my homework, worried when my report cards were not very good, ensured I received a religious education and even raised concerns when I hadn't begun dating at what she considered the appropriate time. Shy and socially awkward with girls, I rarely dated and found it uncomfortable and anxiety provoking. Her prodding made me even more reticent. I preferred television. She allowed me to watch all the television I wanted, which was probably not a great idea, and I came and went pretty much as I pleased without being asked many questions, which allowed me to cultivate a sense of independence. My parents lived their lives as corporate soldiers with a strong sense of commitment and responsibility, but their primary objective was to provide their children with a stable life and good opportunities. In this, they were successful.

Automobile dealers, my father knew, were the heart of the business. My father's first point of order on becoming sales manager was to visit dealers across the country. He and an entourage of zone managers and a public relations director kept a busy schedule, engaged the press and promoted General Motors at the local and national levels. He used those travels to introduce himself, congratulate the dealers on their work, brief them on goals and strategies for the coming year and to become acquainted with their various personalities.

His busy schedule was unavoidable, given my father's insistence on seeing first-hand how the dealers were doing and maintaining personal ties. Dealers liked this, and visits provided a way for them to lobby for more than their fair share of vehicles to sell. At Christmas, unsolicited deliveries of turkeys, cases of wine and seasonal sweets arrived at our home. One year a television set arrived, which my father said was beyond the pale. He instructed the delivery company to return the television, but this never happened. "There was no use trying to return the gifts," he said. "Not only would they not receive them, they would be offended." The television remained in our garage for about two years until one day I accidently plugged our American set into the 220 socket in the living room, and blew it up. The housekeeper had taken the transformer to use with the American-made vacuum cleaner. "Get the television that's in the garage," my father sighed. "They'll never pick it up." It was a 220 Argentine set, and I never had to worry about plugging it in again.

My father also regularly received invitations to *asados* (Argentine barbeques), often at dealer-owned *estancias* or ranches. Nothing matched the *asados*. Always the highlight. This typical barbeque included virtually the entire cow or bull and was consumed with an abundance of bread, salad, french fried potatoes and large quantities of red wine. Other General Motors families also attended the *asados*, which sometimes included equestrian activities of one kind or another, including watching the Argentine version of bronco riding, Polo matches and a modern-day version of Pato. In Pato, two teams composed of four riders each struggled to take possession of a ball covered with six handles and throw it into a netted- hoop at each end of a polo-like field. The riders in control of the ball had to maintain their arms extended as they galloped toward their goal so that their opponents had a chance to wrestle it away. The riders also tossed the ball to each other as they galloped towards the goal. In the original indigenous and gaucho versions, riders played with a live duck in a basket—hence the name!

10
Children Fuse Cultures Easily

Children fuse cultures easily. It happens without much awareness. I did that. Family and quotidian experiences in four countries formed my inner attitudes, emotions, values and views of the world. Only after living in the United States for several years did I fully grasp the extent to which my unconventional upbringing and hybrid sensitivities prevented a clear identification with any one country or culture.

Everyday cultural influences mixed in unique ways, combining the Latin American and the American. I navigated life with this dissonance; in the clouds without grounding is the metaphor that periodically came to mind. It was a while before I discovered that four generations of Poyos before me had lived bicultural lives or that our lives in South America were not that different from the way my father and his brothers had lived in an Americanized Cuba, except that they possessed a clearer sense of nationality. The cultural fusions inherent in our experiences provided advantages and expanded horizons even as they were sources of confusion, disconnection and marginalization. Being in-between often proved uncomfortable for my father, grandfathers and me, especially when feeling insecure about the value of your culture. On the other hand, I learned, when embraced with confidence, "in-betweenness" proved an asset.

My mother loved Hispanic culture and discovered Latin music. My father taught her the *cha-cha-cha* and *merengue* at a Colombian-owned club in Flint. She even experimented a bit with Spanish. She jotted "*mi amor*" and "*mi todo*" on the bottom left side of the correspondence envelopes she mailed my father at boot camp in 1943. More was in store when she met Nana in March 1944 in Cochran, Georgia, not far from Atlanta, when my father trained as an Air Corps navigator. The next year, my mother stayed with her for a longer time while he continued training at Ft. Sumter, South Carolina. During their visits together, she learned to cook Cuban meals and took her first real steps towards learning the Spanish language. In time, she learned Spanish, but it always remained foreign and awkward. Grammar eluded her, an American accent persisted, and many years away from the United States did not affect her underlying cultural attachments to her homeland.

Spanish reigned unchallenged at home in previous Poyo generations, but English dominated ours. Not only did my mother speak English to us, so did my father. He made American choices as often as he could, trying to avoid that in-betweenness. Whether or not I learned Spanish didn't seem to matter much to him. Maybe he just figured we would learn it living where we did; he envisioned us eventually living in the United States, where his experience taught him that Spanish was not helpful, and indeed, potentially harmful. Losing Spanish was consistent with American society's ideas about assimilation, and my father spoke in Spanish only to his brothers and mother. He let loose in Spanish only in moments of frustration or anger, like Ricky Ricardo, but with more colorful language. "*¡Coño!*" he yelled, along with other choice words, when he caught our German shepherd happily gulping down two entire chickens he had dragged off the grill. "*Mierda*," he shouted frequently when things didn't go his way.

According to my mother, I didn't utter a word of English until age six. She attributed that to my Colombian Tía Connie, but the housekeeper probably had more to do with it. She spent more time with me as a child than anyone else. Spanish-speaking domestic workers raised and influenced us in Bogotá, Caracas and Buenos Aires and helped us learn the distinct Bogotano Spanish, Venezuelan-Caribbean Spanish and then the unique Italian-inflected Spanish of Buenos Aires. Only when Nana visited did the household become fully Spanish, and I heard the Cuban version of that same language. Nana's visits reminded us of the reality we often forgot that Spanish had been the Poyo's native tongue for centuries.

Besides the Spanish language, housekeepers taught me most about the cultures of the countries in which we lived. Housekeepers have inhabited most middle- and upper-class Latin American homes since the times of the Iberian conquest when Indians, African slaves and their mixed descendants filled these roles. Later European immigrants joined the mix. Women housekeepers cared for children, cleaned, shopped, cooked, washed and ironed, among other things. They suffered abuses and indignities of many kinds, including sexual abuse from their employers. If married, their husbands often acted as gardeners, chauffeurs or handy men. Latin American families relied heavily on *mucamas*, *criadas* or *muchachas*, as they are variously called—or, maids, as my mother referred to them.

I'm able to visualize Lilia in Bogotá only from a photograph. She formed me in ways I will never know, and cared for me. One day, the ironing woman left the hot iron on the floor while she attended to something in another room. A curious toddler apparently, I wandered into the kitchen and promptly attached my right palm to the surface of a steaming-hot iron. Shrieks brought Lilia running. Despite her fury at seeing the iron on the floor, she carefully peeled my hand from the appliance even before my mother ran through the kitchen door. The only evidence of the incident except for my mother's telling, and the scars still visible on my right hand, is that photograph of Lilia carrying me with a bandaged hand.

Later, Rosa, a young woman of about twenty years old entered my parents' employ and she accompanied us to New Jersey in 1958. Young and with no immediate family, she embarked on the adventure, no doubt curious about the world. She too affectionately cared for us, especially little Cindy and Jeffrey, and even shared their bedroom. When Jeffrey fell out of bed one night and got cut over his eye, she jumped into action. My father called the doctor who lived up the street. At this time, doctors made house calls, and he rushed over as quickly as he could, while Rosa held the gushing, bloodied wound closed with her fingers. Sewed up and bandaged, the next morning I asked Jeffrey, "What happened to you?" I hadn't heard a thing.

Rosa also attended English-language classes and kept us in touch with Spanish when suddenly it had disappeared from our lives. My parents asked Rosa to accompany us to Venezuela in 1961, but instead she returned home to Bogotá. She eventually found her way back to the United States, attended beautician school in New York and married a Colombian. I never saw her again.

In Caracas, a Spanish immigrant named Rita, perhaps in her mid-thirties, joined our household. She too did everything for us, and like Rosa, I took her daily presence for granted. Before leaving Venezuela we stayed at the Tamanaco Hotel, where for a time she came each day and took Cindy, Jeffrey and me to a nearby park. Our sad final *despedida*, when we cried together the day before we departed for Buenos Aires, remains clear in my memory.

A gentle, affectionate and playful couple, Mary (pronounced Mari) and Ricardo Moreno in Buenos Aires, influenced my adolescence day-to-day more than anyone else. They came to our household after two previous housekeepers had not worked out. Perhaps in her early thirties when we met, Mary had come highly recommended within the international community and fit well into our household. She, her mother and two brothers had migrated to Buenos Aires from Santiago del Estero; in Buenos Aires, she had married Ricardo, a *porteño*, as residents of the capital are known. Mary could not have children but she, Ricardo and her mother helped raise her brother's two daughters. Ricardo lived with us too but had his own jobs as taxi cab driver and house painter. On occasion, he helped at the house working in the yard, but he had an injured leg from a car accident and limped, which made that sort of work difficult for him.

When my mother was absent due to social obligations, Mary and Ricardo were there, and I spent countless hours with them. As I got older, we drank red table wine diluted with soda water from a *sifón,* in an area off the kitchen where they had a bedroom, bathroom and a small breakfast area. Ricardo taught me to drive a car and parallel park as he told me stories about the taxi business in Buenos Aires. The car horn, he said, was my best friend. "Never hesitate using it," he insisted. "It will save your life." Most drivers in Buenos Aires lived by that axiom, which defeated the purpose, since it was often difficult to distinguish which horn might be the important one. "Never, never" he told me, "pull into an intersection after the light changes from red to green without waiting for the first car of the oncoming traffic to stop. Three or four will continue through the red light before somebody decides to stop." My older brother could have used that advice. On one visit from the United States, he pulled into the intersection and crashed directly into a car running through the light. The angry driver actually blamed him!

Mary had a strong personality and sense of cultural identity, and lived in our home with confidence. My parents never tolerated any disrespect toward housekeepers, and Mary and Ricardo enjoyed authority in their absence. That was not always the case in some families, where children ordered housekeepers around like slaves, but it never occurred to me to cross them. Mary kept the house clean, but my job, she said, was to keep my bedroom tidy. Her practice of rousing me out of bed on Saturday mornings at 10—at the latest—annoyed me; that was my day to sleep in. "I can't be waiting all day for you to get up," she would say. Often Mary or Ricardo, or both, joined us to watch television when some show caught their fancy. They did not own a set and seemed to survive fine without one. That, I could never understand.

My parents rarely volunteered stories about matters of the day, personal, cultural, political or otherwise, but Mary and Ricardo did. That gave me an understanding of Argentina that I otherwise would not have had. They had an anti-Semitic streak. Not a prejudice expressed in hateful tones, but an ingrained matter-of-fact bigotry typical in Argentina. They relied on popular culture and remedies. When warts broke out on my sister Cindy's hands and the doctors' cures failed, Mary offered a solution. According to my sister, Mary took her to a very modest part of town and entered a house where a *curandera* prepared a concoction of *hierbas*. She wrapped them in a small cloth and tied it closed. "Do you believe in me?" the *curandera* asked Cindy. When she replied, yes, the *curandera* touched each wart with the bundle of mysterious herbs and recited the requisite incantations.

She then gave the little bundle to my sister and told her that as she left the house to throw it over her right shoulder and not look back. "Leave the bag behind with the warts," she ordered. In two weeks, the warts disappeared. That was the first time I thought there might be something to *curanderismo*. Years later, I learned that Blanca Poyo, my father's great-aunt, was a *santera* (Santería priest) and *curandera* in Havana.

Mary could also be irreverent and funny at the same time. To us, of course, but never to my parents with whom she maintained a traditional and formal relationship. She even shared *chismes* (gossip) about my parent's social gatherings. During holidays, my father's Argentine assistant and his wife visited the house for a drink to wish us the best for the season. Mary referred to him as a *chupamedias* (brown-noser) probably because he was the only Argentine employee at General Motors who visited the house. "*Llegó el chupamedias*," she would whisper to us when they arrived for their visits, which we thought was hilarious. Mary and Ricardo and their families were the closest thing we children had to an extended family in Argentina and they taught us to be *argentinos*. I adopted many of their attitudes and values and their country's Spanish-language accent. Many aspects of their way of being remained with me, but not the accent, which took on a mildly Cuban inflection in the United States.

Our cultural experiences included adapting to local eating customs and habits that we carried from place to place. My mother prepared Cuban and Hispanic dishes like *arroz con pollo*, *picadillo* and black beans, *paella*, *bistec cubano* and *tostones*. Occasionally, a Cuban family living in Buenos Aires joined us for a Cuban-style meal. I recall the *arepas* popular in Colombia and the tropical fruits in Venezuela, including mangos, papaya, coconut, *mamón*, *mamey* and bananas. We even had a banana tree in our backyard in Caracas. In Buenos Aires, I ate *bifes de chorizo con papas fritas y ensalada* at least once a week and *paltas* (avocado) from a tree visible from our dining room window. Treats like *alfajores* and *dulce de leche* kept me a little on the chubby side, and I also enjoyed *yerba mate*, a strong tea indigenous to Paraguay, Argentina, Uruguay and Brazil that Mary and Ricardo drank regularly. Mary prepared *milanesas, empanadas de carne*, all kinds of pastas including *canelones, raviolis* and *tallarines*. She also fixed *ñoquis de papa*, one of my favorite. My mother fixed the American fare, mostly during Mary's day off. She especially liked to prepare southern fried chicken and meatloaf, as well as fried chicken gizzards, hearts and livers with rice, which I avoided if I could. Her Missouri ancestors loved the gizzards, she said. She also insisted on celebrating Thanksgiving and cooked the traditional turkey and stuffing.

American popular culture certainly did not elude me while living in South America. Television began for me in Bogotá during the mid-fifties. Our small set had a tiny screen, and we watched the two-hour or so daily broadcasts in the early evening. *Boston Blackie*, a detective show, is the only television show I remember from Colombia. I don't remember seeing many American television shows in Venezuela, but a local show, *Casos y cosas de casas*, a sit-com about newlyweds, did catch my attention. Little did I know that a Cuban, Jorge Félix, was the creative force and star of the television show originally produced in Havana. Venezuelan television began producing the show when Félix fled Cuba in 1961 shortly before we arrived in Caracas.

Ironically, nationalist Argentina was where I mostly imbibed American popular culture and values. On TV, there was a full array of shows from the United States dubbed into Spanish by Mexicans. I especially liked *Combate "con Vic Morrow,"* a weekly World War II drama about a GI squad that roamed the French and German countryside experiencing all kinds of war adventures. *Bonanza, The Rifleman, The Fugitive, Wanted Dead or Alive, The Rebel* and *The Beverly Hillbillies* consumed too many hours of my life. Later, living in the United States, I joked with friends at my surprise to learn that all these television characters also spoke English. Musical variety shows like *Hullabaloo* and *Shindig*, which featured folk and popular rock & roll stars of the day in the United States, kept me glued to the "idiot box," as my mother called the television set with exasperation when I spent a full Saturday or Sunday watching.

The story-telling and morality tales central to these American television dramas, and something about the way a full story could be developed and wrapped-up in half-hour or hour segments, captured my imagination. There were no Argentine shows of that kind. Thinking that perhaps I could produce such a story, at thirteen I wrote a long rambling Cold War tale about a group of American soldiers whose plane was shot down over the Soviet Union—what they were doing there I don't remember. They separated into pairs and the storyline followed each pair as they tried to eludes undetected. Their fate eludes me, but I learned a lot about cities and the geography of the Soviet Union by consulting a map for my story. I don't remember whatever happened to that unfinished manuscript, but it certainly foreshadowed my interests.

British and American films dominated theatres in Argentina, screened in English with Spanish subtitles. When we first arrived, television stations regularly broadcasted American films of the 1930s and 1940s, and surprisingly even television ran them in English with Spanish subtitles. This practice stopped after the military took over. Such films as *Yankee Doodle Dandy* (1942), a musical about the career of George M. Cohan starring James Cagney, introduced me to the world of Hollywood. I enjoyed the movies of Humphrey Bogart and Tyrone Power, particularly popular on Argentine television. I must have seen them all, but my all-time favorites were *Casablanca* (1942) and *The Mark of Zorro* (1940), respectively.

I also frequented inexpensive, popular films at theatres in suburban neighborhoods. On Saturday and Sunday afternoons, they filled to capacity with double features. The *colectivo* at the corner of Roma and Avenida Maipu just two blocks from home transported me to one of the four theatres on the avenue at La Lucila, Martínez, Acassuso or San Isidro. To see the latest and most advertised films—which cost more—I took the suburban train, usually mid-afternoon on Saturdays, to the downtown station of Retiro and switched to the subway that transported me and friends to the corner of Lavalle and Florida streets. Famous for its dozens of movie theatres, Lavalle's blinking marquees lighted the seemingly unending street as thousands of people circulated, reading the theatre marquees and trying to decide which *espec-*

táculo to see. Downtown, I saw the much acclaimed and anticipated films of the era, such as *The Sound of Music, Cat Ballou, Dr. Zhivago, Mary Poppins, Goldfinger, How the West Was Won, The Great Race*, to name just a few.

In 1973, in the United States, I read a book by Chilean author Ariel Dorfman, *Para leer el Pato Donald*. This innovative if somewhat fanciful analysis of Donald Duck as propagandist and icon of American capitalism helped me understand my experience of having left Argentina fully versed in the popular culture of the United States.

Argentine television shows also had their own attraction, but they appealed to different sensibilities. As a teenager, I laughed watching *Operación Ja-Ja*, starring Jorge Porcel, a very heavy-set, popular comedian. Porcel later starred in *Las gatitas de Porcel*, which some twenty years later also appeared on Miami's Spanish-language television. He appeared with scantily clad young women in humorous skits packed with sexual innuendo. Also popular on Argentine television was an all-day Saturday afternoon and evening variety show that featured music, games and comedy. This idea and format also eventually reached US Spanish-language television audiences through the Chilean entertainer Don Francisco as *Sábado Gigante*.

Music from the US and Great Britain dominated youth culture in Venezuela and Argentina during the 1960s. In Venezuela, I remember the Chubby Checker craze and in Argentina, of course, the Beatles, Rolling Stones, Bob Dylan and others. My brother visited from college in the US every summer and introduced me to American folk music with the records of the Kingston Trio, the New Christy Minstrels and Peter Paul and Mary, but mostly I enjoyed my father's great collection of Caribbean and Mexican music on his state-of-the-art stereo system. My parents played Latino music at their parties and showed off their excellent Latin dance skills; one time they won a dance contest on the *USS Brazil* when we sailed from Buenos Aires to New York. Lying on the living room floor listening to their records, I discovered Ernesto Lecuona, Trío Los Panchos, Jorge Negrete, Tito Rodríguez, Pérez Prado, Agustín Lara and others. Harry Belafonte's calypso music kept my foot tapping. The collection also included a wonderful multi-record collection of Latin American music from across the hemisphere issued by Readers Digest that I played over and over. I probably spent more time enjoying that music than rock & roll, which I listened to mostly with friends and at high school parties.

Mary and Ricardo also encouraged me to appreciate Argentine music. They were the only ones who did. Mary loved her country's *folklórico*, the music from the interior where she was born, and Ricardo liked the *tango,* which reflected his *porteño* origins. In the capital city, the *tango* dominated, and international star Carlos Gardel's image even competed with that of Eva Perón on photo displays inside *colectivos* over the front windshield, as well as in other public places. At Mary's insistence, I listened to the folk groups, Los Chalchaleros and Los Fronterizos, who performed with gaucho costumes, guitars, and the Argentine bombo drum. Protest singers of the same tradition, Atahualpa Yupanqui and Mercedes Sosa helped raise my political consciousness in the early 1970s. For a while, I even took guitar lessons to learn Argentine folk, including *zambas, chacareras, cuecas* and *carnavalitos*, but an embarrassing voice and a lack of discipline soon derailed my aspirations. Argentine pop stars, including Palito Ortega and Sandro appeared on television frequently, keeping me posted on that tradition. A stream of international artists also made the rounds in Buenos Aires, including Puerto Rican singer-song writer, José Feliciano, who appeared on television with his seeing-eye dog; Brazilian icon Roberto Carlos; and the famous Italian children's puppet, Topo Gigio. There was much to enjoy.

I attended American-run private international schools, along with mostly American children living abroad, as well as numerous nationals and people of other nationalities. These schools prepared students for university education in the United States, but also created relatively insulated environments that socialized students as Americans.

In 1961, I entered fifth grade in Caracas at Escuela Campo Alegre, founded in 1937 to provide an American-style education through eighth grade. By the time we arrived in Caracas after two and a half years in New Jersey, I had pretty much stopped speaking Spanish. I remember understanding it without a problem, but I didn't utter a word until the school placed me in an introductory Spanish class. Within a couple of weeks, I was speaking fluently, and they reassigned me to a more advanced class, probably thinking I was quite brilliant. It was at Campo Alegre that I remember first liking history and especially the Venezuelan independence war against Spain. Simón Bolívar's military career and his decisive victory over the Spanish at the Battle of Carabobo in 1821 caught my fancy, and from then on, I was always interested in learning about Latin America's wars against Spain.

When my parents discovered that Caracas did not have an appropriate high school for my older brother Sergio, they left him in Atlanta with my father's youngest brother Ernesto and his wife Judy and enrolled him in a private college preparatory school. He could have attended the Escuela Americana with a US curriculum, but it was a primarily Spanish-language institution with a poor academic reputation. My father said it was necessary that my brother stay in the United States, and my mother reluctantly went along. Both agonized over this decision; it was their greatest sacrifice in moving to Venezuela in 1961. My mother only slowly grew used to his absence, but at least she knew that when classes ended in May, he would spend the summer in Caracas before beginning his senior year. This move opened a gulf between my brother's experiences and mine that we have spent a lifetime trying to bridge.

I attended American Community School in Buenos Aires, also known as Asociación Escuelas Lincoln, which enrolled about eight hundred first- through twelfth-grade students when I arrived. According to a US State Department report, the school had the best physical facilities among American schools in Latin America, but the academic program was lacking: "It does an adequate job of North American education but it has not introduced any new techniques in science, mathematics or reading and it is therefore not on par with the best schools in the United States." The school's focus on its facilities over the educational concerns of superintendents and principals reflected the priorities of a very hands-on Board of Directors composed of

American businessmen and one embassy representative who ran the school.

American students were the majority, although the school included students from other countries, such as Indonesia, Israel, Cuba, England and Australia. My father chaired the Board of Directors from 1969 to 1971, and one of his main concerns was the high school students' lack of interest and often their lack of respect for Argentine culture and values, especially those students who arrived from the United States with feelings of superiority and stayed for only a year or two. He particularly worried about American adolescents not understanding the realities of a military dictatorship unsympathetic to modern youth culture, whether American or Argentine. "Don't think you can act here the way you do in the United States," he often responded when students complained. "You are a guest in this country."

Despite the majority American student body, Argentina influenced the school in many ways. In the lower grades, on arriving at school in the mornings, we lined up with our classmates for the raising of the Argentine flag, and, after school, we did the same as it was lowered. We frequently sang the Argentine national anthem, as we had also done at Campo Alegre with the Venezuelan anthem. The elementary and junior high at Lincoln included a bilingual curriculum. Mornings, we attended classes in English with an American curriculum, but afternoon classes were in Spanish and taught in Argentine format. Many American kids in sixth and seventh grades did not take the Spanish classes seriously, which reflected the ugly side of American exceptionalism, many of the kids even treated the Argentine teachers disrespectfully.

I preferred the Argentine curriculum. I liked the Argentine teachers and particularly Argentine history; this was reflected in my better grades in those subjects. As in Venezuela, the independence era occupied an honored place in the Argentine curriculum. In the pantheon of Latin American independence leaders, I admired José de San Martín. He led victories over Spanish forces at the Battle of San Lorenzo in 1813 and the Chilean royalist army in 1817. San Martín's famous conference with Bolívar in Guayaquil, where he selflessly turned command of his army over to the Venezuelan general and returned to

Argentina to avoid sparking a divisive rivalry between the two leaders, confirmed his greatness for me. San Martín and Bolívar entered my consciousness long before George Washington. For American parents, including mine, the fact that their children studied Argentine history, participated in flag ceremonies and sang the national anthem merely meant the school was meeting the Argentine government requirements. For me, this represented a formative emotional engagement with Argentine identity and history.

High school, which began in eighth grade, was different: the curriculum was exclusively American. That is when I received my first taste of the exceptionalism central to historical narratives of the United States. I heard nothing more about Argentine or Latin American history, but a teacher from the United States ensured that I learned about George Washington, Thomas Jefferson, John Adams and the "extraordinary and unique" nation they established. History was my favorite subject, but the text and teacher's triumphalist tone seemed overdone, and I slowly developed a suspicion the United States was an arrogant and braggadocio nation.

Despite the high school's mission to keep US students Americanized and to favorably influence non-US students, the faculty was diverse and offered differing perspectives. Locally hired teachers came from many backgrounds. Walter Damus, a German immigrant, taught world history and geography and a French teacher, Martha Ruegg, was originally from Alsace-Lorraine. I enjoyed Damus' section on European history and especially his wonderful impersonation of Bismark. Anglo-Argentine Irene Heyartz and Jewish immigrant Naum Mittelman taught English and Chemistry, respectively. Joseph Czarnik, a Polish-American immigrant originally from Chicago, taught math. Argentines Beatriz Magaldi and Haydee de Lozada taught Spanish language and literature courses. Luis Donato "Profe" Laurita and Herminia Granitto taught physical education and coached the sports teams.

I learned soccer from Profe. I knew little about the sport before arriving in Buenos Aires in 1963. Baseball is what I played while living in Tenafly and Caracas. The attractive blue baseball uniform with the name "Adams" (a Tenafly local retail store) emblazoned across the front appealed to me more than the game itself; it made me feel important, and for some reason I especially liked how those socks cushioned my feet and reached all the way to my knees. In bed at night, I listened to New York Yankee games on a transistor radio, and my father even took us to a couple of games at Yankee stadium in the Bronx. I rooted for Mickey Mantle, Roger Maris, Yogi Berra, Bobby Richardson and Cletus Boyer, and I especially liked Hector López from Panama, he was the only Yankee with a Spanish surname. My brother Sergio and I collected baseball cards that came in bubble gum packages, and we eventually had the entire 1960 New York Yankee team. Many years later, when I went to university, my mother sold them for next to nothing at a school fundraiser in Buenos Aires. Sigh.

Venezuelans also shared enthusiasm for baseball, and it was easy to continue following the American leagues in Caracas newspapers and magazines. My father even subscribed me to a baseball magazine with team and individual photos delivered weekly from the United States. But in Argentina, a country with little baseball tradition, the sport was difficult to follow. For a time, I listened to the World Series games on short-wave radio and regularly followed professional season games in box scores, as well as the light coverage in the sports section of the *Buenos Aires Herald*. I also played on the high school softball team and the summer baseball league for American kids.

In Buenos Aires, it did not take long for me to become an enthusiast of Argentine *fútbol.* In physical education and in pick-up games with friends and eventually on the school team, I learned the game. A national obsession, *fútbol* elicited infectious enthusiasm. Stadiums erupted into celebrations accompanied with synchronized *cánticos*, or chants and songs. I watched first-division league games on weekend television, especially Club River Plate, the team from our part of town, but I only went to one professional game.

My father never liked soccer much; baseball and golf remained his favorite sports. Because he thought the stadiums were too dangerous, he never took me to a match. He felt vindicated when in June 1968, before my departure for the United States, the worst soccer tragedy in Argentine football history occurred at River's stadium in a match against its perennial rival the Boca Juniors. Something sparked a stampede of fans trying to leave the building. Those rushing toward Exit 12 found it closed and locked. Frightened fans, pushing to get out, smothered and crushed seventy-one people against the metal gates. Television coverage showed bodies strewn on the sidewalks and hysterical people screaming for their loved ones.

Authorities never revealed why that gate remained closed, but the tragedy spoke to the anxiety that always surrounded River-Boca games, exacerbated by the undercurrent of class antagonism between fans. A traditionally working-class neighborhood close to the old port, La Boca is the location of the country's most famous soccer stadium, La Bombonera, which hosts perhaps the most famous Argentine soccer club. Not all fans of the two clubs based their loyalties on class identity, but the symbolism was always prominent in their match-ups.

The first World Cup competition I remember was in 1966 when Argentina and England played a hard-fought semi-final match in London, which I listened to on the radio. Argentina lost 1-0 in a competition since referred to as "*el robo del siglo*" (the robbery of the century). The referee showed a red card to Argentine Captain Antonio Rattín, a Boca Juniors star, for seeking clarification of a call. Rattín refused to leave the field, and the police escorted him off. Playing against ten men, England scored, went on to the finals against Germany, and won its only World Cup championship. Fully engaged with the game and as infuriated as all Argentines with the outcome, I became an unconditional fan. Later, after leaving Buenos Aires, I cheered Argentina on to two World Cup victories in 1978 and 1986.

Administrators, including the superintendent and the elementary and high school principals, usually came from the United States, as did the academic counselors and a number of other teachers, but Argentines staffed the school offices and housekeeping departments. Profe, who coached softball, basketball and soccer, did more than teach physical education. He modeled positive values and a life of integrity. Although over time he learned some English, he taught only in Spanish, the only one who did (except the Spanish teachers). No one else at the school did as much as Profe to build relations between Lincoln and Argentine schools and organizations. While Lincoln school kept me connected to the United States, the thoroughly bicultural and bilingual international environment helped develop a transnational identity that has always remained with me.

⁂

The pre-Vatican II Catholic church emphasized universality rather than parochialism and my socialization in this faith also contributed to my cosmopolitan perspectives. Still, I feel annoyed when churches display national flags; this mixing of nationalism with universal religious values has always bothered me. Identical masses always in Latin, whether in Colombia, New Jersey, Venezuela or Argentina, provided a certain comfort and belonging with a universal community of believers. Catechism in Venezuela and later CYO meetings in Argentina kept me conversant with the basic tenets of Catholic belief and practice. Nevertheless, Catholicism remained more a cultural than a spiritual experience.

Not very devout, my parents never introduced faith into our household conversations; it remained in the background, a private matter for each of us. Church going seemed to be more of an obligation than a commitment for my parents; we did not even offer a prayer at meals, and neither did I later in life. My mother grew up a non-practicing and unschooled Presbyterian. Although catechized as Roman Catholic in high school, my father was also non-practicing. He remained emotionally distant from the Church for most of his life. This was common in Cuba, but our family's revolutionary masonic background contributed to this attitude. My father's family only rarely attended Mass, and when they did, my grandfather remained at the back of the church with his arms crossed, while the rest of the family sat in the pews. He stood there as if daring God to have a go at him and, according to my father, he considered priests in their cassocks effeminate, suited to care for the spiritual needs of women and children, but certainly not to be taken seriously by men. Late in life, my father attended Mass every morning, but more than once commented that his family's masonic influences had affected his efforts to express his faith fully.

Like many Catholics, I always had my quarrels with the Church and especially wondered why God was so distant and inaccessible in spite of the Church's claims to the contrary. I was never a good Catholic, if that is to be defined as adherence to doctrine, Mass attendance and engagement with parish communities, which is certainly a solid definition. Nevertheless, like a good Catholic, I assimilated fear and guilt and thought much about good and bad, and right and wrong. For me, as a youth, Catholicism resided mostly in the senses, in empathy and emotion, not in the mind. The nebulous mystical realm inspired me to attend church regularly until age sixteen, but then I began to intellectualize what I believed. Faith became more difficult.

My mother converted to Catholicism in Bogotá, a devoutly Catholic country. She had my brother Sergio and I baptized, and then my two younger siblings who were born in Colombia. At the appointed time, I made my first confession and Communion in Bogotá. On a bench next to my classmates, I waited my turn with the priest in the confessional. Darkness enveloped the church except for candles, candles everywhere. The look of anxiety on my classmates' faces, and my own I suspect, underscored the seriousness of the mystery at hand. Wandering through the church, my eyes encountered a marble Christ on one knee with a cross on his back. Poor guy, I thought. I turned my head toward a niche containing the Virgin standing over even more flickering candles representing the prayers of the faithful. Then I spied our First Communion teacher looking at me disapprovingly. Bowing my head, I gripped my rosary tightly.

"Forgive me, Father, for I have sinned," was what I would say in a few minutes and then recite my list of sins. At seven years old, I could not think of too many sins, but I still felt burdened. Then, the priest would absolve me and give me my penance of five Hail Mary's and ten Our Fathers. I tried to remember how it went: "Our Father who does art in Heaven, hollow be thy name…" Got it. I reviewed the prayer again. "Not *does* art; not *hollow*—hallowed," I corrected myself. But, before leaving the confessional, I would also have to recite the Act of Contrition, professing my sorrow for having sinned. I could never remember that one very well. It began with "Oh my God, I am hardly sorry for having offended thee," but then in a panic

I opened my Communion book and reviewed the prayer. "Heartily, not *hardly*," I corrected myself. It was my turn. I rose slowly, walked to the booth, pulled the curtains closed, kneeled and could barely make out the priest through the little screened window. "Forgive me, Father, for I have sinned," I began.

The next day I arrived at the church for my First Communion wearing a brand-new grey suit that matched all the other boys and carrying a large candle with both hands. The girls all had on matching white dresses. A choir gave the occasion a solemn tone as several scores of children prepared to receive Holy Communion for the first time. As Mass began, I went over my checklist of preparations. I had not eaten breakfast as instructed nor sinned since confession the prior afternoon, at least not that I remembered. The moment arrived, and I walked in the line of children forward to receive Holy Communion. We walked slowly, and I anticipated the moment God would enter my body. "How could a little piece of round bread *be* Christ, anyway?" I thought. As I drew closer, I remembered the instructions: open my mouth and extend my tongue slightly. The priest said "*Cuerpo de Cristo*" (in Latin). I responded, "Amen." After receiving the host, I was careful not to chew. Apparently, it would be painful for Jesus. It just melted on my tongue the way the teacher had said it would. I crossed myself, returned to the pew and kneeled with my classmates. It tasted just like bread. I waited for something to happen. I only noticed that a tension had lifted after the much-anticipated event. I waited some more but felt nothing else. Communion only affected adults; many looked serious, some held their faces in their hands and some even had tears running down their faces. Maybe only adults felt God.

In Venezuela, we remained a church-going family. I went to Sunday school and took my Confirmation, choosing the name Santiago, James. As an altar boy, I became particularly enthralled with the pageantry of the liturgy, even though I had no idea what was being said. Everything about Latin seemed mysterious, and I recall the moment of consecration as particularly moving. As my booklet, *How to Serve Low Mass*, reminded me, "You are now at the most solemn moment of the Mass—the Consecration—and you should try to realize as best you can what is about to take place." It emphasized, "Let your exterior reverence show your real internal feelings." Kneeling behind the priest as he faced the altar with his back to the congregation, I waited for him to genuflect. That was my signal to ring a little gold bell with my right hand. Then as the priest raised the Host towards the sky, I raised his chasuble with my left hand and again rang the bell. When the priest placed the Host back on the altar, I released the chasuble and rang the bell for a third time. We did the same thing when the priest now raised the chalice with the wine. The Pater Noster followed, ending with "*Et ne nos inducas in tentatinonem.*" I responded: "*Sed libera nos a malo.*" The priest followed with, "*Per omnia saecula saeculorum. Amén.*" "*Amén,*" I would repeat. The priest finished with "*Pax domini sit semper vobiscum*" and me with "*Et cum spiritu tuo.*" After Mass, I rushed to get breakfast, since we could not eat on Sunday mornings before taking Communion.

My first real concrete awareness of the Church's global reach was in Buenos Aires, when we still lived at the Claridge Hotel. Pope John XXIII had fallen critically ill. Newspapers and television news tracked his decline, and on June 3, 1963, he passed away. In the next days and weeks, I followed the funeral and the papal conclave that elected Pope Paul VI. The pageantry and ritual associated with the entire process of Pope John's death and the appointment of his successor not only impressed and captivated me, but for the first time provided a concrete glimpse of the Church's universality. Only something as grandiose and universal as the Catholic Church, I thought, could be worthy of representing God's word to the world.

Our family's engagement with the Church changed in Argentina. My parents' responsibilities to work and community increased, and they both became more involved with weekend social activities and especially golf on Sundays. We attended church as a family less frequently, but I continued to go on my own. Unlike in Colombia and Venezuela, where we attended Mass with many Americans, in Buenos Aires I went to neighborhood churches in San Isidro and Olivos. The music and congregational responses echoed off the walls in those large cathedral-like churches, and the excessively long sermons always emphasized personal salvation and the dangers of hell. This may be why at age thirteen or fourteen I began thinking a great deal about death and the afterlife. Death fascinated and terrified me at the same time. I also wondered why God never responded to my requests for clarification about these matters. Contemplating nonexistence was a bit overwhelming, and I became particularly attracted to the crucifix with the hanging Christ evoking a kind of mysterious inevitability.

These existential struggles were mostly a private matter. The only serious question I ever remember posing to my mother about God was one evening when my father quietly but hurriedly packed his bag and prepared to leave for Atlanta. His brother Ernesto had died suddenly at the age of thirty-three. The youngest of the four brothers, Ernesto was the only one of the four to remain in Atlanta, where he had attended Emory University, worked in the insurance business and married my aunt Judy, the daughter of an Atlanta businessman. They had two daughters, Lisa and Gail, who were five and two when my brother Sergio arrived at the house and found our uncle dead on the living room floor. He had spoken to Uncle Ernesto on the phone less than an hour earlier, asking to borrow his car for the day. I had met my uncle for the first time that I remembered the previous year on a family visit to the United States. He was very attentive and genuine with me, and I remember thinking how much he looked like my father. The brothers spoke in Spanish, which warmed my heart. Hearing them speak their childhood language seemed so intimate somehow, especially since they never spoke to me in Spanish.

I recall my father's drawn and sad face, and he did not say a word as he left the house for the airport, nor did he say much about what happened when he returned about a week later. After my father's departure, I asked my mother why God would take away such a young and vibrant man. She did not know, and I wondered even more about death.

This loss occurred for me without reference to extended family and community, from a distance, without seeing a body or attending a funeral. All theoretical, really. Without community, faith floats in the ether, lacking substance, and is easily subverted. For the first time in my life, intellect challenged faith, a questioning that has never ceased. The devout Catholic seeks the integration of his faith and his reason, but for me they were in ongoing dialogue and conflict. Sometimes faith won arguments, but the intellect took charge most times. They never integrated and coexisted easily. My parents did not say much more about my uncle, but this first awareness of a death in the family left me wondering about this mysterious God. I felt terribly sorry that I would never see Uncle Ernesto again.

After this, my relationship with religion became more distant and I finally walked away after an incident in Buenos Aires during my regular Saturday afternoon reconciliation. After confessing to my regular litany of sins, the priest asked if I was sure that I had covered everything.

I thought for a moment and said, "Yes."

"Isn't it true," he asked, "that at your age you are sinful with your body? Tell me about that," he invited.

Taken aback that he should question me like that, I did what all adolescents should do in such a situation: lied. "I don't know what you're talking about, Father."

"Come on, now, I know you've had certain thoughts and touched yourself. . . . "

His words sounded like a plea for a lurid story. A creepy feeling overcame me, and I left the confessional embarrassed and angry. I never returned to the confessional. Shortly after that, perhaps less from that experience than my changing adolescent interests and my still lingering questions about Uncle Ernesto's sudden death, my attendance at church all but stopped.

Despite this distancing, the Church had formed me in many ways, and I maintained a Catholic identity with a universal take that reinforced the reality of my formative transnational experiences.

Vacations north every two years kept me engaged with the United States as a concrete rather than theoretical place. During those excursions, my father always worked at the General Motors offices in New York City for two weeks, and then we would spend two more weeks visiting family. We had no immediate family in New York, but visited Nana and her second husband, Alvin, in Philadelphia, Uncle

Ernesto and family in Atlanta and my maternal grandmother in Clio and then later Houghton Lake, Michigan, where on those occasions my mother's two brothers and their families joined us.

Our Pan American Airline flights always landed at New York's Idlewild Airport. Although renamed John F. Kenndey Airport in 1963, we continued for many years to refer to it as Idlewild. Architecturally and technologically modern, the Pan American terminal had interesting sculptures, a large fountain outside, air conditioning and doors that swung open automatically. As my gateway to the United States, the act of arriving at Idlewild reminded me of the wonders I would surely encounter in the following weeks.

From the airport, we would go directly to the Manger-Windsor Hotel at 100 West 58th Street at Avenue of the Americas. I found the city's traffic and hustle and bustle always exhilarating, and my mother, siblings and I spent a lot of time at Central Park just a block from the hotel, where we strolled and visited the zoo. While we enjoyed the park and visited friends in Tenafly, my father worked briefing his superiors about matters in Argentina.

New Yorker's gruff and utilitarian demeanor and endearing accents stood out. I always returned to Buenos Aires mimicking the accents and happy to return to what in my tender years I considered to be a more sophisticated city. One day in New York, my father asked me to buy new padlocks for our travel trunks. I went to a hardware store down the street from the hotel and asked the attendant for two locks.

He promptly threw two packs of cigarettes on the counter, saying, "Here ya'are, kid."

Puzzled, I looked at him and repeated, "I need locks, not cigarettes. Padlocks."

"Oh, why didn't you say so, kid? I thought you wanted two packs of Larks."

We both laughed, and he gave me the locks.

I always got a kick out of seeing a man dressed as a Viking on 42nd street outside the Port Authority building. The towering man, with a helmet, shield and lance, walked up and down the street shouting incomprehensible things. People just walked past him as if he didn't exist; each time we passed there, I stopped and stared at the spectacle for a while. This kind of performance is commonplace today but was exotic, I think, in 1964; certainly, for a kid living in Buenos Aires, where the Viking would have been arrested in short order.

On another occasion, the whole family went shopping, and my father decided to take a cab back to the hotel rather than bring all the bags we were carrying onto the subway. When we reached the Manger-Windsor, the cabbie opened the trunk and retrieved the shopping bags. I took mine and started into the hotel as my father paid the fare, but then I heard a commotion. I turned and saw them yelling at each other and thought the confrontation might end in a fistfight. Then the cabbie threw some money at my father, got into his car and screeched away.

"What happened?" I asked.

"He thought the tip wasn't enough and he threw it at me," he said indignantly. "He thought he deserved more for having to get out of the car, open the trunk and hand us our bags," he complained. "The hell with him! Only in New York!" he added for good measure. Such a disagreement, had there even been one, would have been handled in a more civilized manner in Buenos Aires, I remember thinking.

Consumer culture in the United States always produced in me anticipation and excitement. When visiting my grandmother in Michigan, we ate hamburgers and drank iced-cold rootbeer in mugs at an A&W drive-in restaurant. On our drives from New York, we spent nights at a Holiday Inn or Howard Johnson, the elite motels of the day. Either was fine with me. The food seemed so luxurious, the rooms bright and fancy and the swimming pools were a lot of fun. Large grocery stores with carefully packaged foods had everything, not like in Argentina where people bought their produce, meat and dry goods at different stores. Department stores likewise had everything in incredible abundance, and on those visits, my mother bought me enough pants, shirts and shoes, among other things, to last me until our next visit two years hence.

In Argentina, American clothes carried status, but according to my mother, they were also cheaper and better quality. I also thought Argentine candy could not compare with American chocolates, such as

Snickers, Mounds and Hershey bars. One year, we visited our friends in Tenafly and went directly to the television room. "You will be in for a surprise," our host said. He handed me a remote and told me to push the power button, and the television came on. I could see a cable that went around the wall to the television and saw how it worked. Then I saw color on the screen, which I had heard about but was amazed to see. In the United States, everything seemed clean and orderly. I never saw walls with graffiti, except in the subways of New York.

I grasped the cultural chasm between Argentina and the United States during a visit to the 1964 New York's World Fair when I was thirteen. Uncle Jorge, on "home leave" at the same time from Brazil, where he directed General Motors Acceptance Corporation in Sao Paulo, joined us at the fair. His Brazilian girlfriend, Leah, a Pan American Airlines stewardess, came along. Of the many pavilions, General Motors' *Futurama* highlighted the technological prowess of the United States. Seated in moving chairs, we passed elaborately produced 3D models of what life would look like in the future, in the depths of the oceans, in futuristic cities and even on the moon. The exhibit also explored what the future held in the world of transportation. When I read about the General Motors' 1939 *Caravana* in Havana so many years later, I immediately thought of the *Futurama*. They had the same purpose: to promote the technological wonders of the United States.

That evening, a different and much more alluring aesthetic awaited me. Uncle Jorge asked me to join him and Leah for a flamenco show and dinner at the Spanish Pavilion. Though I had only vague notions of what flamenco was, I said yes. But what of my attire? I was wearing a T-shirt, shorts and sneakers. Not to worry, my uncle said, and off we went. Enchanting guitars, powerful dance and emotional songs created a breathtaking world. I had never heard anything like it; the soulful *cantos* remained in my heart for days. Even now, flamenco drives straight to my soul and mesmerizes me as it did that first evening I encountered it in 1964.

Then, we went to the Toledo restaurant, an elegant place requiring a reservation and coat and tie. The *maître de* whispered something to my uncle and then quickly went to the coat check. He returned with a coat and tie. "The smallest size we have," he said. The jacket fit big, reaching my thighs. We rolled up the sleeves and the tie looked odd over my T-shirt. I felt like a circus clown, but the outfit passed muster. The dinner, my uncle had assured me, would be very exclusive, and it was indeed. I can't recall what we ate, but the good food, professional waiter and the song-and-dance around the selection and pouring of wine remains vivid. When the waiter brought two glasses, my uncle asked for a third.

"The boy is too young, in New York anyway. *En España sí, pero aquí no*," he declared.

"*Ah, sí, vale*," my uncle muttered. "Okay, then, two glasses but put mine right between us, and I'm sure you won't be offended if he sips a taste now and again," he said with a wink. "He has only had Argentine wine, and its time he tasted good Spanish wine."

"Of course, it would be a crime if he didn't taste our wine," the waiter winked back. "I'm sure I won't even notice," he whispered with a smile.

After the meal, we sipped coffee and the waiter arrived with a flan that he set aflame with his lighter. An unforgettable delicious dazzling dessert. That night at my uncle's hotel, I thanked him, especially for the flamenco:

"I loved it."

"You should," he said, "it's our ancestors' music," and he settled back in bed, pulled an airline sleeping mask over his eyes, inserted ear plugs and turned off the light.

These vacations were fun but evoked some conflicting feelings and perceptions about the United States. That day and evening at the World's Fair in the heart of New York City, the stark contrasts between Anglo-American and Hispanic pavilions stood out. The Hispanic flamenco spoke from the soul. The American exhibits felt cold, distant, technological. My uneasy feelings about these contrasts grew stronger later. I thought of Argentina as the product of ancient and sophisticated Mediterranean civilizations that guided their societies with tested wisdoms. US capitalism inserted itself in the world with crude pecuniary interests and little respect for tradition and the past. American self-centeredness and claims of exceptionalism put me off, especially as expressed in self-congratulatory and narcissistic ultra-patriotic markers of which I was always very much aware. By age fourteen or fifteen, I thought of the United States as a nation not morally or culturally equipped for world leadership. American-sponsored schools in South America sought to connect me with the United States, but the reality is that Venezuela and Argentina won me over. As diplomats like to say, I "went native," and much later when I applied to the US Department of State for employment as a Foreign Service Officer, it became clear that the interviewers distrusted my political instincts and, perhaps, ultimately, my loyalty.

Americans in Buenos Aires more often than not spoke about the country that hosted them in condescending ways. At gatherings of the General Motors "family," conversations frequently revealed these American attitudes of superiority. An incompetent Argentine government, self-serving labor leaders, complaints about public services, maids that could not be trusted, lazy gardeners and a generally ignorant population usually topped the list of problems these Americans had with the country. Even the American kids, especially those who lived in Argentina for a short time, looked down on their Argentine peers. They frequently referred to Argentine youth as *caqueros* (greasers is the only word that comes to mind in American slang), particularly those whose clothing styles were decidedly local and who used *gomina* to slick their long hair straight back on their heads, which was quite common.

Eventually, I heard some of my thoughts about the United States and Americans legitimated in the writings of José Enrique Rodó, the early twentieth-century Uruguayan modernist writer and philosopher. Oh, I thought, I wasn't the first to think this. In my university literature class, I read Rodó's classic *Ariel*, written in 1900. Rodó rejected the utilitarian and materialistic assumptions of technological progress exemplified in American values; these were criticisms Ricardo often expressed about the United States when I sometimes joined him for a glass of wine. *Arielistas* viewed the United States as uncultured, indifferent to notions of truth and beauty, and drawn to unrestrained acquisitiveness and accumulation. They contrasted the US' impersonal society with Latin America's personalist aesthetic in tune with spiritual and humanistic traits and traditions. Like Rodó's disciples, my heart belonged to the South, but somehow I knew I could not escape the North.

11
The World Isn't Fair

Introverted and overly sensitive, I enjoyed being alone in our large comfortable homes in Buenos Aires. I filled the hours with plenty of television. In my bedroom, I spent time inventing games, reading newspapers and news magazines, as well as daydreaming about what the future would bring. The solitude itself lead to questioning and a growing desire to know about the outside world. As I grew up, I accepted, rejected or tried to refashion my ideas according to my needs. At first, things were the way they were. Then, there were questions: "Why this landscape, and not another? Why here and not there? Why rich, why poor? Where do I belong?" These questions eventually took me on a surprising journey of discovery involving my sense of place and belonging in the world.

I first recognized human social distress and injustice for what it was on our sea voyage to Venezuela in March 1961. Even my privileged and insulated life in South America did not protect me from the inevitable realization that the world was not fair. My parents remained strangely silent about such matters, but perhaps religious faith or just an observant and sensitive nature inherited from my mother forced me to notice and react. When the *SS Santa Paula* docked at the Dutch islands of Aruba and Curacao, standing on the deck I saw tourists aboard the ship throw coins into the water below. Diving into the filthy oil-slicked water, teenage boys, and even younger ones, retrieved them. The boys surfaced triumphantly, holding the coins in their fingers and motioning for the tourists to throw more. It reminded me of a zoo where seals dove for fish tossed in by keepers. Why didn't tourists just give them money rather than encouraging them to risk their lives?

Before sunlight a couple of days later, the ship docked at La Guaira, the port for Caracas. I awoke and excitedly raced up to the ship's main deck and scanned the scene. Across the docks beyond the cranes, trucks, crates and dozens of working men, I noticed a town of makeshift shanties made of tin, cardboard and whatever else people could find for shelter. I just stared for a while until my father joined me and I asked with some consternation, "Is this our new home?" No, he reassured me, Caracas was in a valley across the mountains. I felt relieved, but this proof of Latin America's social reality did not disappear on the other side of the mountains. Similar shantytowns hugged the sides of the mountains that ringed Caracas, and every major rainstorm sent raging waters down the sides of hills taking with it many of the fragile structures. Television news routinely reported on the numerous deaths associated with these rainstorms.

Life in Venezuela was the polar opposite of my experience in Tenafly, New Jersey. In 1958, we settled into a comfortable house at 2 Glenwood Ct., in Tenafly, a small suburban town just across the George Washington Bridge from Manhattan. Sergio enrolled at Tenafly High School, I attended Maugham Elementary and Cindy went to Mount Carmel Catholic School. Still too young for school, Jeffrey remained at home. This white upper- and middle-class village existed free of the poverty and racial strife evident in many sectors of American society. I had no awareness of the era's civil rights activism, which certainly did not intrude on that homogeneous little town.

Life for me involved riding my bicycle freely throughout Tenafly and to school, exploring the nearby woods, trading and "flipping" baseball cards with friends, going to the town center to buy sweets, and generally enjoying a carefree life. The only hint that all may not have been well with the world were the pint-size UNICEF milk cartons we carried during trick-or-treating on Halloween night to raise money for the poor. My parents voted for President John F. Kennedy, the symbol of a new generation assuming leadership in the United States with idealistic and optimistic plans for the future. Kennedy also won our classroom election at school. Had I remained in Tenafly, I surely would have imbibed the American narrative of exceptionalism and embraced the self-congratulatory, hyper-nationalist rhetoric so common in the United States. Thankfully, I avoided that fate, but not the troubling realities in South America and their existential implications for my life.

∽ ∽ ∽

I reached the age of reason in the early 1960s, and so, the polarizing Cold War arguments of the times shaped and marked me. Emerging from the devastation of World War II, the United States and the Soviet Union vied for the hearts and minds of their citizens and citizens of the world: Capitalism vs Socialism, Democracy vs Dictatorship of the Proletariat. People chose sides. A time arrived when I awakened to the strong political and social tensions around me, and the strained relationship between Latin American nations and the United States became evident.

I knew nothing of the intense political struggles in Colombia during the 1950s. I learned later that in 1948 just a few years before our arrival to Bogotá, students from across Latin America, including a young Cuban student radical named Fidel Castro, attended an anti-imperialist conference called to protest a meeting of hemispheric foreign ministers gathered to sign the charter of the Organization of American States, the regional version of the United Nations. During this conference, popular Colombian Liberal Party leader, Jorge Eliécer Gaitán, was assassinated, sparking *El Bogotazo*, three days of bloody rioting in the capital, which unraveled Colombia's already fragile political system. An uncontested national election the next year installed as president Conservative Party candidate General Gustavo Rojas Pinillas. Many radicalized Liberals joined small bands of communist guerrillas in the countryside, initiating an extended period of political unrest in the country known simply as *la violencia*.

My father never told me anything concrete about the political violence that contributed to our eventual departure from Colombia in 1958, but the travel diary of a young Argentine medical student named Ernesto Guevara Lynch gave me some clues. Intent on discovering

Latin America, Guevara and a friend traveled from their hometown of Rosario on a motorcycle, on buses, and later hitchhiked through Chile, Bolivia and Peru, planning to complete their adventure in Venezuela. When they reached Iquitos, the two medical students caught a riverboat on the Amazon River for a two-day journey to a leprosarium in San Pedro near Peru's jungle frontier with Brazil and Colombia. They stayed for two weeks, learning about the realities of the disease and making friends with the medical staff and the lepers themselves, with whom they played soccer and socialized. When they made plans to continue their journey, the community built them a raft on which they intended to travel to Manaus, from where they would make their way to Venezuela. It did not work out as they had planned. After a couple of days on the river, they ran out of food and abandoned the idea. Instead, they made their way into Colombia and arrived in Bogotá.

It was July 1952, Guevara described a dark political climate in Bogotá in a letter to his mother: "Of all the countries we have traveled through, this is the one in which individual guarantees are most suppressed; the police patrol the streets with their rifles on their shoulders and constantly demand one's passport." After he was arrested for making fun of a police officer who asked to see his documents, Guevara and his friend made their way to Venezuela. Colombia, he said, had "an asphyxiating climate, which Colombians can stand if they want, but we're beating it as soon as we can."

At that time, the young traveler and future guerrilla fighter was not on anybody's radar, but my father did see first-hand some violent consequences of the political repression Guevara observed. In August 1956, a disaster struck in the heart of Cali, an important city of about 250,000 persons 185 miles southwest of Bogotá. Years later, I saw in my father's collection of photographs images of damaged cars and trucks, some with large rocks sitting on their dented roofs and hoods. Presumably taken for insurance purposes, the photos revealed a dramatic event, but it was in a *New York Times* article that I learned the story. A seven-truck military convoy loaded with dynamite and gasoline that was parked for the evening in front of a railroad terminal and close to several businesses, including General Motors and Ford, ignited during the night. Explosions rocked the city, destroying the terminal and razing eight city blocks, including hotels, cafes, hundreds of small shops and a military headquarters and barracks. The blast destroyed dozens of cars parked on the streets, and windowpanes shattered within a three-mile radius. Debris covered the streets and buildings. The explosion even blew off the doors of St. Peter's Cathedral, thirteen miles away. More than 1,000 people died, many asleep in their small working-class residences tucked away in this mostly commercial district. While authorities never discovered the cause of the explosion, many in the press believed the seven trucks, each carrying five tons of dynamite that could not have exploded spontaneously, had been sabotaged. They pointed to recent guerrilla activities in the area and the increasing resistance to Rojas Pinillas's dictatorship.

My father traveled to Cali to survey the badly damaged General Motors agency and reported on the condition of the hundreds of damaged vehicles. What he saw had a sobering effect on his perceptions of what lay ahead for Colombia. My only memory of Colombia's troubles was driving through town one day and coming upon a military roadblock. A soldier approached the car and told my father he could not pass. I was too young to have any idea what was happening, nevertheless that encounter remained lodged in my memory, especially the soldier's rifle.

Images of Fidel Castro's frenzied speeches on Venezuelan television, though my parents never discussed them, remained imprinted in my mind and marked the moment when I first sympathized with Latin America's plight. On April 15, 1961, Cuban exiles flew B-26 bombers out of Nicaragua and began bombing Cuban airfields. This was the beginning of the long-awaited CIA-sponsored invasion of Cuba. About 1,300 exiles landed on Cuba's southern coast, but faced 20,000 Cuban troops that quickly encircled them. The CIA's plan to provide the Cuban exile invaders with US air cover while they secured a beachhead went awry when President Kennedy—who had just taken office and inherited the plan from the previous administration under Dwight D. Eisenhower—withdrew overt US involvement. Without support, about 1,180 exile fighters finally surrendered several days later. In the aftermath of this crisis, on May 1, Castro jubilantly celebrated the victory, proclaimed the Revolution socialist and declared that instead of giving each Cuban the vote, the Revolution would give each one a rifle. In October 1962, Cuba again dominated Venezuelan television channels and newspaper headlines as the United States and the Soviet Union confronted each other over nuclear missiles on the island.

These events had a lasting impact on the Western Hemisphere for the following decades, and we encountered its reverberations at different times in our daily lives in South America. Too young to understand what had precipitated the Cuban Revolution, much less able to assess its implications for Latin America; I only remember my feelings about the sensational television coverage in Caracas. I had a vague sense that the Revolution represented something good for Cuba, an impression as it turned out shared by millions of people in Latin America who recognized the Revolution as the conscience of the people, a government determined to face the region's intractable poverty and suffering. My father never discussed what was happening in Cuba with me, probably assuming, as adults often do, that children are oblivious to events outside their immediate domain, but I was becoming aware of the political violence associated with Latin America's colonial legacy of authoritarianism and extreme social inequality. We experienced the turmoil and revolutionary agitation that plagued Colombia, Venezuela and Argentina, and eventually I understood the relationship between that turbulence and Latin Americans' embrace of the Cuban Revolution.

The consequences for South America of Castro's triumph in Cuba first appeared in Venezuela. I remember gunshots and explosions in the distance occasionally interrupting my play outside our house on Calle California in Caracas, but only years later did I learn that

Cuban-inspired-and-supported guerrillas sought to overthrow the government. Cuban efforts to undermine the Venezuelan government began soon after fifty-year-old President Rómulo Betancourt, a social democrat, had replaced the almost decade-long dictatorship of Marcos Pérez Jiménez that ended in January 1958. Elected president just a month and a half after thirty-three-year-old Fidel Castro marched into Havana in January 1959, Betancourt, a seasoned politician of many years involved in reformist politics, did not like Castro. Just weeks after the Cuban revolutionary victory but before Betancourt's inauguration, Castro accepted an invitation from students in Venezuela to visit their country. Thousands of admirers turned out to greet him, in dramatic contrast to the thousands who in 1958 had jeered and spit at Vice-President Richard Nixon and attacked his car while he rode through the streets of Caracas.

During his visit, Castro asked Betancourt to divert Venezuelan oil to Cuba. Betancourt did not trust the young revolutionary and neither did the Venezuelan military establishment, and they refused his request. Betancourt preferred to cooperate with President John F. Kennedy's Alliance for Progress and continued to ship Venezuelan oil to the United States. Intended as a response to Cuba's call for socialism in the hemisphere, the United States promised economic resources for Latin American governments willing to embrace reform instead of revolution, including significant land reform. In August 1961, Ernesto Guevara, now known as Che, represented Cuba at the Organization of American States' economic conference at Punta del Este, Uruguay, where the United States unveiled Kennedy's plans for Latin America. In his speech at the conference, Guevara denounced the proposal as intentionally vague and designed to raise the hopes and confuse the millions of Latin Americans living in poverty.

Guevara had other plans for the region. Intent on sparking revolution throughout Latin America, in early 1962 Guevara hatched a plan called Operación Andina and sent agents to Bolivia to promote guerrilla operations there, as well as in Peru and Argentina. His recruits established a guerrilla unit in the northwest Argentine province of Salta on the border with Bolivia. Guevara planned to join them at the appropriate moment and take charge. Even before this, the Argentine had his eye on Venezuela, where Betancourt's relationship with Castro continued to deteriorate. Venezuelan radicals wanting to follow Castro's example received support from a growing Communist Party, and with Cuba's material help and training launched urban and rural guerrilla movements. Frequent assaults on government buildings, military installations and banks routinely left police and military personnel dead.

Cuban intrusions into Venezuelan politics provoked a break in diplomatic relations in November 1961, and Betancourt supported expelling Cuba from the Organization of American States and isolating Castro economically. In fact, a month after the break in relations, Kennedy and his wife Jackie visited Venezuela. I remember well her appearance on television where she gave a Spanish-language speech in which she called for greater social justice across Latin America. She impressed many Venezuelans to no end. While the political nuances of what was going on in Venezuela eluded me, awareness of the turmoil and violence did not.

Appalling social conditions were at the heart of the turmoil in Latin America. During the post-war era, industrial policies in Latin America accelerated a dramatic rural to urban migration of the region's poorest, especially to the capital cities. Throughout urban Latin America, poverty-stricken populations fended for themselves, squatting and creating neighborhoods known in different countries as *ranchos*, *barriadas*, *favelas*, *colonias* or *villas miserias*. Those migrants who managed to secure jobs in the cities actually fared better than they had when they had lived in the countryside, but the new industrial economies could not absorb most newcomers. Many workers viewed these shelters as temporary while they sought economic opportunity and stability, but moving on was usually an illusion. Industrial policies really just transferred the poor to cities, where they became visible to the affluent classes like never before.

In Caracas, kids my own age and younger walked the streets without shoes and even shirts, cleaning car windshields and hustling for money. One day while walking home from school, a group of barefoot kids surrounded me on the sidewalk and half-heartedly wrestled me for my watch. Startled, I swung my book bag at them and ran while they laughed and jeered. I looked back just in time to see them flipping me their middle fingers. The fright passed quickly, but I didn't feel angry, just troubled. Why did so many children have so little and yet I had so much, I wondered? I remembered the kids diving into the squalid waters in Aruba.

Even the cosmopolitan and sophisticated city of Buenos Aires could not hide its similar problems. In Argentina, rural employers increasingly replaced the city-bound migrants with workers from the poorest northwestern provinces, such as Jujuy or Salta, or even immigrants from Paraguay and Bolivia. Many of them also eventually ended up in Buenos Aires, populating the already established "temporary" *villas* that became permanent despite their precarious legal status, lack of utilities and poor living conditions. The poor continued to migrate, and in the mid-1960s about 280,000 people inhabited "*villas de emergencia*," their official designation in metropolitan Buenos Aires.

Perhaps a majority of people survived in what economists and sociologists refer to as informal economies. On the suburban trains, from the exclusive Barrio Norte neighborhoods where we lived to the Retiro station downtown, children my age sold candies and other merchandise. They walked up and down the aisles setting their products on the arms of the train seats hoping someone would buy something. Frequently, on my way downtown to see a movie, feelings of empathy inspired me to leave money beside their merchandise. Whenever my family went to a restaurant, an adolescent or young man with a rag usually appeared and directed my father to a parking spot on the public street. He opened my father's door and announced he would watch the car and give it a good cleaning. After dinner, my father gave a tip. The *sereno* was another informal job. Riding a bicycle late at night, the *sereno* rode through the neighborhood blowing a distinctive four- or five-toned flute to let families know he was on patrol. Presumably, thieves also heard the whistle and they moved on to other neighborhoods. During Christmas holidays, *serenos* collected their *aguinaldos* house to house. People invented a living in countless ways, but the children always caught my attention. I empathized with them.

At the San Isidro Golf Club in the summers, I sometimes played golf with the boys who fished balls out of the water hazards for tips. The kids were my age; they lived in slum-like neighborhoods near the club. When the course closed for maintenance on Mondays, caddies and ball boys could play as long as they did not interfere with maintenance activities. Sometimes they invited me to play with them, and it didn't take me long for me to stop accepting their betting propositions. My infrequent efforts at golf could not match the skills they had developed from a young age, and after a time I realized that they probably rubbed their hands together greedily when they saw me coming. These encounters often provoked more moments of introspection about privilege and disadvantage. "There but for the grace of God go I."

My closeness with Mary and Ricardo also at times evoked feelings of concern. They had showed me first-hand what it meant to start from scratch in Argentina. They bought a small *solar* (urban lot) in an undeveloped outlying district of Buenos Aires without drainage or running water. I saw first-hand how Argentines survived the country's long-term economic travails. Cement block by cement block, Mary and Ricardo built their home, laying the next one whenever they had saved enough money to buy it. Seeing their small one-room structure with a tin roof, an obligatory outside grill for *asados* and an outhouse some distance away, I felt guilty. They built their home with pride, but I could not believe this was all they could afford! These were the only adults I knew who had so little. I learned not to take for granted all that I had.

Their family survived by pooling work and resources and remaining close-knit. They all contributed to their goal of achieving housing security. Mary's brother, his wife, two daughters and mother lived in a modest rented apartment while Mary worked her job as a live-in domestic. Her brother worked as a mechanic in a small shop and only earned enough to pay for transportation and a few groceries. Since he had no other employment prospects, he remained at the shop, hoping for things to improve. Ricardo's mother lived in a Perón-era rent-control apartment downtown, and his sister lived in Chicago and sent money to the family when she could. They not only pooled their money to build a modest house, but also sent the two daughters to a private school to ensure a better future for them.

My parents never treated Mary or Ricardo disrespectfully, that I knew, but certain household protocols made me uncomfortable. My parents enjoyed occasional formal Sunday mid-afternoon family lunches. Generally, my father arrived home late from work during the week, and only my mother joined him for dinner at nine or ten, Argentine-style. We ate much earlier in the kitchen, accompanied by my mother or Mary. So Sunday lunches were the time for the family to dine together. We dressed for those ritual occasions with shoes, nice slacks and shirts, and sat in the dining room to a formally set table with the best china and silverware. That's when Mary really became a servant, which I thoroughly hated. Somehow, this role seemed different from her everyday presence in our lives. It did not fit her strong personality or her sense of dignity. My mother rang a table bell to signal Mary to serve lunch or clear the table. How Mary felt about those moments I didn't know, but I felt humiliated for her. I did not relate to Mary as a servant, but she was a servant and this made me feel awkward. When I complained about this formality without mentioning Mary specifically, my parents explained that one day we would appreciate knowing social and table etiquette. Fortunately, this initiation into high-bourgeois culture happened infrequently, but they were right. It came in handy.

Outside a thirty-foot fence that separated our school sports field from railroad tracks and the banks of the Río de la Plata, at some fifteen feet below a small community of people squatted in huts made of wood, tin and other material. They built as close as possible to the edge of the long-abandoned railroad tracks so the tide and waves of the river would not reach them. Families lived in these tenuous shelters, and they became part of our normal landscape as we played on the sports fields during physical education and baseball or soccer practice. That small community was a constant reminder of the social inequality of the country in which we lived.

The Barrio Norte neighborhood of San Isidro not far from where I lived included La Cava, one of Buenos Aires' largest and most notorious shantytowns, where thousands of poverty-stricken people lived. On Saturdays, I played baseball, and on the way to and from the fields of the Goodyear Tire plant in Hurlingham, the *colectivos* passed La Cava. I wondered what was there and one Sunday I found out. Two American Jesuit seminarians who conducted monthly CYO classes at a convent in San Isidro invited me and several others to accompany them on an errand to the slum. At La Cava, we walked along unpaved paths, past modest homes made of a variety of material. Cinderblock homes were the sturdiest, but most were made of tin, wood and some even of sturdy cardboard. Women, holding their children, watched us and with friendly smiles nodded as we passed. We stopped at a door where the seminarians handed a woman an envelope that I presumed to contain money, perhaps for a family emergency. The very different world in that *villa miseria* left me saddened, but awakened.

A chance encounter one evening in early 1967 further piqued my curiosity about the Argentina's social challenges. Three friends and I purchased a case of *cerveza* Biekert, Argentina's most popular beer, and went to an old abandoned, rotting wooden pier on the banks of the Río de la Plata in La Lucila. We walked about a third of the way down the pier, sat, opened our beers and began our carefree teenage banter. That is all the evening would have amounted to, except for a man who was sitting at the end of the pier. The scruffily dressed man rose to his feet and made his way toward us. Maybe he had been asleep and our laughing woke him. As he got closer, we saw that he was about sixty, with a scraggly beard and a smile that revealed he was missing numerous teeth. Wary, at first we remained silent and tense, not knowing what to expect, but then he simply wondered if we would share one of our beers. I handed him one.

After a minute, he sat down and quietly asked, "*¿Son ingleses?*"

"*No, estadounidenses*," someone replied.

He immediately turned talkative and told us that while he did not like the United States, he held nothing against us. During the next hour and a half or so, he narrated his life story, with former President Juan Perón as the central protagonist. I knew that Perón and his wife Evita had done many things for the poor, but knew no one who had anything nice to say about them. "Bad for Argentina," was what everyone said; even Mary and Ricardo could not abide them. They said he only helped the unions, not the real poor. The man that evening very emphatically insisted that Perón had given him the best years of his life, including work, a decent place to live and enough money to enjoy a vacation now and again. It did not last. After Perón's removal by the military in 1955, his steady job disappeared and he ended up with nothing. Only Perón cared about the poor, he insisted, and the military were a tool of the rich.

As labor secretary of a military government in early 1944, Perón with the help of his wife had organized the working poor into labor unions that provided a political constituency and a path to the presidency two years later. During the Perón administrations, unionized workers secured better wages, social security, vacations and other benefits that transformed Argentine politics forever. That old man on the pier spoke with passion about Perón. He finished several beers, thanked us, wished us a good evening and went on his way. For some reason a Chalchaleros, song came to mind on that occasion. Entitled "El Arriero," the chorus spoke to the injustices in Argentine society. "*El arriero y las vaquitas,*" it said, "*van por la misma senda. El arriero y las vaquitas van por la misma senda. Pero las penas son de nosotros y las vaquitas son ajenas. El arriero va, el arriero va.*" The cowherd and the cows drive along the same road. But the suffering is ours and the cows belong to someone else. So goes the cowherd.

~ ~ ~

At sixteen, I knew little of the deeply institutionalized social and political rifts in Argentine society created during Perón's presidency. Labor unions achieved real and enduring power. Even after Perón's overthrow, union power remained intact and presented the military with a dilemma whenever it sought to restore Argentine electoral politics. No one doubted that free and fair elections would return Perón to power. To avoid this, the military banned *peronista* candidates in the 1958 election and again in the 1963 electoral campaign underway when we arrived in Argentina.

The low-key 1963 electoral season, with bright and colorful political signs and graffiti that seemed to cover every inch of Buenos Aires' buildings and walls, took to the presidency Arturo Illía, a nondescript country doctor of the middle-class Radical Party. Perón's followers demonstrated their political clout anyway, voting "en blanco," that is by submitting ballots with no preference for any of the candidates listed. Without a strong constituency, Illía only attracted 25% support to win the election over a right-wing candidate, former General Pedro Aramburu. The *peronista* blank protest vote garnered 19% of the vote, leaving Illía without much backing and certainly no political mandate. Recognizing the difficulties of ignoring such an important constituency, Illía in 1965 agreed to allow *peronista* candidates to run in the midterm congressional elections. A *peronista* governor won in the important province of Mendoza and set the stage for more *peronista* candidates in 1967.

The first real direct question I asked my father about politics was on June 28, 1966. On that day, television screens went blank and then returned with a waving Argentine flag and the sounds of martial music. Tanks rolled out from the military headquarters at Campo de Mayo and surrounded the Casa Rosada, the presidential palace, not far from our Buenos Aires home in the Olivos neighborhood. Soldiers escorted Illía out of his office, and the next day the military junta closed Congress, dissolved the provincial governments and banned all political parties. The head of the Argentine army, General Juan Carlos Onganía, became president.

"What's this mean?" I asked my father, genuinely alarmed.

To my surprise, he brushed the question aside with a simple, "Don't worry, the country will be better this way."

I later learned that the conspiracy had not been a well-kept secret, which perhaps explains his nonchalance, but he did not want to discuss it. Neither did anyone else. Even in school, silence prevailed: no class conversations or evidence that anything at all had happened. In our circles dominated by business and diplomatic interests, the military dictatorship offered promising improvements and created a new political landscape. At some point, I grasped that at its root the military takeover was aimed at keeping the *peronistas* from returning to power.

The rise of the military government marked the beginning of a sustained era of radicalization, including in the military, organized labor and the political left and right. Unlike the coup against Perón in 1955, in which the military organized new elections within two years, the 1966 Revolución Argentina embarked on a more ambitious plan for the military to stay in power for a prolonged period while the generals sorted out the nation's problems.

During the Argentine coup, the military easily suppressed half-hearted student resistance at the University of Buenos Aires. Anti-military working-class demonstrations in Córdoba's city center resulted in one dead demonstrator, but overall no one was prepared to resist. President Onganía declared a Law of National Defense that defined economic development and national security as the government's primary priorities and moved the country toward moderately freer markets, repression of uncooperative unions and suppression of emerging guerrilla groups.

During the next year, events further awakened me to the politics of poverty in Latin America. During 1967, the English-language *Buenos Aires Herald* and *La Nación* reported frequently on Che Guevara's guerrilla operations in the Bolivian hinterland. After various failed efforts to foment revolution in various countries, Guevara finally decided to take his stand in Bolivia and launched a guerrilla operation in November 1966. His goal was to ignite many Vietnams in Latin America, including in Argentina, but his almost year-long operation didn't inspire support among Bolivian peasants, who saw him and his Cuban fighters as strange foreigners. The Bolivian army tracked him with counter-intelligence and technical training from the United States. The Argentine press reported daily as the military closed in during the first week of October 1967, which I followed with interest. A romantic figure who spoke for Latin America's poor, I hoped he would escape somehow, but he did not. On October 9, the newspapers reported on Guevara's capture and quick execution. My interest in Cuba grew after this, and I especially watched for articles about the Revolution in the press. I even did a report on Cuba in my high school Spanish literature class. As my political conscious formed, I grew accustomed to a country governed by the military. After a while, military rule seemed perfectly normal, but somehow still unacceptable.

12
Fixing the World

In anticipation of graduating from Lincoln High School in Buenos Aires in June 1968, I told my father I wanted to stay in Argentina for university, perhaps attend Universidad Católica. I had visited the university a couple of times with a friend and liked it.

"Out of the question," he said. "A future in Argentina won't be easy without some kind of American business connection. Only access to dollars means security in Latin America. If you want to return to Argentina after college, you need an American education . . . a degree in Business Administration and a job with a multinational corporation. Then . . . it might be possible. Besides, the United States is home."

I didn't argue with him. I never argued with him, at least not then. He disabused me of the idea of staying in Buenos Aires. I visited annually for several years, but never lived there again.

In any case, getting into university for me was not a foregone conclusion. University admissions officers in the United States were unconvinced of my potential for university work. I disliked high school and fared poorly academically. Mediocre grades and a poor showing on the SAT exam resulted in more than a dozen rejection letters. Fairfield University in Connecticut, Miami University in Ohio, Rollins College in Florida, Emory University in Atlanta, the University of Georgia and a number of others judged me unworthy. I often wondered why my early education was so uninspired. Eventually, I concluded that I simply had no interest. My parents had not attended university and viewed education primarily as a way of acquiring practical vocational skills. There was little intellectual engagement in our household. No dinnertime conversations about politics, art, music, literature or religion stirred my imagination or sparked a sense of wonderment. General Motors consumed my parents' lives.

Our comfortable homes did include my mother's art collection. In addition to her own art, over the years she collected works from Cuba, Ecuador, Colombia, Argentina and Uruguay, but she never spoke of how she acquired the pieces or why she bought the works. We never went to museums. Although they both loved music, we never attended concerts or symphonies. Once we did go to the Teatro Colón in Buenos Aires, one of the world's great opera houses, on the invitation of one of my father's business contacts. At that time, it was not commonplace for mothers or fathers to read to their children from infancy on, at least not in our family, and so I did not grow up in a culture of reading. There were few books in our home. When my father did read for pleasure, it was mostly light mysteries, Mickey Spillane especially. When I was eleven, he bought me *The Hardy Boys* mysteries for young adults, which I read voraciously and thoroughly enjoyed, but not much more after that. School libraries did not attract me, and I used them only when class assignments made a visit unavoidable. I did not develop an appreciation of learning simply for the sake of learning. The Poyos were never intellectuals; they have always been a practical people focused on the everyday demands of making a living. Even José Dolores preferred revolutionary action to theoretical musing. Only later did I discover compelling reasons to look for solutions beyond the practical and pragmatic.

Yet in hindsight, I realize that I had some interest in learning, evoked during Uncle Jorge's infrequent visits. This inveterate raconteur opened me to the world of intellect and cultural appreciation; my adventure at New York's World's Fair was just the beginning of a lifelong engagement with him. Consistent with his interest in languages, when I was thirteen he gave me a Webster's English Language Dictionary and told me to always have it by my side. I still have it.

"Study it!" he ordered. "Increase your vocabulary so you can express yourself well."

I used it all through college, but unfortunately cannot say I grew up studying it. While our only occasional meetings did not immediately spark in me a love of education, they planted seeds of curiosity that eventually bloomed.

∽ ∽ ∽

In 1968, the only college that accepted me was the University of South Carolina—at the bottom of my list. My father had recommended I apply there as a fall back after I received a couple of rejections. Where he learned of the school, I don't know, but a backwater state university in a conservative state appealed to him. It would insulate me, he must have thought, from the ongoing political unrest in more liberal colleges. He knew of the student activism, and disruptive demonstrations that were taking place on campuses across the northeast and California, but South Carolina would be different. Little did he understand that many in my generation wanted to change the world, even in the American South.

The United States in 1968 seemed a daunting place to be. It was the year of Martin Luther King's assassination and that of presidential candidate Robert Kennedy. Inner cities in the United States, including Harlem, Watts, Newark and Detroit, were going up in flames as black rage poured out in the face of continuing racism, poverty and police brutality. Argentine society in the 1960s even under military rule seemed civilized in comparison. And protests against the United States war in Vietnam rocked campuses across the country.

When I arrived in Columbia, South Carolina in August 1968, the Democratic Party convention was taking place in Chicago. It was my first glimpse of American politics in action. Ignorant of how party conventions proceeded normally, I watched the clashes of police and demonstrators in Chicago's streets. Protestors of every stripe condemned the war and delivered countercultural messages of all kinds, demanding freedom from everything and everyone. Police battled demonstrators while inside the convention hall the party's delegates lined up behind the presumptive nominee Minnesota Senator Humbert Humphrey, President Lyndon Johnson's vice-president. A more disciplined Republican convention nominated Richard Nixon. He promised to end the war "honorably," and seemed the better bet, but I was not old enough to vote. In any case, only American citizens could vote, and I didn't feel American. Four years later the war raged on, and this time I felt compelled to vote for Senator George McGovern, who had promised an immediate withdrawal of American troops from Vietnam.

For my first Thanksgiving in the United States, I visited my brother Sergio at Fort Benning, where he worked as an artillery instructor. We did not discuss the war, but the visit did bring the issue closer to home. I worried about his potential deployment. In Columbia, I had numerous conversations with draftees who did their basic training at Ft. Jackson and frequented the bars around the university. Seeking drink and entertainment, many spoke of their dread and their opposition to the war. A conversation with a married draftee, probably in his late twenties with two children, plucked out of his work and family life to fight in Vietnam, particularly bothered me. He thought the war was useless, but felt helpless. "Stay in school," he advised.

Rather than ending the conflict, Nixon escalated the war as a strategy to get the North Vietnamese to enter peace talks. US troops entered Cambodia on April 30, 1970 to destroy North Vietnamese forces that regularly transited through that neutral country into South Vietnam. Demonstrations exploded on university campuses across the country. On May 5, at Kent State University, Ohio National Guardsmen fired on protesting students and killed five. Ten days later at Jackson State College in Mississippi, three black students died protesting racist policies in the city. According to the authorities, the police were blameless.

I was among the students who responded at the University of South Carolina when the Student Emergency Coalition for Academic Freedom called a demonstration and boycott of classes to protest the Cambodian invasion and the Kent State killings. I'm not sure how I became involved, but I did. During my first two years in the United

States, my growing sense of disquiet about the poverty and the inequities I had witnessed was transformed into anger. I concluded that the Vietnam War was simply a symptom of existing political and socioeconomic structures that had been created to benefit the few. These structures needed to be transformed if humanity hoped to eradicate injustice. With less selfishness, new ways of doing things and fewer wars, humanity could make the world a better place.

My frustration at having left Buenos Aires to land in this strange place contributed to my rebelliousness. The military takeover in Argentina would have been a good excuse for anger and action, but when I was fifteen, it never crossed my mind to join protests. Now, I acted. About three hundred of us walked in a "death march" that ended at the historic center of campus, known at the Horseshoe, named for the arrangement of the university buildings around an attractive tree-filled commons. We marched quietly around an outdoor Awards Day ceremony that included the swearing in of a new student body president. Settling down on the grass behind the well- dressed attendees in their lawn chairs, we listened respectfully to what the new student body president had to say. We left unimpressed.

The next day, hundreds of us skipped classes and gathered at the Horseshoe to memorialize again the dead students, this time at the main campus flagpole. As we listened to speeches, nervous university officials cited three non-students for speaking without proper permissions and forced them to leave campus. We wanted to lower the US and South Carolina flags to half-mast to commemorate the dead students, which provoked a scuffle with a group of conservatives who opposed the idea. They grabbed the ropes to prevent the flags from being lowered. A standoff ensued while the police monitored us, until the university president finally ordered the flags lowered to avoid violence. We then marched to the student center, known as Russell House, and joined a sit-in that had been organized by the Student Emergency Coalition in reaction to an entirely different issue.

During spring 1970, reports of rampant drug use on the campus had prompted the State Law Enforcement Division (SLED) to monitor activities at Russell House. Undercover agents—often students themselves—roamed the building while university officials randomly checked identification cards to ensure only students entered the building. Considering SLED actions a violation of student privacy and freedom, the Student Emergency Coalition organized the sit-in, which coincided with anxieties students felt over the events in Cambodia and at Kent State. The two student constituencies joined forces.

When we arrived at Russell House, our anti-war group joined the one hundred students already inside the building. Even so, the drug controversy did not particularly motivate me. After all, drugs were illegal and the state did have an obligation to enforce the law, but this issue and the war became fully enmeshed. University officials closed the building and tried to coax us out with a combination of promises to consider student demands and threats of dire consequences. No one left. Finally, around mid-afternoon, the university president called the governor's office for assistance. In short-order, seventeen SLED agents, fifty highway patrolmen and one hundred national guardsmen entered the campus and surrounded Russell House, angering most of the 1,500 students now gathered outside. A large bus commissioned as a paddy wagon arrived and was met by students chanting, "Sieg, Heil! Sieg, Heil!" Highway patrolmen started single file up a ramp to the second floor, where we had gathered. Students blocked their way shouting, "Kent State, Kent State!" Others threw cans, and at least one student was clubbed to the ground while the police pushed their way forward with their batons at the ready. "Pigs off campus!" students chanted.

Inside the building, everyone was angry. Why did they need the National Guard and Highway Patrol to repress a peaceful student protest on university grounds? We listened to speeches from the student leaders and broke into occasional chants against the war and about academic freedom. A little after five, the head SLED officer entered the building and warned that students who did not abandon the building in the next five minutes would be arrested. With the helmeted police lined up on the ramp, I agonized and did a bit of soul searching. I wanted to stay, but I knew my parents, who lived so far away and were facing their own problems, would never understand. My nineteen-year-old idealism conflicted with my sense of responsibility to my parents. Nothing to be gained by staying, I figured. The point had been made. Obviously, I was not angry enough to cause my father distress. With about half the protesters, I reluctantly walked out of the building as the police took photographs. In the next days, I berated myself. I had committed to action but had not honored my convictions.

True to their word, after a few minutes the police entered the building, arrested and escorted the remaining forty students, including my roommate, to the waiting bus. An aspiring poet with a flair for the dramatic, he leaned out the window with his fist raised, while I joined chanting students surrounding the bus. The police pushed protestors out of the way as the bus moved slowly forward. Some students threw cans and finally a few rocks at the police and soldiers as the paddy-wagon bus left the campus accompanied by police vehicles and the National Guard bus.

In the meantime, a national anti-war coalition had organized a massive demonstration in Washington, DC for that weekend, Saturday, May 9, to protest the Cambodian Campaign that was extending the Vietnam War. I joined my roommate who was out of jail on bail, his girlfriend and another friend for a drive to Washington in her convertible Volkswagen bug. Approaching the capital on Interstate Highway 95, we passed dozens of military trucks carrying troops. I wondered: have they been deployed to protect the government from us? What a wild idea. We flashed peace signs, and many responded in kind, but in a few hours, they would be prepared to confront us if matters got out of hand. We later learned that in the early morning hours that Saturday, as we slept in our parked car, Richard Nixon shocked protestors when he impulsively visited the Lincoln Memorial with his valet, doctor and several secret service agents and spoke with protestors already gathered for the day's events. I admired his moxie, but reports described a very frustrated president who did not think students understood his policies.

In the morning, we made our way to the Washington Monument and looked down across the famous reflecting pool toward the Lincoln Memorial, where the thousands of mostly student protestors had gathered in solidarity against the war. Speeches from the steps of the memorial had begun early and went on all day. People relaxed on the grass, smoking pot, while others danced to the driving rock & roll music. Dozens of Frisbees pierced the air while some naked protesters frolicked in the reflecting pool. Under the trees, and sometimes right there on the great lawns, there was much evidence of the "free love" movement I had heard so much about. Every political group imaginable had showed up. Hippies, Yippies, Black Panthers, Progressive Party Maoists, SDSers, Young Democrats and countless others pressed their ideas, but most were young white students demonstrating their opposition to the war.

I witnessed violence only late in the day. As the crowd thinned, police on horseback began moving demonstrators off the Washington Monument grounds. When we resisted and shouted at them, the horsemen started across the field with their batons swinging. We retreated. One galloped by and hit my friend in the back, leaving a big bruise. We left the area quickly, jumped into the car-and-returned to Columbia that night. As exciting as it was, I never imagined that my first visit to Washington, DC would have occurred under such circumstances.

After we returned to campus in Columbia, on Monday, May 11, students gathered for another demonstration, this time to protest the state of South Carolina's criminal prosecution of the students who had been arrested at Russell House the previous Thursday. We students believed that those arrested should face the university disciplinary committee, not state criminal prosecution, but Governor Robert Evander McNair wanted to make an example of the student leaders. We met at the Johnathan Maxey monument on campus to hear the latest from organizers who had been made aware of a Board of Trustees meeting in the administration building to consider the question. Several hundred of us moved *en masse* to the building. A group of students went up the stairs and pushed past the campus police officers guarding the entrance. Dozens of us followed them into the building. Police immediately escorted the trustees out of the building to the jeers of hundreds of students congregating outside. Governor McNair again dispatched state police and the National Guard to the campus and surrounded the building. In a frenzy of anger, a number of students broke into the treasurer's office and destroyed desks, chairs and anything else they found. They also tried to break into the university records office, but they could not breach the strong doors. At this point, I realized this form of protest was not for me. A sit-in demonstration made sense to me, but I did not want to be involved in random destruction and vandalism, especially of the records of thousands of students and alumni who would need to access them throughout their careers.

Many of us left the building, and after a while, everyone else did too. We then focused our attention on the hundreds of National Guardsmen occupying the campus. Governor McNair took charge of the university, declared a state of emergency and instituted a campus curfew from 9 pm to 6 am until further notice. Speaking through megaphones, state authorities ordered students to the dormitories or off campus. We regrouped at the Horseshoe, and the National Guard followed. They lined up across the grounds, fixed their bayonets, placed masks over their faces and moved to disperse us with pepper gas. The evening turned into a cat-and-mouse game as guardsmen in formation and free-wheeling state police pursued hundreds of us who refused to comply. Some students even secured gas masks at the local Army Surplus stores, and the confrontations continued late into the night before I retreated to the dormitory. Others left the campus altogether.

The next day, Governor McNair agreed to meet with five student representatives, which included my roommate. A state vehicle picked them up at the dormitories about seven that evening and took them to the capitol, where the governor waited. Some 1,000 of us marched to the capitol steps and waited. The student representatives had five demands: amnesty for all students arrested during the previous week; the removal of SLED officials and police from Russell House; that the university condemn violence against students at Kent State University; denounce US military operations in Laos, Cambodia and Vietnam; and that Governor McNair speak to the students waiting on the steps of the capitol. The governor rejected everything and told the student leaders they had no legitimacy, that they represented only a small fraction of the student body. Most, he said, just wanted to get on with their studies.

In meeting with students and offering nothing, Governor McNair simply aggravated the situation. When the student leaders joined us on the capitol steps almost an hour later and condemned the governor for refusing to negotiate, we broke into boos and chants that continued until 8:30 pm. Finally, a university official reminded students that the university intended to enforce the nine o'clock curfew and advised those wanting to return to dormitories to do so or prepare to remain off campus until the next day. We made our way back to the campus, but the mood was ugly and almost two hundred of us gathered in front of the high-rise dormitories known as the Honeycomb Towers, where I resided. Chants against the curfew broke out at 9 pm, and more students joined the protesters, many who had not been compelled to join by the original grievances, including some of the fraternities' members who lived just across the way. They too resented the curfew and urged the protesters on, bringing cases of empty Coke and beer bottles to the demonstrators. I moved up a hill with the crowd toward the heart of the campus, but the police appeared almost immediately. Students pelted them with their missiles, and the chanting grew louder.

Then, a moment of truth. As I thought about throwing a bottle, I saw a projectile hit a cop. I hesitated. Who would I hit? Did he deserve to be injured or even killed for doing his job? The thought came and went in a split second, but it was sufficient for me to abandon the idea. I urged those around me not to throw bottles, but the fully enraged crowd threw them with determination. I remained with the protesters, and we were soon on the defensive. Along the main street that ran beside the Towers, guardsmen appeared in formation, while the state police charged *en masse* with batons in hand. Gas filled the air again, and we retreated quickly.

Police beat and arrested the unfortunate students they caught, while the rest of us headed back into the dormitory building. We locked the large plate glass entrance doors and pushed furniture against them, but angry officers with black tape covering the numbers on their badges smashed through the glass and swiftly entered the building. I headed up the stairs to my room while police chased students to their rooms on the first and second floors, beating and arresting several. Behind my locked door, I watched from the porch as national guardsmen surrounded the building and lit it up with a spotlight. A flag with Che Guevara's image hung from one window, Jimi Hendrick's rendition of *America* filled the night air and wafting pepper gas still stung my eyes. That evening, police and the National Guard arrested another eighty students and badly injured numerous others. At least one had to be hospitalized.

The guardsmen stayed through the night and occupied the campus for the final three weeks of the semester. The next evening as I slept, three police officers entered my room without knocking and shined a flashlight in my face. They asked my name and demanded I tell them my roommate's whereabouts. After his arrest at Russell House, my roommate had also participated in the takeover of the administration building. Now, he faced a second arrest warrant for destroying property in the administration building and returning to campus from which he had been suspended pending hearings. "Haven't seen him since the Russell House takeover," I told the police officer. The next day, my roommate called to tell me he had gone home to New Jersey and had no plans to return. He asked that I ship his belongings via Greyhound. I did, and never heard from him again.

May's events greatly disturbed state and university officials and, not willing to take a chance, the university operated under the governor's state of emergency declaration until the first week of June. National guardsmen occupied university buildings during classes and final exams and even stayed on to guard the campus Naval Armory throughout the summer. To finish the semester on a lighter note, my friends and I attended a final rally to see film star and anti-war activist Jane Fonda, who arrived in Columbia to participate in a Vietnam Veterans against the War rally at the gates of Fort Jackson, one of the US Army's largest training facilities. She had heard about the events at the university and offered to speak to the students. Since holding the rally on campus was out of the question, we gathered at nearby Maxey Park on the edge of campus. I sat down close to the front of the crowd, where a lone microphone stand stood, and waited patiently until someone finally stepped up and made the introduction. Suddenly, a young woman in a T-shirt and jeans sitting right next to me stood up and made her way to the microphone. Much to my astonishment, it was Jane Fonda. I leaned over to my friend and whispered, "She certainly doesn't look like Barbarella," the sexy, mostly unclad protagonist Fonda had played in a French-Italian science fiction movie released in 1968. As we disbursed after the event, several cars displaying Confederate flags drove down Blossom Street alongside the park and threw tear gas canisters at the crowd.

Although I grew up in a country where militarized police with machine guns routinely guarded banks and patrolled the streets, this was the only time in my life I had actually confronted furious and often raging and out-of-control police with batons, pistols, rifles and gas. At first, we had felt secure in our right to protest and engage in peaceful demonstrations and sit-ins, but our resistance to authority had quickly transformed us into a real threat. We became the state's mortal enemies, which justified their repressive action. The older police officers, though not generally the younger National Guard soldiers, seemed to take our resistance personally and responded with violence. The experience taught me that even a nation committed to freedom of speech and association could become a police state in an instant. Challenging power in this way involved risking one's own life. One had to go into such activities with open eyes and a clear head, which I had not. What happened at Kent State could have easily occurred in South Carolina, with hundreds of armed police and soldiers chasing students around the campus for hours. My naiveté about the power of "rights" disappeared in the face of the overwhelming display of force that semester at the university.

Those events in May 1970 had a decisive impact on my thinking. Not until arriving in South Carolina did I wonder what obligation I might have to make the world a better place. The police and National Guard occupation of the university campus disturbed me enough to spur my street activism, but it didn't last. My life had not been marked by discrimination or repression, and my anger was intellectual not experiential. This moderated my actions if not my thoughts. Deeply ingrained fury rooted in lived grievance is less easily controlled. I had the luxury of returning to school in September, determined to learn and better understand, and I actually received good grades for the first time in my life. I changed my major from Business Administration to International Studies, with a History minor.

"What will you do with that degree?" my father asked.

"I don't know," I said, "but I'll learn about the world and its problems."

"That won't put dinner on the table," he warned.

I was at a loss, but my determination to explore the questions that had engaged me since that first protest outweighed my father's objections. He relented, and although at the time I was not aware of what this would mean, I turned toward an academic life.

Courses in International Studies, US and Latin American history and economic theory shaped me during the next two years. It did not take long to see that American history in high school had been thoroughly sanitized. I could no longer trust what I thought I knew. University courses offered critical and challenging perspectives that gave me a clearer understanding of the Vietnamese struggle as part of post-World War II Asian and African popular rebellions to dismantle European colonialism. National liberation movements set out to replace the colonizers in India, China, Algeria, Vietnam, Burma, Mozambique, Rhodesia, Congo, Angola, South Africa and elsewhere. Instead of supporting the anti-colonial trend in the world, the United States simply tried to replace Europe as a new colonial bulwark in the name of capitalism, democracy and resisting socialism, the ideology most liberation leaders embraced.

With the North Vietnamese leader Ho Chi Minh well positioned to unify his country, the United States took over from the French. I considered US actions in Vietnam and Cambodia to be imperialistic and immoral, and I vowed never to participate in that war, even if it meant going to jail or leaving the United States. "This is not my fight!" I insisted. Fortunately, my resolve was never tested. I often wondered if I would have had the courage to stay true to my convictions. Student draft deferments through college saved me from the draft, and by the time I graduated, the draft lottery had fallen below my number of 113.

~ ~ ~

An imposing building with a domed roof and tall columns, McKissick Library sat at the top of the university's Horseshoe. It was the first research library I had ever encountered. For some reason, long lines of card catalogs, books shelves everywhere and dozens of students busily unearthing knowledge of all kinds excited me. Although small by state university standards, the library certainly contained more than sufficient resources for the many term papers required in my international studies and history courses. During those many hours at McKissick, my love affair with books, libraries and archives began. The solitary work suited my personality and temperament, and, in some ways, reminded me of the hours I had spent alone as a kid in my bedroom inventing games and daydreaming. Only now, I had books. I actually enjoyed writing term papers, reminding me of the adventure story I wrote as a kid in Argentina. Each semester my research assignments took me to new places and eras, and taught me just a little bit more about the world.

Post-war US aggression in Asia, I discovered, was just the current manifestation of long-standing American policies that had already been implemented across the Americas, driven by capitalist expansion. These policies began with the moment of the nation's independence. Reinvigorated Anglo-American advances into Native American territories during the century that followed independence, half-destroyed cultures and ways of life that had existed for millennia. The Louisiana Purchase in 1803 facilitated this expansion, and each westward step made the United States thirsty for even more land. Spanish Florida was not exempt from this drive to expand, which culminated in the United States coercing Spain to cede the region in 1819. Unfortunately, Latin American independence movements did not transform the region's colonial legacy, and fragile economic elites and weak divided governments ruled the new countries. This suited US interests. Especially vulnerable Mexico lost its northern province of Texas to American settlers and interlopers in 1836. Ten years later, the United States annexed Texas and from 1846-1848 conducted a full-scale war against Mexico to gobble up half that country's national territory from New Mexico to California.

After the US Civil War, the liberal and capitalist Anglo-American northeast set a path toward economic domination of the more traditional Latin American south, establishing enduring but unequal interactions between the regions, culminating in wholesale US economic penetration of Mexico and the Spanish-American War. Then came US occupation of Cuba, Puerto Rico and the Philippines in 1898 with its consequences for my own family. Interventions in Latin America continued unabated in the twentieth century with occupations of various durations in Cuba, Panama, Mexico, Nicaragua, Haiti and Dominican Republic before World War II. After the war came the CIA overthrow of the elected government in Guatemala in 1954, the attempted overthrow of the Cuban government in 1961, an invasion of the Dominican Republic in 1964 and ongoing support for military governments in South America beginning also in 1964. The United States was an imperial nation, just as Britain and Spain had been and before them, Rome. It was not so unique or exceptional, after all. The hypocrisy and false moralism is what bothered me most. Why not call it what it was? The latest world empire.

At the University of South Carolina, exiled Cuban political scientist Nestor Moreno took a critical but academic approach to the Cuban Revolution, and another exiled professor, Eulalia Lobo from Brazil, taught an especially fascinating course on her country that introduced me to the origins of European colonialism and economic dependency in Latin America. That was when I first learned of the concrete reasons for Latin America's social inequality and rampant poverty. The realization that it stemmed originally from the political, economic and social structures of Spanish and Portuguese colonialism shattered my illusions: Rodó's defense of Latin America's essentially elitist and reactionary ideas in the name of Hispanic values and anti-Americanism could not hold. Elitist politics, reinforced with American economic interest, seeded Latin America's problems. Elites in both regions contributed to the enduring and unrelenting poverty in Latin

America. That was what I thought about the Western Hemisphere two years into my new major.

Events in Chile during the early 1970s further challenged me to think about my beliefs and commitments. In 1970, socialist candidate Salvador Allende won the presidency and promised to resolve the nation's poverty. His platform included giving peasants land and alleviating the challenges of the slums. I took him seriously, followed developments closely and wrote a senior thesis comparing the economic development policies of the left-wing Allende government with those of Brazil's right-wing military dictatorship. I remembered the poverty and misery I had witnessed growing up in Latin America and, of course, became intensely interested in Allende's planned transformation of the Chilean economy.

I visited Buenos Aires in December 1970 for the Christmas holidays. My mother picked me up at the airport with the GM driver and looked shocked as I exited the customs area sporting almost shoulder-length hair.

"You should have gotten a haircut before coming," she said.

"I did."

Not pleased, she mumbled something about what my father would say. Sure enough, that evening when he arrived from work he looked livid, but kept his composure.

"Why are you wearing your hair so long?"

"That's the way I like it," I said.

Things went from bad to worse. I told him about my involvement in anti-war activities, my admiration of Allende and my growing interest in socialism.

My father's silence about world affairs ended when mine did, and our relationship changed. For the first time we talked, but not fruitfully. It was contentious and even antagonistic. Foreign business investment provided profits, political leverage and cultural openings in Latin America for Americans, creating a new form of colonialism, I lectured. To his chagrin, I added that those Latin Americans who facilitated American expansion acted as imperialist agents and certainly did not advance the best interest of their countries. They privileged their own personal interests at the expense of their nations'.

He grew angry at what he properly took to be a criticism of his career and raised his voice, "You don't know what you're talking about!"

Committed to a capitalist culture of corporate conformity and material abundance, my father believed this sort of capitalism would eventually transform Latin America, indeed the world, into modern economic systems resembling the US system. He knew this was a long-term proposition and that liberal capitalism was not a popular ideology in Latin America, which made his job very difficult.

"Capitalism," he said, "is human nature. People only work to benefit themselves and their families. And for them to progress, you need to give them the proper incentives. Otherwise, they'll take shortcuts and do just what it takes to get by . . . which doesn't make for progress. Communism, even socialism, takes away incentives to work, to produce, make progress."

"But, Dad, that's just propaganda . . . "

"Communism is all for the State, not for individual people and families. . . . " he continued. "Everything they want is for the State, and they need to have government decisions in everything."

"But, Dad, capitalism is inhuman, makes for inhuman, unhealthy work and just exploits most people to make a few people rich."

"Well, yes, there's problems and injustice, but that's life. . . . Capitalism is the best system we have, even with its flaws."

For my father, the capitalist workplace was like a ladder on which employees competed in a never-ending climb to the top. An indispensable tool on this corporate climb was a *martillito* (little hammer). When those below on the ladder of success tried—as they certainly would—to reach, grab and pull you off the ladder to clear the path for themselves, a *martillito* could be handy to crack and dislodge grasping hands tugging on pant cuffs and ankles. Such declarations he made only in jest, but he accepted that life was not easy or fair and that one had to fight for his bread. He also believed fervently in his corporate mission with General Motors.

"Latin America," he insisted, "needs the economic investment and knowhow of the industrial nations to overcome its backwardness. That's the only way it will ever stop depending on the United States and Europe."

"Dad, if given a chance, people can learn, improve themselves and act justly. Given a chance, people will do what's best for the majority and not just to make a few people wealthy."

"Gerald, you've got your head in the clouds. . . . You've got to be more realistic."

My dad and I spent many fruitless hours arguing about such things, which of course reflected the sharply differing interpretations that existed in Latin America itself about the United States' economic presence. How could my father simply ignore the injustices around him? I thought. He was a good man, I knew, but how could a man of good conscious be so complacent, so uninterested in the fate of the poor living all around us?

Back at university, professors Moreno and Lobo spoke to me in Spanish and took me under their wings. During my last semester, Moreno encouraged me to take an MA degree in Latin American politics at South Carolina and offered me a graduate assistantship. Lobo said that I would do better taking an MA degree in Latin American Studies at the University of Texas at Austin. She had taught there for a year as a visiting professor and said it was the best place in the country to study Latin America. I followed her advice, and she wrote me a strong recommendation that overcame my chronically low standardized exam results. In the fall, I was headed for Austin, Texas.

My first day at the University of Texas in January 1973, I visited the extraordinary Latin American library, which eventually was named the Nettie Lee Benson Latin American Collection. In one of three modern-elongated structures with glass walls that stood low to the ground, known as the Sid Richardson complex, the Latin American Collection had as many volumes just on Latin America as many libraries' entire holdings. I have been fortunate to live most of my adult life near this most comprehensive library of its kind in the world.

Daily newspapers and weekly and monthly magazines from across the region covering the latest events kept me going there almost every day. Roaming the open book stacks became a favorite pastime in a collection especially strong on Mexico, the Andean countries, Río de la Plata and Brazil. Its Rare Books room included extraordinary holdings dating to the Spanish conquest of Mexico. I took a student assistant job at the library and knew Nettie Lee Benson herself, the director and force behind this enterprise. She enjoyed telling stories of the early archival collections she obtained in Mexico and of her continued archival acquisition trips across Latin America. She was an extraordinary woman. The library and its holdings highlighted for me the diversity of human endeavors and convinced me that historical studies offered the best path for understanding the confusion of the world around me. History, I thought, considered everything: how people made a living, their culture, economy, politics, social relations, psychology and even their sexual practices. I chose to focus on economic history in my graduate program.

Much to my dismay, Allende's government fell into deep trouble quickly. American policy worked to cripple the Chilean government, but the administration also had a hand in undermining itself. The United States supported Allende's opposition, including secretly funding strikes that paralyzed the economy and intimidating countries and international organizations willing to help Chile. But it was also the case that Allende badly underestimated the challenges of attempting a radical economic transformation in a democratic context without a large electoral mandate. September 11, 1973, when I returned to my apartment after classes, I learned from the evening news that the Chilean military, with the support of the country's upper and middle classes, and the encouragement of the United States, had assaulted the presidential palace. Footage of fighter planes bombing the building left me stunned and furious. After the bombing, soldiers entered the palace and found President Allende dead. He had shot himself rather than surrender.

The military followed this up with savage repression of pro-Allende loyalists and anyone else with leftist beliefs. Soldiers herded thousands into Santiago's largest soccer stadium and summarily executed hundreds. The new military head-of-state, General Augusto Pinochet, referred to this as a necessary national cleansing to save Chile from godless communism. During the next years, thousands more died at the hands of military thugs; it was an experience that haunted me for a long time. The Argentine generals followed this example in subsequent years.

Among those forced to leave Chile was Radomiro Tomic, leader of the Christian Democratic left, who polled third in the 1970 presidential election. In January 1974, he arrived in Austin as a visiting professor. I immediately enrolled in his course, expecting to hear about Allende's heroic effort to bring justice to Chile. Instead, I heard of a deeply divided Unidad Popular coalition that the president was unable to control, that had led to chaotic policies and opened the door to the coup. As Tomic detailed events, I became convinced that democratic transitions to socialism were virtually impossible, given the forces always arrayed against such efforts. Even Tomic voted to impeach Allende in the end.

This was a crossroads for me. US imperialism and economic injustice across the world became my primary political point of reference. I lost confidence that industrial capitalist elites of any stripe had any interest in resolving Latin America's pressing social problems or even that democracy meant anything, given the hostility of the United States and its close relations with Latin America's military establishments. The moment arrived when I thought Che Guevara and Fidel Castro had the right ideas about fixing Latin America. Like many people of diverse political persuasions, I too became radicalized. As I sorted out my adolescent reactions to life's realities, radical actions to end abject poverty and provide dignified lives seemed appropriate and urgent. Intense anti-communist feeling permeated the communities in which I lived, but I could not help wondering why it was that communists like Guevara and Castro wanted to help the poor while anti-communists did little to relieve their misery. I thought I had an obligation to advocate for a better world. This was both exhilarating and a burden, and later this experience helped me better understand José Dolores Poyo's radical career.

Even though I wore my hair long as a form of protest, I had little interest in the American counterculture and the New Left. I especially rejected cultural activist Hippies and Yippies for what I thought was their hedonistic, obsessive libertarianism and their naïve demands for unfettered freedom and expression. They seemed provincial lacking knowledge or apparent concern for anything outside their own society, except, of course, Vietnam. Socialism attracted me, not the cultural revolution of Abbie Hoffman and Jerry Rubin, two "intellectual" icons of those movements. The United States needed a social, not a cultural, revolution. The country lived with racism, lack of health care, unequal education, unaffordable housing, inadequate nutrition and packed prisons, and, for the most part, accepted these deficiencies in the name of individualism and freedom. In the context of the United States, I admired the Democratic Socialist Michael Harrington whose book *The Other America* opened my eyes to the great social problems in the United States itself, and I applauded Senator Ted Kennedy's 1972 book *In Critical Condition: The Crisis of America's Health Care,* a devastating analysis of the private health care insurance system. I could not understand why the richest country in the world refused health care access to significant sectors of its population.

On the other hand, the great social initiatives of the 1960s, such as President Lyndon B. Johnson's Civil Rights Act of 1964, the Voting Rights Act of the following year and the Great Society legislation gave me hope. It seemed the country was developing a social consciousness. Perhaps a liberal democracy could dedicate itself to the greater good, I thought. It did not last. Monies were diverted from social concerns to the Vietnam War, and a resurgent right-wing movement led by ideologues such as William Buckley and Barry Goldwater cared more for egocentric individualism than justice. They did what they could to dismantle the nation's social safety net. I became increasingly dismayed with a liberal capitalist system that seemed more concerned with accumulation of wealth and protecting private property than the common good.

I also concluded that democratic socialist ideas had limited relevance in Latin America. Chile's experience suggested that democratic socialism could only flourish in a Latin America absent pro-American local elites. Perhaps the region needed radical solutions, and for the first time I read *The Communist Manifesto*. From there I turned to *Das Kapital*, but was not intellectually prepared for it and soon put it aside. I did better with Vladimir Lenin's and Leon Trotsky's various political tracts, especially Lenin's *Imperialism. The Highest Stage of Capitalism*. Anarchist texts also interested me for a time, having read Peter Kropotkin's *Mutual Aid*, but it all seemed too utopian. The communist newspaper, *The Daily Worker*, the Socialist Worker's Party newspaper *The Militant* and propaganda materials from the Socialist Labor Party kept me thinking about the need for alternatives to liberal capitalism, which I did not think could ever serve the common good. My reading revealed a preference for activism and solutions over ideology, and my theoretical understanding of Marxism remained superficial; economic determinism, class struggle, equality and internationalism were at its heart. That was enough for me.

Romantic revolutionary rhetoric inspired me. It promised justice, but the violence inherent in this kind of approach to change bothered me. Not even willing to throw bottles and rocks at the police during the demonstrations at the University of South Carolina in 1970, I struggled with the idea of revolutionary violence, which really did not suit my temperament. I hadn't even been in a fistfight, but after a while, I accepted that violence was legitimate in certain circumstances, especially when authoritarian political systems made peaceful reform impossible, as in much of Latin America. Launching objects at police and National Guard doing their job in the context of a university demonstration in the United States did not make much sense, but people in Latin America had the right to respond to military dictatorship and violence. I accepted the need for the action-oriented approaches of Guevara and Castro in their countries.

The fact that a handful of rural-based insurgents in Cuba could build a national movement and defeat a dictator backed by the most powerful country in the world was astonishing. In Lee Lockwood's compelling and extended 1965 interview, *Castro's Cuba, Cuba's*

Fidel, Castro expressed himself in ways that inspired me. "What is the philosophical foundation of free enterprise?" Castro asked. "That the most competent, the most able, the most audacious will triumph. . . . And he has to achieve it in competition, in a war to the death with everybody else, in a pitiless struggle for existence. . . . It assumes that man is capable of acting rightly and correctly only when he can derive an advantage or a profit." On the other hand, he noted, "We Marxists have a much better concept of man. We believe that man is able to act uprightly out of reasons of moral character, out of feelings of love and of solidarity with his fellow man." In a nutshell, that's how I felt in 1974. What I saw growing up in Venezuela and Argentina was my evidence. Castro spoke the truth and then offered concrete ideas about how to resolve Cuba's and Latin America's problems through economic diversification, educational advancement, universal health care, agricultural reform and nutrition for all in ways radically different from business as usual in the south. Although his ideas were grandiose, they made sense to me; these were ideas that could easily have gotten me killed in Buenos Aires, had I pursued my university career in Argentina.

When I had left Buenos Aires in 1968, I hoped to eventually return to live there. On completing my MA degree in 1974, I made plans to join my parents in Montevideo and apply for a job teaching history or social studies at my alma mater, Lincoln School. I remembered my Chicago-born math teacher, Mr. Czarnik, who had gone to teach at Lincoln and made a life for himself in Buenos Aires. Perhaps I could do the same. The idea sounded promising, but life intervened in unexpected ways, as it often does. I traveled to Montevideo to evaluate the possibilities, but found myself thinking of Betty Kay. Our relationship had grown strong the previous year, and after a month in Montevideo, even before crossing the river to visit Buenos Aires, I decided to return to Austin. The heart is a hard master to disobey—we were soon married.

My path took a very different turn. Instead of heading to Buenos Aires, still with much trepidation and self-doubt about my intellectual and academic preparation, in August 1975 I started a doctoral program in Latin American history at the University of Florida, where I could study Cuba. It seemed to me that Cuba's example of radical action and change provided significant and immediate solutions to the problems of entrenched poverty and inequality. I could not hope to grasp the Cuban Revolution's inspiration and rationale without looking into the country's historical aspirations, challenges and traumas, especially its independence wars and its legacy as the object of US imperialism. One of the Cuban Revolution's fundamental ideological propositions insisted that the turbulent events of the 1950s and 1960s brought to fruition in Cuba what the US had prematurely sidetracked with its occupation of the island in 1898. I hoped to investigate this idea academically, but also somehow—I didn't know how—first-hand on the ground in Cuba.

13
The Turmoil of Ethnic Politics

If radical politics and socialism transformed me so did ethnic awareness, very unexpectedly. My Cuban heritage provided a measure of connective tissue with this University of Florida community. At some point, I remembered an overnight train trip a decade earlier from Buenos Aires across the Argentine pampas to Córdoba, halfway to the Andean mountains, with my high school sports program for a week-long tournament. We competed in softball, basketball, soccer, track and golf. Our competitors' families in Córdoba hosted us in their homes. One morning while sipping coffee and munching on a *media-luna*, the host mother asked me about my background. I explained our complicated past, mentioning that my father was Cuban and my mother American. She thought about that for a minute and said, "*Ah, como* 'Yo Amo a Lucy.'" I thought about that for a minute—the comparison with the TV show had never occurred to me! "*Sí, precisamente*," I told her. Mostly I thought the comparison humorous, but when I encountered Cubans in Florida, I remembered the conversation.

Was I Cuban, I wondered? I had never lived in a Cuban community. I never recited Martí's poems as a child, which many Cuban children did. My father danced like a Cuban, but he never taught me. No Cuban ever mistook my Spanish as coming from the island, and I lacked points of reference to Cuban places and spaces. I was unaware of the many particular markers that defined Cuban culture. In college when I saw Cuban films, I learned about Cuban ways, but when I saw Argentine films, I recognized and laughed knowingly about the uniquely *porteño* expressions.

Despite my overall ignorance of Cuban culture, the seeds Nana had planted blossomed among warm and accepting Cuban friends in Gainesville. They simply considered me Cuban—a different kind of Cuban to be sure, but a Cuban nevertheless. The fact that I was not born in Cuba nor had ever been there mattered little; once a Cuban, always a Cuban, was their subliminal message. For the first time since leaving Argentina, I found myself again speaking Spanish every day and engaging with a community of people I related to culturally. I felt an emerging sense of ethnic solidarity, but not without a learning curve.

The United States in 1968 left me with even greater desire to go home to Buenos Aires. Only a couple of months after arriving at the University of South Carolina, I had disturbed my father with a litany of complaints and, as my letters criticizing the United States became increasingly despondent, he grew impatient. He was unsympathetic to my whining. Never one to coddle, he expected me to sort it out. My mother finally asked me to stop writing him about such things, and my letters dwindled to half-page obligatory notes assuring them I was fine and thanking him for the monthly check to cover living expenses. This took me to emotionally precarious places. If Argentina was not my real home, as my parents contended, and a permanent return to Buenos Aires was not in the cards because of limited economic possibilities and the dangerous political situation, I had to figure out my place, somehow. As my father had in the 1940s, I began exploring the North.

In the United States, it seemed culture, language and skin color mattered more than class. Most white people, the skilled working classes and even assembly line workers, thought themselves middle class. Poverty seemed closely aligned to skin color, or language, or culture. White rejection of blackness or any other non-white skin tone had historically forced ethnic and racial minorities in the United States to seek refuge among their own. In my first university history courses, I learned that the United States' much-celebrated version of democracy had always systematically segregated, oppressed and excluded anyone outside the Euro-American mainstream. Whites invented identity politics at the moment of the nation's birth when they refused to honor their declaration that all men were created equal. Africans endured slavery and segregation; Native Americans suffered ethnic cleansing and imprisonment in reservations; and Asians faced immigration exclusion before anyone else. Latino Americans were not yet on the radar, or in the history books. The Declaration of Independence was a farce, and democracy was an illusion.

I had never thought much about the significance of racial and ethnic differences in human societies, but the turmoil of identity politics in the United States during the 1960s and 1970s challenged me to understand human relations as more than a matter of class. Shocked at the depth of race hatred infecting English-speaking white Americans, I began a journey through the ethnic crucible when I asked myself why whites defined their identity and security in contrast to blackness. Deep racism had also haunted Latin America's historical development, but in the United States, the starkness of formal racial segregation that daily sinned against the dignity of people of color, as well as the boastfulness of white supremacy, shocked me. In Argentina, I simply never experienced the kind of raw racial animosity I saw and heard in South Carolina and Georgia.

My father viewed his own corporate interests in opposition to the organized working classes—the unions—but he never made an issue of race or color. As a child in Bogotá, a black Colombian couple lived next door, and their son, Tito, was my friend and playmate, but after that, my world was completely white. Tenafly, New Jersey did not have African American residents that I saw. In Venezuela, I perceived people as rich or poor, not as blacks or mulattoes, although a relationship between those constructs certainly existed. For me, they were simply Venezuelans. Buenos Aires' population was almost completely white; the rare blacks seen on the streets were usually foreigners, Brazilians or US Embassy Marine guards. In the early nineteenth century, perhaps a third of Buenos Aires' residents were black, but they had mostly disappeared. Some scholars say they assimilated into the large white European immigrant culture, while others claim they became cannon fodder during the wars of independence. Both are probably true. Argentina still has a small black population, but it is mostly invisible.

I have to confess that I unwittingly participated in racist behavior back in Buenos Aires. Inspired by *The Little Rascals* (Our Gang) films that regularly ran on Argentine television, a group of us began putting on humorous skits between classes or after school. These included demeaning impersonations of the show's African American characters "Buckwheat" and "Farina," whom we mocked the most. We even spoke with stereotypical black accents. It is disconcerting how US-style racism infected teenagers in a South American community without blacks in the 1960s half way across the world. Somehow, I did not recognize this for what it was. I thought it harmless fun and, only after arriving in South Carolina, did I fully understand how this behavior derived from a deeply brutal system of race oppression.

~ ~ ~

The first state to secede in 1860 from the United States, South Carolina a century later remained deeply and unapologetically racist. Only in the fall 1963 did the University of South Carolina accept its first three African American students—the last flagship university in the South to do so—but only after bitter legal battles, a court order and armed guards escorted the students to class. A local radio station denounced the university, arguing to a mostly sympathetic audience that the integration of schools was not academic freedom but rather academic prostitution. Integration proceeded slowly and, in 1970 during my second year at the university, only 279 black students attended the school of some 15,000.

It did not take long for me to see white racism in action when I attended a football game in 1968 with my new roommates, who were from Georgia, Tennessee and Delaware. Thousands of Gamecock fans roared with approval when the South Carolina team charged onto the field. The band struck up "Dixie," and a student ran alongside the team waving the Confederate battle flag. The sound of "Dixie" and the flag waving continued throughout the game, especially when

South Carolina scored or fans otherwise celebrated their play. I knew this to be an insult to blacks, but for my southern roommates, who simply sang along, this was well within their normal experience. Football did not interest me, and I did not go to any more games, but later in the semester, I attended basketball games of the then-nationally ranked all-white Gamecocks and saw the same spectacle of waving Confederate flags and the sounds of "Dixie." Besides that, it was not lost on anyone that the all-white football, baseball and basketball teams systematically excluded representation of the state's almost thirty-percent African American population.

During October, I saw on television African American track stars Tommie Smith and John Carlos at the Olympic Games in Mexico City raise black-gloved hands and lower their heads during the United States national anthem while receiving their medals to protest racial injustice in the United States and across the world. I thought they acted courageously and with good reason, but most did not. Students in the dorm television lounge booed their acts of defiance. The American press criticized them, and the Olympic authorities expelled them from the games. The next year, racial confrontations became deadly across the United States after the FBI launched a repressive assault on the armed Black Panther Party founded in 1966 to defend African Americans and protest the poverty in their communities. The repression ended in the deaths of many Panthers in southern California and Chicago, for all practical purposes crippling the organization.

One day as I walked in the student union, I ran into a teach-in sponsored by the campus organization AWARE. Titled "White Awareness Week," the teach-in on racial realities in South Carolina included lectures, folk singers, workshops and testimonials by black students. The AWARE chairman explained that the goal was "to tell it like it is" because the "mass media isn't." The week's activities, he said, would help "educate whites and change the racist society which exists today." I had already seen the segregated and poverty-stricken African American communities in Columbia and in Atlanta. They reminded me of the poor in Argentina, and I understood what AWARE wanted to do, but the event included something I did not expect: a first-year commemoration of a tragedy that had occurred at South Carolina State University in Orangeburg, an historically black college. South Carolina State students told of their efforts to desegregate a bowling alley near their campus. When they entered the building, they were ordered to leave, which they did. The next day, they tried again, but this time security guards assaulted them. The following night, several hundred people gathered in front of the bowling alley, and police arrived to control the angry chanting crowd. Scuffles broke out, and police opened fire with shotguns and rifles, killing three and wounding twenty. The police blamed students for inciting a riot and claimed they had heard gunfire before turning their weapons on the crowd. Investigations revealed no evidence of weapons involved other than those of the police, but the city had held no one accountable.

Perhaps it was the anger about racism discussed that week at the teach-in that led the Association of Afro-American Students to demand the university ban "Dixie" and the Confederate flag at sports events. The student newspaper, *The Gamecock*, in an open letter to the university president declared these symbols, "a tribute to a movement that sought to destroy the United States . . . a tribute to the peculiar institution that enslaved human beings . . . and [they] offend normal sensibilities." During "White Awareness Week," the organization requested permission to burn the Confederate flag in effigy at a formal ceremony. University authorities denied the request, pointing out that it was against state law to burn the flag, but agreed to take their request banning the symbols under advisement. A barrage of letters to the *The Gamecock* denounced university officials for even considering such a thing, and certainly the governor and state legislature would never have allowed it. One clueless letter writer claimed that "Dixie" was much beloved and embraced by a large majority of Carolinians and that it was only a radical minority who had wanted to burn the Confederate flag and introduce the question of banning the song. "Why would this group want to burn a Confederate flag? To stir up hatred?" Hatred, indeed.

On Friday, February 18, white students associated with AWARE went ahead and burned a Confederate flag in front of the president's home. The next day, as I was entering the undergraduate library, I saw a group of black students huddled together next to the reflecting pool in front of the building. They laid a Confederate flag on the ground, soaked it with a liquid and ignited the banner. Dozens of white students arrived on the scene from the nearby fraternities and surrounded the black students, yelling and cursing at them. At least a dozen police cars responded to an alert, and I observed four officers dressed in riot gear emerge from each vehicle. They separated the students and escorted the black students off campus. The police averted violence, but a tense racial climate prevailed on the campus for the rest of the semester.

During the summer break in 1970, I stayed in Atlanta with my brother Sergio and his wife. She worked for a real estate company and found me a job on a construction site. The bosses were all white and the workers black, all except me. On my first day, the foreman assigned me to James, a tall heavy-set African American man of about forty years. He looked at me as if to say, "Why stick me with this little skinny white kid?" Instead, carrying a large jackhammer, he ordered, "Follow me. And, bring the wheelbarrow." We entered the ground floor of a five-story commercial building, still only a skeleton without exterior walls. James stopped at an area with pipes jutting through the concrete floor. The pipe installation had to be re-done, and we were to open up a small section of the concrete foundation. Easy enough, I thought, as James placed the jackhammer under his round protruding gut and began the noisy task of breaking up the concrete.

After a while, he stepped back and told me to remove the debris. He watched as I filled the wheelbarrow to the top and then chuckled when it tipped over on its side as I tried to lift it.

"You can't fill it to the top . . . ," he said matter-of-factly, without ridicule or judgement, " . . . unless you got muscles," he added with humor.

"Yeah, I get it," I responded with some embarrassment and lifted the wheelbarrow upright.

I filled it again, but this time only half way. With considerable effort, I pushed and emptied it at the edge of the building and returned to find a new pile ready to go. I repeated this several times and got the hang of it but not before wrenching my back.

At our first break, James asked, "You ever work construction before?"

"No," I answered, sheepishly.

"This kind of work will make a man out of you," he said.

I nodded.

Back on the job, he asked, "You want to try the jackhammer?"

"Sure . . . "

It did not go well at first. The hammer bounced all over the place until James showed me how to place my full weight on it so it could penetrate the concrete. We continued in this fashion and by the end of the day completed the job.

"Great first day," James said as I left with swollen, blistered hands, a sore back and a headache, but also a real sense of accomplishment.

The next day, with my body hurting as never in my life before, I joined a group of workers with wheelbarrows and, in a non-stop circular fashion at a good pace, we transported cement from the mixing truck to fill a large hole in another area of the same building's foundation. This went on for an hour before we heard the break-time whistle and took a well-deserved rest. For me, it was just in time.

Unfortunately, the construction job only lasted about a month. When I had begun the job, the site foreman had told me never to sign anything, but I had no idea what he was talking about. Eventually, two white organizers approached me during a break and insisted that I had to join the union to keep my job. Not connecting the dots, I naively signed the union card, and at the end of the day, the foreman fired me. I had fallen into the middle of a dispute between the union and contractors about hiring students as non-union workers in the summer. My job disappeared, but the following week, a major citywide strike closed down construction sites anyway. What the African American workers thought of my presence I never knew; perhaps they thought me some kind of scab. I sat by myself during break times and at lunch. Only James occasionally joined me as I picked up a sandwich from the food truck. If nothing else, I earned James' respect, which meant a lot to me, since at first he had wondered whether I was up to the task.

I returned to campus more conscious of black students, and I pitched in when an African American ran for president of the student body during the spring semester of 1971. I helped the Association of Afro-American Students and various white organizations distribute flyers across campus, including dormitories and the nearby bars I frequented. Much to everyone's shock, the African American won the election. An amazing breakthrough, I thought, but it soon became clear that few students had actually voted; only the most motivated wanting to make a strong statement. The election did not represent a transformation of the campus, but it did send a message that activists with well-organized goals could make a difference. The activism of African Americans at the University of South Carolina was a local reflection of the powerful national movement of ethnic awareness and pride that arose to fight the legacy of centuries of denigration and oppression. Change arrived only when they had engaged in civil rights activism and the solidarity of identity politics. I admired their determination.

I found that living in South Carolina could also be a source of grief for anyone who was different, not just for African Americans. During my first year, I had joined the Latin American Club, attended parties and dances, and played on the university soccer club with half a dozen Latin American friends. My American friends and those from Venezuela, Ecuador, Aruba and Peru remained in distinctly different circles. I never met any US Latinos in South Carolina; I had not even heard of such a thing. Interested in helping better integrate me into the United States, my brother Sergio had told me about his experience in a fraternity at Emory University, which he had very much enjoyed. He suggested I check the fraternities out at South Carolina. So I attended one fraternity mixer and took along Ignacio, a Venezuelan friend. Like me, Ignacio was a second-year student, but unlike me he was short, dark and with a distinct accent. He dressed in a suit while everyone else, including me, wore slacks or jeans. We mixed with the fraternity brothers and guests and went our own way. As I enjoyed a beer and conversation, I suddenly noticed across the room something odd in the way a group of fraternity members were engaging Ignacio. At first, they joked with him, and he responded with good humor, but the jocular mood seemed to have shifted, and he looked uncomfortable. I made my way toward him and heard someone make sarcastic compliments about his suit. Then things turned ugly, when a tall and muscular bully asked if he could try on his suit jacket and began tugging it off his shoulder. I arrived at Ignacio's side and asked the bully what he was doing. He ignored my question and continued urging Ignacio to let him try on the suit jacket. I advised Ignacio in Spanish to leave and that I would join him shortly. He knew why, and he did. Boiling angry and with a couple of beers of courage, I cursed the ringleader and challenged his racist attitude.

"We were just having some fun," the bully said as he grabbed my shirt and threatened to "beat the shit out of me."

"Go ahead," I told him, "but you're a moron."

A couple of his fraternity brothers intervened, and I left to catch up to Ignacio.

How could they treat Ignacio in that way? I understood that my physical appearance made me acceptable, but not my friend's. White, no accent and knowledgeable about what to wear for the occasion, the good ole boys welcomed me into their company as long as I accepted their racism and did not defend my unwelcome friend. This was my first realization that Americans viewed Latin Americans as inferiors, much in the same way they viewed blacks. What Ignacio experienced was not an isolated case, an aberration, one racist fraternity boy. I saw that Latin Americans were not immune from the deeply engrained psychological impulses behind the black-white divide in American society.

When I later learned of my father's similar experiences in the United States in the 1940s, I asked why he hadn't warned me. It had not occurred to him. After all, I was an American and would not face the same challenges, he said. "Anyway, things have changed."

"They haven't. And why'd you put up with it?"

"There was nothing I could do about the racism back then," he explained. "What could one lone Cuban do? I just tried my best to get along."

Twenty-five years later, I enjoyed the luxury of not having to accept racism. And I could remain with my Latin American friends as well as maintain friendships with Americans who didn't display racism. My background of privilege gave me the freedom to act from my values and not from some required sense of conformity. My father's need to secure his family financially drove his conformity, and ironically, the economic benefits of that very conformity gave me the freedom to take my own path.

Learning about race and ethnicity became even more personal, when I arrived at the University of Florida and encountered Cubans. Something drew me to them almost immediately. Some Cubans could be innocently (or perhaps not) pretentious, as I learned a couple of weeks after arriving in Gainesville from Texas. Hungry for Mexican food after two years in Austin, one day I spotted a taco restaurant. The Cuban owner took my order and shortly brought me a plate replete with piping hot tacos, rice and refried beans. The rice and beans tasted good enough but the meat in the tacos had the distinctive flavor of Cuban *picadillo*—my first taste of Mexican-Cuban fusion. Not only that, but the taco lacked even the tiniest *picante* kick. On my way out, I asked if the cook was Mexican, knowing fully he was not. The owner exclaimed proudly, "*No, chico, mi mujer cocina. Es cubana, mejor cocinera que los propios mexicanos*," claiming his wife cooked Mexican food better than even the Mexicans. Later I learned that I had encountered a *cubanazo*, an arrogant nationalist. Good thing for him that most people in Gainesville did not know how a Mexican taco actually tasted.

I encountered humble Cubans too, not boastful at all. When seeking daycare for my newborn son, Noel, the Cuban grapevine recommended two wonderful elderly sisters, Luisa and Tata, who cared for about five children at their home. I usually picked up his older brother, Jeremy, after school, but in a pinch, they also cared for him when necessary. They loved the children so thoroughly that after a while, little Noel thought we were the babysitters and cried when we picked him up after work. They spoke no English, so they helped inculcate Spanish into Noel's world from almost the day he was born.

Politics was my greatest source of potential conflict with Cubans, especially the activist Cuban American students who held anti-Cuban rallies and demonstrations at the drop of a hat. I did not frequent their events, but instead spent time with three unforgettable Cuban friends: Professor Andrés Suárez, who became my dissertation advisor, and librarians Rosa Mesa and Salvador Miranda. Sra. Mesa, as I called her, directed the Latin American Collection at the University of Florida Library, where I worked as a full-time library assistant while taking two courses per term, studying at night, changing diapers and rocking Noel to sleep at three in the morning on more than a few occasions. Sra. Mesa had worked at the Cuban National Library before the Revolution, and her husband Danilo Mesa served briefly in Castro's first government.

Salvador Miranda arrived in the United States as a young man in 1960 and volunteered with the exile Brigada 2607 that landed at the Bay of Pigs in 1961. As the Latin American bibliographer at the library and knowledgeable in Cuban historiography, Salvador saved me countless hours, as did Mrs. Mesa. They broke the stereotype of Cuban exiles as shrill unthinking anti-communist zealots. Despite their condemnation of communism in no-uncertain terms, they spoke from their experience, maintained determined but rational critiques of the Cuban Revolution and listened to different opinions without personal rancor. They had my back as I struggled, often overwhelmed, through my doctoral program.

Professor Suárez was an aide to Justo Carrillo, leader of the anti-Batista group called the Montecristi Movement, which campaigned to get Colonel Ramón Barquín, a progressive activist who had earlier attempted a coup against Batista, out of prison and take control of the government before Castro arrived in Havana. This failed, and Suárez left Cuba. As a young man in the 1930s, he had flirted with Marxism, but his personal experiences with the authoritarianism of Cuban communists had helped change his mind. In the United States, his well-received book, *Castroism and Communism,* demonstrated him to be a thoughtful not ideologically rigid critic of the Revolution, which made him *persona non-grata* in Miami. We got along well, and when the time came for me to go to Cuba, he supported me. He refuted what he considered Cuban Marxist influences in my doctoral dissertation, but respected my perspectives and conclusions. Years later, I would come to appreciate his critiques more than I had at the time. When I ran into personal problems that delayed the completion of my degree plan, he did all he could to help me return to finish my Ph.D., which I did. He was the only professor since my undergraduate years with Professors Lobo and Moreno with whom I felt a personal and cultural affinity.

In 1978 in Austin, where I went to write my dissertation, I had joined a group of Cuban students in forming a chapter of the Brigada Antonio Maceo (BAM). Founded on the east coast in 1977, BAM proclaimed a very controversial idea that disturbed most Cuban exiles. Aware that the Revolution enjoyed full support of the Soviet Union and that the United States had abandoned plans to overthrow the regime with military force; we called for a reevaluation of exile attitudes. Weary of the almost decade and a half of anger and violence, BAM called for dialogue. BAM put forward new perspectives on the homeland that most members had been forced to leave as children and adolescents. What perhaps seemed so black and white to the older generation was more complicated to younger Cubans, who saw things with more nuance. Our emerging ethnic identity in the United States during a particularly turbulent period, and the complexity of world events, especially in Latin America, challenged us to question the entrenched opinions held in our communities. We rejected the aggressive stances and simplistic Cold War sloganeering of our elders and preferred analysis and informed debate. Most exiles saw us as traitors, plain and simple.

Our group met for several years, and I had the opportunity for the first time to meet with Cubans of my generation who had progressive ideas and who were interested in understanding the realities of the Revolution. All but two members of the group were the sons and daughters of Cubans who had fled the Revolution. We met regularly, organized film showings and discussions, hosted Cuban dinners and most importantly found ways to go to Cuba. Those were intense times, and more than once our BAM chapter received threats, presumably from members of the Cuban American community in Austin who rejected visits to Cuba and dialogue with communists. These friends welcomed me into their world and shared memories of their homeland. I learned much about the island's culture and the people's way of being, which helped me prepare for my first visit to the island in 1979.

Visits to Nana in Miami exposed me to full-throated Cuban culture in action. Nana's path to Miami was circuitous. After leaving Cuba in 1942, she remained in Atlanta until her fourth son, Ernesto, started school at Emory University. Then she "found," in her words, a second husband. Three years her senior, Alvin did not speak a word of Spanish, and Nana's English remained always rudimentary. Originally, from Louisiana, Alvin was a postal official, and Nana moved with him when he transferred to Philadelphia. When Alvin retired in 1958, they moved to Havana, but their timing could not have been worse. The revolutionary victory, the rise of anti-Americanism and open confrontation between the two countries prompted Alvin's quick return to Atlanta, but Nana remained to protect her home until the political situation forced her to leave.

Her dream of living out her years in Cuba had crumbled, but she still had Ernesto, his wife Judy and two granddaughters Lisa and Gail in Atlanta. Always frugal, Nana and Alvin had saved sufficiently to purchase an apartment complex with six units. He managed the property and returned to work as a bookkeeper while she got a job as a cafeteria worker not far from where they lived. She prepared and served food, and even washed dishes. Proud of her work, she took me to the cafeteria and introduced me to her fellow workers.

Nana tragically lost Ernesto in 1965; it was the greatest shock of her life, more even than the loss of her first husband. Despite the pain and tears, she remained strong and kept her attention on Judy, Lisa and Gail. For the rest of her life she remained close and loving with them. When Judy remarried, Nana gave her enthusiastic blessing; she also consented without hesitation when Dick, her new son-in-law, adopted the girls and changed their surname. Nana wanted the family to feel close and united. She loved "Díque," and in order to communicate with the family, she took English classes twice a week late into life. "*Estoy tomando clases*," she wrote "*más que nada para aprender a escribir algo; así puedo escribirles a* Judy, Lisa y Gail." With class registration free for people over sixty-five, she could not pass it up. Her teacher could not believe she was eighty. "*Se quedó asombrado*," she said proudly.

On the other hand, Nana felt ecstatic when in 1966, Uncle José, Aunt Connie and their four boys moved from Colombia to Atlanta. After a few years, my uncle transferred to Miami, and she and Alvin followed. They sold the apartment complex and purchased a duplex in Miami, where they lived until their deaths. When I put them on the Greyhound bus at the downtown Atlanta station for Miami, she insisted on getting there an hour early. "*Se llena; hay que hacer cola*," she said. I carried their two bags to departure post number four, and we were first in line between the two black lines designed for the queue. During the next forty-five minutes, at least thirty people, all African Americans, lined up behind us. Right on schedule the bus arrived, but stopped perhaps ten feet beyond the passengers. The crowd surged toward the bus as the door opened and the driver announced, "Only four seats available." He took the ticket of the closet person, and at that point, Nana raised her voice and declared, "Line here! Line here!" She repeated it even more loudly when no one paid attention.

Finally, people turned in amazement to see who was making the disturbance. Alvin was a mild-mannered, quiet southern gentleman, but even without English, Nana could make herself heard and understood. She always said that in Cuba people spoke up to get along, and when my father one day in a public place told her not to speak so loudly, she set him straight in no uncertain terms. That was how she spoke in Cuba and that was how she would speak in the United States! Then a young man standing next to us said half in jest, trying to help Nana out, "Let the old lady on before she has a heart attack!" "Come on, let them by; they're old," the bus driver added. As with the Dead Sea in "Exodus," the crowd split, opening a lane. Nana quickly gave me a big hug, grabbed Alvin's hand and walked through the people onto the bus. "Hey, man, you've got one tough granny," the guy told me. I spotted them through the window and waved. "Yep!" I said, and thanked him.

∽ ∽ ∽

"*Vamos a la bodega*," Nana declared when I arrived in 1971 on my first visit to see her in Miami. "We'll buy bistec to eat with rice and black beans. And if they have *plátanos*, we'll buy those too, for *tostones*."

Nana always prepared this simple culinary delight for me, but I had to do my part and accompany her to the Bodega Tropical. She dragged me along, not because she could not manage with the groceries; she did that well enough, making the journey each morning, walking from her duplex in Westchester down 39th Street to 97th Avenue. As we strolled, she greeted her neighbors sitting on lawn chairs on the front porches of duplexes that extended down the street, stopping occasionally to chat and introduce me, her *nieto*. They were all Cuban in this neighborhood that Nana enjoyed. At the end of 39th Street, she crossed Bird Road at the light to the bodega. Her main purpose in taking me was to show me off. Although she always wondered why I wore my hair long, like a "hipper," she certainly had no qualms about introducing me to the neighbors and at the store. She accepted people as they were.

"*Ven acá, chica, te quiero presentar a mi nieto*," she said loudly and with pride to the cash register attendant.

In the middle of checking someone out, the attendant stopped what she was doing and turned. A cheerful and plump woman of about fifty answered, "*Ay, qué lindo, encantada*," and offered me her hand.

As I extended my hand, she enveloped it with both of hers and held it tight, gushing to Nana about how tall I was (all of 5'10 ½") and how *americano* I looked—as if I wasn't even there. "*Y qué lindo, habla español*."

"Yes, he looks just like his father, Sergio, the one who lives in Argentina," Nana responded. "Sergio was blonde as a boy in Cuba," she said with some satisfaction. "*Gerito* came from college to visit me. . . . He is attentive, *y me quiere mucho*."

The attendant then looked back at her customer, another middle-aged Cuban lady who all the while smiled and was thoroughly engrossed in the conversation. "*Chica, pero mira, qué cosa más grande*," the attendant said to the lady. "Her *nieto* came to visit her from college. He speaks Spanish, and looks very *americano*," she exclaimed as if the woman had not just heard the entire conversation.

"*Qué bueno, felicidades*," she said to Nana. All the while, the groceries sat unattended on the counter, waiting to be processed, and two other customers were now waiting to check out.

I took Nana by the arm and gently directed her into the store toward the meat counter to buy the *bistec*. Before we arrived, the butcher stepped from behind a skyscraper of packages of Goya brand black beans. As he made his way to the meat counter, my grandmother found another opportunity to introduce me.

"*Qué hubo, Paco, te quiero presentar mi nieto. Vino a verme*."

"*Sí, sí, oí, mucho gusto, hijo*," he said.

"*Es muy atento conmigo y le voy a preparar un bistec. ¿Tienes tres?*"

"*Sí, cómo no, señora. La carne es fresca*."

He scooted behind the counter while Nana went for the *plátanos*. She examined each carefully in search of the green ones, which were the best for *tostones*. After finding two and placing them in the tote bag she took to the bodega each day, she found her cigarettes, those short, strong ones Cubans called *negros*. A pack lasted her almost two weeks, since her smoking ritual consisted of one cigarette a day as she washed the dinner dishes. The sight of her standing over the kitchen sink, scrubbing the pan, a cigarette hanging from her lips like some Bogart impersonation, flashed through my mind.

As we made our way to the check out, Nana asked me to get a six-pack of "Boodweiser," which is what Alvin liked. We would each drink one before dinner while we watched the "Lawrence Welk Show," perhaps the only television show she and Alvin liked. Then she would give us another with dinner while she sipped on a Coke. After dinner, she prepared an *arroz con leche* (rice pudding) with the leftover rice for the next evening's desert. Before reaching the counter, she picked up a new *cuaderno* for her English homework. Her English never seemed to improve much, but each evening after dinner she worked diligently on her written exercises and, to her delight, we reviewed her work together.

I reached the counter with the beer just as she began another conversation with a friend who had just entered the bodega. The attendant also joined in when she saw me and said, "*Allí está el nieto*," and we went over familiar ground. The butcher brought the meat; we had everything. The attendant offered her hand again and told me how happy she was to meet me, but I told her we would certainly return the next morning. "*Qué bueno*," she said. As we moved to the exit, I spotted a newspaper stand close to the counter with free newspapers. I picked up a copy of *Patria*, one of the more popular papers published in Miami that passionately opposed the Cuban Revolution.

"*Vamos, Gerito*," my grandmother said, "*tenemos mucho que hacer en el jardín con* Alvin." My afternoon was full too!

I liked the Cuban Miami of the 1970s; it was vibrant, as if on steroids, buzzing with that fast-paced and distinct Cuban music, from traditional *sones* and *boleros* to Willy Chirino and the emerging rollicking sounds of Gloria Estefan and the Miami Sound Machine. I never passed up visiting the Cuban bookstore Ediciones Universal and typical restaurants La Carreta and Versailles on Calle Ocho (Eighth Street). Nana loved the beach, so we often went to Miami Beach or to Key Biscayne. She spent at least a month during the summers at Hotel Cardoso in Miami Beach's art deco section on Ocean Drive and 13th Street, long before the area became gentrified and fashionable. Directly across the street from the beach, it was an inexpensive somewhat rundown but clean hotel that Gloria Estefan bought many years later and turned into a high-end accommodation. Nana bathed in the ocean twice a day: once in the early morning and once in the late afternoon so as not to "take too much sun," as she liked to say. During the day, she often sat on the hotel's front porch with other guests and a couple times a week attended dances in a hall not far away. She always said the Jewish widowers were gentlemen, usually spoke a word or two of Spanish and liked to dance. Uncle Jorge lived in the apartment next to Nana's during her last years. He remained there until his death, where I visited him occasionally, listened to his stories and kept up with what was happening in Miami.

∽ ∽ ∽

I possessed an unconventional sense of Cuban Americanness that resided in family memory and history and later in my knowledge of the Key West Cuban community experience, but not from having migrated from Cuba to the United States. Exploring this early Cuban story in Florida helped me realize that our family had long-standing connections to the United States, which my father and his brothers claimed as evidence of our Americanness. This Cuban Americanness helped me sort out my ambiguous identity, come to terms with my displacement from Argentina and find a place in the United States.

Evidence of that traditional community remained when I first went to Key West in 1975. José Dolores Poyo and thousands of Cuban immigrants participated in converting the small fishing village of Key West into a major cigar-manufacturing center and the largest city in Florida at the end of the nineteenth century. A statue of José Martí dedicated in 1932 still graced Bayview Park and the historic San Carlos Institute building founded in 1871, which had been the Cuban community's most important civic and education center, still existed on Duval Street though it sat empty and closed. Tourists regularly gathered on the waterfront to enjoy beautiful sunsets and jugglers, mimes and other entertainers along with food vendors, at the same site where thousands of Cubans, including my family, had arrived from Havana beginning in 1868 to escape Spanish persecution.

I stopped my car at a phone booth as I drove into Key West and checked the directory. No one with the Poyo surname lived in Key West anymore, but I did find Ana Alpízar, no doubt a relative from the Poyo-Alpízar line. She lived on Bahama Street, more an alley than a street packed with small and modest wooden cottages known as shotgun houses originally built for the cigar workers in the late nineteenth century. Confirming the address, I climbed the couple of steps onto the small porch of one small house and knocked. A tiny elderly woman opened the door, and I introduced myself. She smiled when she heard my surname.

Ana stepped out of the house and closed the door behind her. She offered me a seat on one of several wooden chairs on the small porch. She was in fact Raoul Alpízar Poyo's widow, grandson of José Dolores Poyo and author of the biography I had recently read. She knew my great-grandparents Pancho Poyo and Louisa Skillin in Havana. She proudly told me about Bahama Street, known to Cubans as *Callejón de Poyo*, and pointed to a funeral home at the end of the street. "That is the house where José Dolores lived." She told me that Raoul idolized his grandfather, as did all the Poyos of that generation.

Ana also told me that a relative of my great-grandmother Louisa, Carmen Isabel Delgado, still lived there. I knocked on the door of a middle-class home and introduced myself to a woman about fifty-five-years old. "Is Carmen Delgado available?" I asked. She considered me with suspicion and then with some hesitation announced that her mother-in-law was ill and suffered from dementia. I apologized for troubling her but, just as I turned to leave, I heard from the interior of the house, "*¿Quién es? Oí algo de Poyo*."

An 86-year-old-woman appeared at the door behind her daughter-in-law and demanded, "Who are you?"

"Luisa Skillin was my great-grandmother," I answered.

"*¡Mi tía!*" she exclaimed! She pushed her daughter-in-law aside and grabbed my hand saying, "*Pase, pase*," and walked me into the living room. "I have so many questions," she said.

"Me too," I responded.

Descended through my great-grandmothers's sister Rosa María Skillin, Carmen Isabel was born in Ybor City, Florida in 1896, the same year my grandfather was born in Key West. She married and moved to Key West in 1920 and raised a son. She filled me in on the Skillin family genealogy, demonstrating full control of her faculties. This was my only encounter with her, but she and Ana Alpízar left me with a sense of the Poyo family's connection to this town and its historical Cuban American community. I realized that I did indeed have an extended family.

The next year, I made a second visit to Key West with a colleague. We visited the abandoned San Carlos Institute. A delegation of the elderly club officers greeted us and offered me a formal welcome, as if I were a returning native son. As descendants of the traditional Cuban community, they knew of José D. Poyo and his role in founding San Carlos. That's when it occurred to me that Key West was my family's original American space. San Carlos contained a partially destroyed archive, which turned out to be the Cuban consular archive of Key West. The consulate had occupied offices in the building, and the archive remained there after the United States and Cuba broke relations in 1960 and the consul refused to return home. Later, when the institute closed, homeless persons sometimes broke into the abandoned building and used the archival paper to start small fires to stay warm. Over the following years, I participated in efforts to preserve the archive and getting it microfilmed.

∽ ∽ ∽

Latin American history remained my primary interest, but I found myself spending more and more time thinking about these Florida communities as part of a Cuban American experience that extended long before the mass arrival of Cubans after the triumph of Fidel Castro in 1959. Curiosities about immigration and ethnic history prompted me to take a course at the University of Florida with Professor George Pozzetta, who specialized in Italian-American history.

"Americans," he explained, "expected my Italian forbearers to embrace a distinctly white Anglo-Saxon Protestant culture (WASP), but in our era many white ethnic groups in the United States—including Irish, Jews and Italians—actively questioned and resisted this proposition." Pozzetta introduced me to the idea of immigration and ethnic history and its many nuances and I took it on as a minor field in my doctoral program.

In Key West, I learned of a deeply rooted community, something I had never experienced in my youth. In South America, my parents never even spoke about belonging to a particular locality, just the United States. The idea of our family having descended from this Key West Cuban multiracial working-class community—a very different world from mine—fascinated me.

As I thought about a doctoral dissertation based on this community, I tested out immigrant and ethnic themes and wrote a term project on Cuban politics in 1870s Key West. With Pozzeta's encouragement, I published my first academic article, which appeared in the *Florida Historical Quarterly* in 1977. More articles followed on Cuban nationalist activism, labor organizing, anarchism and journalism in Key West and Tampa. Passion for the subject drove my research, along with a growing conviction that the history of Cubans in Florida needed to be included in the state's and the nation's historical record. I came to see this work as an act of political and social activism like that of historians of the 1960s and 1970s who were writing about traditionally neglected sectors of US society, including women, African Americans and labor. In Latino scholarship, a new generation of especially Mexican-American scholars from Texas to California had already led the way in writing their histories. Some had found jobs in the nation's universities, organized Chicano studies programs and organizations, and created supportive communities.

Initially, while Cubans in Cuba appreciated my work, it did not really enjoy an academic home in the United States. My research occupied a marginal place within historical writing on Cuba and did not fit comfortably into the growing but mostly social-*sciency* writings about Cuban exiles in the United States in the post-1959 era. As far as I knew, there was no scholarly community interested in Cuban American history before 1959, as such, at least not until I received an invitation in 1984 to present a paper at an interdisciplinary seminar on Cuban American Studies in Boston. Scholars identifying as Cuban exiles made most of the presentations, and for the first time I met many leading social science scholars working in the emerging field of Cuban American studies.

Mine was the only presentation on Cuban historical communities in the nineteenth century. I introduced the idea that post-1959 Cuban American communities had to be considered in light of this much longer historical record. This experience encouraged me to carve out a niche for myself exploring the Cuban historical communities within the context of a broader Cuban American story and gave me the confidence to call myself a Cuban American scholar. I settled into my career writing Cuban American history while following the trajectory of the Cuban Revolution and teaching Latin American history.

14

Pressure Cooker

During the 1970s, I studied, became politically radical, struggled to find my place in the United States, married and began raising children. I also remained emotionally tied to my home, Buenos Aires. Travels there each Christmas for a month between semesters during my undergraduate college years kept me connected. Back in the United States, I kept up with the news, often feeling depressed or nostalgic, while my parents lived their every day in a country that not long after my departure in 1968 began a downward spiral into political, economic and humanitarian crisis. Argentina entered an extended period of economic crisis in 1972, reflected in automobile industry trends. Overall cars sales had grown almost every year from 1959 to 1973, but matters changed as economic stagnation and accelerated inflation took hold. Prices increased while consumer income declined. The industry as a whole, including the American companies GM, Ford and Chrysler, showed financial losses beginning in 1972. The total number of vehicles sold in 1978 fell to 1966 levels.

Matters got even worse after that, and became particularly difficult for my father as competition for automobile market-share grew fiercer. General Motors fared poorly in comparison to Ford, its primary competitor. Without overall better products, GM could not hope to challenge the market leader.

My father told me that when he recommended additional investments to improve automobile quality, the New York office advised him his job was to sell existing products. The truth was that in Argentina, Ford produced the best quality cars of the American companies and established unassailable brand recognition through strong investments in public relations. Ford also maintained a high profile in matters of social responsibility, which GM apparently considered superfluous.

❧ ❧ ❧

Even before the onset of economic recession, political repercussions stemming from the 1966 military coup complicated Argentina's future. On May 29, 1969, while living with my brother in Atlanta just after completing my first year at the University of South Carolina, I heard news reports of a popular uprising in Córdoba, Tucumán and other cities in Argentina. Military units and police attacked protestors in the streets, and at least a dozen demonstrators died before the military finally crushed the uprising in Córdoba. It marked the beginning of activist opposition to military rule.

The following month dissidents organized demonstrations in Buenos Aires after hearing that New York governor Nelson Rockefeller would visit as part of a fact-finding tour of Latin America on behalf of President Richard Nixon. The government banned the protests and called out some 20,000 police and troops to protect the visitor and most US companies in Buenos Aires. Police defused a bomb near the IBM headquarters, but protestors succeeded in setting off explosions at nineteen Minimax supermarkets partly own by the Rockefeller family, including the one where my mother shopped. Since protestors had little possibility of assaulting Rockefeller directly, a commando group assassinated one of Argentina's most powerful labor union leaders who had advocated for a conciliatory approach with the military government. Rockefeller immediately cancelled all scheduled meetings with labor leaders, but followed through with sessions that included government, business, agricultural and students leaders.

The Rockefeller Report reflected these Argentine experiences when it said that, "Rising frustrations throughout the Western Hemisphere over poverty and political instability have led increasing numbers of people to pick the United States as a scapegoat and to seek out Marxist solutions to their socio-economic problems." I scoffed at the notion that the United States was a scapegoat. It was clear that American policies supported military rule and the status quo in the region. The report warned that one communist country already existed among the twenty-six nations of the hemisphere, and the future could bring more if the United States was not careful. "And a Castro on the mainland," the report declared, "supported militarily and economically by the communist world, would present the gravest kind of threat to the security of the Western Hemisphere."

Facing escalating violence and little public support, the military liberalized their hold and returned the country to democratic rule in early 1973. Elections reflected a major realignment of political power not seen in eighteen years. No longer able to repress the *peronistas,* the military allowed them to field a presidential candidate. *Peronista* leader Héctor Cámpora won the election handily and immediately initiated a dramatic and predictable shift in the country's political and economic direction. A now much older and ailing Juan Perón returned to Buenos Aires and, in a highly choreographed political drama, Cámpora resigned the presidency in favor of new elections.

Perón became president. Things did not go well. *Peronista* populist economic policies redistributed national wealth, but increased wages, price controls and social welfare deepened economic problems. Spreading civil conflict unnerved the country and affected foreign corporate communities, including my family, which kept me in a constant state of unease. Hundreds of guerrilla actions shook the country in 1972 and increased throughout the following years. Bombings, bank robberies and assassinations of military personnel, politicians, government officials and collaborationist union leaders kept everyone on edge. The most lucrative targets were foreign and local business executives. At the end of 1973, the conservative pro-business journal, *The Review of the River Plate*, in an editorial entitled "The Destruction of Capital as Policy," declared that all of Argentina seemed to have bought into the nationalist notion that foreigners were at the root of all its problems. "Argentina is now engaged upon a full scale witch-hunt . . . the witches are foreign companies which, simply because they are what they are, are condemned from the start, whatever they do or however they behave."

Systematic actions against businessmen began in May 1971, when Cuban inspired Ejército Revolucionario del Pueblo guerrillas seized Stanley Sylvester, manager of the Swift Meatpacking Company and ransomed him for $250,000. During the next two years, guerrillas received millions more from such corporations as the Bank of Boston, Coca-Cola, Amoco, Fiat, Kodak, the British-American Tobacco Company, Firestone and Esso, totaling some 23-million dollars in ransom.

In June 1973, General Motors received a serious threat of violence against top executives, including my father, unless the firm rehired one thousand laid-off workers in a weakening economy. A company spokesman made it clear, "We are not complying," which placed everyone in imminent danger. At first, General Motors stepped up its security operations at the plant but also assigned twenty-four-hour security details at the homes of American executives and provided escorts to and from work. For some time, my family lived with machine-gun-toting security guards in the garage of their home. One evening my sixteen-year-old brother, Jeffrey, returned home late and tried to sneak into the house undetected. The guards heard him and charged out of the garage with their weapons ready to fire. Fortunately, he identified himself in time and quickly went into the house.

Finally, the risks became untenable and, in January 1974, my family and the entire American executive staff of GM moved to new offices in Montevideo. Henceforth executives commuted to Buenos Aires on Monday mornings and returned Friday evenings. GM took the occasion to restructure its operations in the southern region of Latin America. My father became regional sales director for Argentina, Uruguay, Paraguay and Bolivia.

Well-known columnist, Mariano Grondona, noted in *Mercado* that Argentina had under the *peronistas* become a "democracy of fear," where all business executives constantly looked over their shoulders half-expecting to be sequestered at any moment. "The executives are on the front lines," he explained. They experience the "personal terror of kidnapping and economic terror of the ransoms, fear of being foreigners and of not being a foreigner." My father had more than once complained of the times his father in Havana had spent the night at the car distributorship protecting it from revolutionary groups interested in "liberating" vehicles. In some ways, my father faced a similar situation in Buenos Aires. The political violence in Argentina throughout the 1970s and the all-out assault on foreign business interests and personnel worried us all. For me the situation highlighted obvious contradictions. I feared what might happen to my father, but this fear competed with my sympathy with socialist revolution, highlighting my dilemma between the personal and the political. In any case, regardless of what I thought, it all seemed unavoidable as long as Latin America's social problems confronted Cold War impositions from the United States. I could only pray my family would be safe.

The sixty-percent majority of Argentines who elected Juan Perón in 1973 had hoped he could bring a modicum of peace to the nation. His idea for a social contract between capital and labor had seemed workable enough and perhaps might have led Argentina to some viable economic and social compromises and a reduction in violence. Unfortunately, just the opposite happened. Perón could not unify his divided political movement and, worse still, he died the next year, leaving his wife Isabel as president. In 1976, the nation's deepening political and economic crisis finally prompted the military to remove her and returned to power.

My parents uncharacteristically corresponded about the overthrow of Isabel Perón. In mid-1976, my father wrote, "Life continues pretty much the same, going back and forth to Bs. As. [Buenos Aires] to push the Dealers and my boys to at least try harder, for conditions are completely depressed . . . there's really very little one can do under these conditions." My mother, who rarely mentioned politics, wrote from Montevideo, "I don't think there is any chance of going back across the river, at least, for a good long time." She missed Argentina and looked forward to the day she could resume a normal life with her friends in Buenos Aires. "The government is going to have to prove that they have everything under control before GM would take the chance of moving Americans back. Even the Peronists are happy about this takeover as it [the country] was certainly going down the drain. Madam President was milking the country dry. . . . I guess the most they will do is to send her into exile with all her millions of dollars."

The following month my father said, he had no "complaints about this new 'right' government. . . . The democratic left all were so busy lining their own pockets that the people are pretty happy with law and order again. Like I've always said, not all people can have a working democracy. They just can't handle it." Continuing to make his case about Latin American military governments, in July he wrote, "Don't make the mistake of thinking that people in Uruguay, Chile and Argentina are worse off than before. People's governments are the best if they are for the people, but pretty sad if it's only a lot of words in order for a few to live off the people. In the long run these military governments are keeping order, doing things, and probably if they last long enough will do more for the people than what they had before, but it takes time and unfortunately that's what nobody wants to do: wait." He often pointed to the Chilean military's economic successes as an example of what a military regime could accomplish in implementing US economist Milton Friedman's liberal trickle-down economics; of course, he did not refer to the thousands of lives sacrificed during the military's rule in the country.

My father was right, of course, the Guevara-inspired guerrillas and *peronistas* had made as much a mess of things as the military, but what transpired in Argentina after my parents' return to the United States was beyond what they and I would have ever imagined. Even before Isabel Perón's overthrow, the Argentine military had already developed plans for a massive repression to rid the country of all dissident voices, armed or not, using torture as its tool of choice. This repression made previous military governments look like child's play. Certainly, Onganía in the 1960s and those before were quite benign in comparison. In the fashion of the Chilean military throughout the 1970s, the new Argentine government launched a "dirty war" that killed and "disappeared" thousands of mostly leftist Argentine youth, *guerrillas* and otherwise. On taking power, one general said that the military would have to kill 25,000 subversives and 20,000 sympathizers. Another 5,000 deaths would be "mistakes." It was not far from the truth.

I kept my poster of Guevara on my home-office wall, which my father saw on one visit.

"After all that has happened, why do you have *him* on your wall?" he asked.

Our thinking was so incompatible; I wasn't able to convey my reasoning. Guevara had failed, but the repressive military regimes had done much worse, offering only death and continuing poverty. I remained drawn to Guevara's vision. It challenged the notion that poverty and social ills were inevitable, hoping to create a region where people lived with dignity and relative equality.

My father simply shook his head and said, "Professors!"

All of this had its impact on my mother. For several years in the early 1970s, I knew she was having difficulty coping. The day-to-day anxiety and tension of life in Buenos Aires had affected the entire family, especially my mother who feared for her husband's assassination or kidnapping but also for her children when rumors circulated that the guerrillas might target the school. The move to Montevideo in early 1974 had brought some measure relief, but my father and his colleagues spent Monday through Thursday nights in a Buenos Aires hotel with security guards escorting them back and forth to the General San Martín plant. Also, my father's promotion to regional sales director required him to travel regularly to Bolivia and Paraguay. With my father gone and my mother separated from her friends and community in Buenos Aires, she felt isolated.

My mother kept a comfortable apartment overlooking a beach and marina on the Río de la Plata, but anxious and depressed, she drank excessively; it was not an uncommon malady for overseas corporate wives. In addition to the stressful conditions, years of attending cocktail parties, entertaining at home and late afternoon happy hours caught up with her and she struggled with drink forever after. Jeffrey left for college the summer of 1974, and now all her children lived in the United States. She had a hard time adjusting as her children left her one by one. No other family remained to help fill the void, but she tried to stay busy.

"I haven't been writing [letters], as I have been holding a sale for charity [at the American school], and have been terribly busy," she wrote in November 1975. "I am just finishing up the accounting and . . . it takes two months of hard work to get it all done. We sold over 16 million pesos." Concerned about her, my father wrote, "Let's hope she can hold on until I get moved to another job where I won't have to travel so much and be with her more."

One disconcerting and painful side effect of living abroad for my mother involved the distancing of connections with her birth family. My mother learned that the mostly privileged and middle-to-upper class communities we lived in did not normally include extended families—grandparents, uncles and aunts, cousins. Truncated families had to be self-sufficient and not dependent on extended relations for emotional and structural security, and they could expect to see family only on relatively short visits to the US. Those economically, socially and racially homogeneous and artificially constructed corporate worlds abroad promoted US economic and political interests, but did not in any sense constitute authentic American communities. It was in those communities that I grew up, so for me it seemed normal, but not for my mother.

On leaving Flint and leaving the country, she slowly lost touch with the very close relationship she had shared as a young woman with her mother. If her few surviving letters are any indication, she had provided her mother with strong emotional support. During the war when she was away from home with my father, she wrote her mother regularly, but also her two brothers. She complained when they did not write back. As the family's emotional hub, she felt an obligation toward them. Our only week-or-two visits every couple of years to Michigan provided important times of visual and physical reaffirmation of familial bonds, but the stay was too short to keep relationships strong over time.

Inevitably, the distance and time took their toll, especially in an era when telephone calls cost too much and letters were the only form of communication. When letters in both directions became less frequent, she learned to live without her extended family. My mother's photo album documented her active social life as a young woman in

Flint. She enjoyed her friendships immensely, but they too faded from her life. She missed the funerals of her grandparents, with whom she had lived for a time during her mother's bout with tuberculosis; she lost touch with her four aunts with whom she had been quite close; her only uncle Roy, for whom she had a special affection, also faded. Although my mother never spoke of these losses in her life, I'm sure the distance grieved her.

My mother especially mourned the death of her mother in December 1974. My grandmother grew ill from an addiction to prescription medications for undiagnosed body pains that left her virtually helpless. Suffering from dementia, her husband could do little for her, so my mother spent the entire summer with them that year. In her mother's chest-of-drawers and closet, she found dozens of empty and half-full bottles of pills prescribed by many different doctors. For months, she had pleaded with her mother to institutionalize herself, but she refused and it all came to a head when one night while she slept, her demented stepfather entered her room and tried to climb in bed with her. That was all my mother could take. She called her brothers and said she was returning to Montevideo and, despite their protests, left.

That December, my sister and I arrived in Montevideo for Christmas, and Mary and Ricardo visited from Buenos Aires. We settled in for a weeklong reunion and celebration, but the day after our arrival, my mother received a phone call from her younger brother Robert telling her that their mother had died. In a contentious conversation, he shamed her for leaving. Shaking and in tears, she refused to attend the funeral. I volunteered to go in her stead. "No," she said. "We will have our Christmas together as planned." She and her brother never resolved their anger, which left my mother heartbroken. Her commitment to an international corporate life had weakened her ties with her parents and siblings, and left her feeling guilty. As a result, she learned to rely almost exclusively on the extended Poyo family for her sense of familial connection to the world.

Around 1976, my father received word that General Motors planned to transfer him to South Africa, where the company also faced many difficult challenges. Before he agreed, my mother became even more ill. After a lifetime of smoking and recent stress, she had developed throat cancer. She returned to the United States and took a room at the Clinton Inn in Tenafly, New Jersey. My sister withdrew from her college semester to care of her. Each day, they traveled into New York City for chemotherapy while my father remained at his job in Uruguay. After some soul searching, he asked for a transfer to the New York office. He knew this might end his career, but he had no choice. My mother had stood with him his entire career, and now he would put her interests first. They bought a house in Closter, New Jersey, and both made a transition back to a country where they had lived for only two and a half of the previous twenty-seven years. Thankfully, she survived the bout with cancer and made some progress controlling her drinking.

❧ ❧ ❧

Life remained lively for my parents. In early 1978, GM announced a major corporate restructuring that included integrating the highly independent overseas division into the domestic corporate structure. The New York offices closed and overseas operations personnel moved to Detroit. Later in the year, GM announced its plan to discontinue manufacturing operations in Buenos Aires within sixty days. That left 4,000 workers unemployed and 180 dealerships across the country without automobile stock. Official reasons cited low sales and a stiff competitive environment that included ten other automobile companies. After fifteen years, my father's career with Argentina ended.

15
Pilgrimage

Socialist politics and my newly acquired claims on a Cuban American identity inspired my trip to Cuba in March 1979. Besides wanting to learn about family, I needed to see the Revolution first-hand. Cold Warriors depicted communism as an evil system with no redeeming features, one that was created by power-hungry men for their own purposes. I wondered whether a stereotypical Stalinist country awaited me in Cuba, but had grave doubts that liberal democracy could solve social inequality. Intellectual and philosophical objections to eastern European communism did not overcome my conviction that Cubans could learn from communist mistakes and create a more humanistic experience. It was imperative to try, for the sake of millions of people, particularly in Third World countries condemned to starvation and lack of adequate health care, sanitation, housing and education. The truth is that I hoped to discover a new kind of communism: not Soviet or Chinese communism, but a more pragmatic and solution-oriented communism in tune with the needs of the people and not party elites. Fidel Castro and Che Guevara had promised as much.

Even Cubans in the United States who told me of their first-hand experiences with the Revolution did not deter me. Like my grandmother, they had lost livelihoods, properties, a way of life, their country. Not just elites, but middle- and working-class people had fled Cuba in the aftermath of revolution, unwilling or unable to adjust to the radical collectivist experiment. Even significant numbers of Afro-Cubans who had initially celebrated the Revolution, by 1980 could no longer tolerate the difficult conditions and had fled. All of this I knew, but I wanted to see whether the vast majority of Cubans who stayed had embraced ideological commitments, placed collective goals above individual ambition and built a nation for the common good. Exiles told me no; Cubans were slaves, they insisted. Could these traumatized and angry exiles take an impartial view? They would never admit to anything good about the Revolution. I needed to see for myself.

The day after our arrival in Havana, we headed to Santiago on a Cubana de Aviación plane, a Soviet Yakovlev Yak-40 aircraft with unsettling and strange grinding sounds. From there, our ten-day pilgrimage began on a large comfortable bus that slowly and with many stops toured us back to Havana. The memorable cross-country trip gave me a wonderful sense of Cuba's topography, from the Sierra Maestra mountains to the llano across which we traveled. We visited the Moncada barracks in Santiago, where Fidel Castro initiated his revolution against the Batista government on July 26, 1953. His ill-fated attack on the barracks with about 135 fighters armed with sporting guns against 1000 well-armed defenders hoped to spark a generalized rebellion against Fulgencio Batista, who had overthrown the democratically elected but thoroughly corrupt government of Carlos Prío Socarrrás on March 10 a year earlier. Poor planning and even poorer execution doomed the attack. Castro turned himself in and was jailed. Imprisonment and a much-publicized trial gave him a national platform to disseminate his ideas, and he wrote his famous manifesto "History Will Absolve Me" in prison. An amnesty in 1955 allowed him to go to Mexico and begin his revolutionary career in earnest.

The main attraction at the Museo de la Revolución in Havana is the Granma, a yacht Castro purchased in Mexico to transport eighty-two fighters, including Che Guevara, to Cuba in November 1956. How this small vessel carried that many men across the seas for seven days is beyond me; they were a courageous band. The force landed on Cuba's southern coast near the Sierra Maestra Mountains, but

Batista's army lay in wait. When the fighting ended, only about fifteen men, including the Castro brothers and a wounded Guevara, managed to escape. They reassembled and continued into the mountains to recuperate and reorganize. During the next two years, the small band gathered a rebel army, which in January 1959 marched into Havana and took charge of Cuba. The museum includes triumphalist exhibits that narrate the entire story of the revolutionary struggle in minute detail.

Our itinerary also included stops to honor independence war heroes. The Museo Antonio Maceo in Santiago honors the fiercest of independence war generals. We visited José Martí's tomb at Santa Ifigenia cemetery not far from where he died in battle at Dos Ríos in April 1895. In Holguín, Camag ey, Santa Clara and Havana, tours through the old sections of towns provided a taste of their colonial constructions, architecture and overall ambiance. Especially impressive was Havana's colonial district, including Plaza de la Catedral, the Plaza de Armas, the imposing colonial Palacio de Capitanes-Generales from where the Spanish-era governors had ruled the island, and the Morro Fortress that sits across the harbor on a hill above the city. "My ancestors walked these streets," I could not help thinking.

The Revolution's social accomplishments were also on display, such as the universal health care policies, with emphasis on primary and preventive care. In the middle of a rural district a little ways on the road from Holguín to Guardalavaca (on Cuba's northern coast), we visited the Mario Muñoz Rural Hospital, a 100-bed facility with a large maternity ward. The hospital placed a lot of emphasis on preventative care and with its three ambulances provided vaccinations, health workshops and other services throughout the district. During the seventh or eighth month of pregnancy, women living in isolated areas moved into the hospital ward for the duration. Doctors explained that rural infant mortality rates had dropped dramatically after the hospital opened. Extraordinary, I thought. Cuba was the only country in the Western Hemisphere, except perhaps Canada, that guaranteed people healthcare services without question.

A free educational system from primary through university has produced the most literate population in Latin America. A revolutionary move against illiteracy began in 1961 designated the "The Year of Education." In April of that year, secondary schools closed and children formed brigades of *alfabetizadores* who after some training set out to remote areas of the country with a hammock, blanket, paraffin lamp and a flag. Using highly politicized teaching manuals, *brigadistas* set to work offering rudimentary reading and writing instruction, which, if not fully effective in actually instilling the skills, certainly introduced the idea of education and transformed people's sense of possibility. This was accompanied by an overhaul of the public school system and abolition of the private schools to which the middle classes and elites had sent their children. In the next years, illiteracy in Cuba disappeared, and virtually all children attended school. Unlike in Venezuela and Argentina, I did not see children on the streets begging and hustling or selling candies and other merchandise rather than attending school.

In Camagüey, we visited the Palacio de Pioneros, an extracurricular camp for kids modeled after similar institutions in the Soviet Union. The *palacios* provided children with vocational education that complemented their regular academic studies. A delegation of three girls perhaps twelve years old greeted us as we entered the grounds. Along the camp's main street stood the rest of the children in two rows at attention dressed in their distinctive pioneer uniform of red pants or skirts, white shirt and red bandanas around their necks. One of the girls then recited a José Martí poem, made a revolutionary speech, and the children in unison completed the welcome with a revolutionary exhortation: "*¡Seremos como el Che!*" (We'll be like Che.) Cuba's highly organized, ideological indoctrination system introduced school children to revolutionary norms at a young age, but it also ensured all children attended school.

In one of the *palacio*'s activity centers, young girls sewed and made dolls while boys learned to use shortwave radios, among other things. Not the height of gender equity, I quipped, but our guide assured us girls could use the radios too. The educational system's vocational focus reflected an interest in ensuring that education combined intellectual and practical learning. The *palacio*'s fully racially integrated *pionero* population was a breath of fresh air compared to the many segregated schools in the United States. Before the Revolution, only about half of Cuba's children attended elementary school and about twenty percent enrolled in secondary school, but this increased to one hundred percent in elementary school and almost fifty percent in secondary school after the Revolution. Unlike in most of Latin America where so many children never attended school and worked, hustled or begged for a living, in Cuba school attendance was universal.

In Santa Clara, at the Universidad Central de Las Villas, which opened in 1952, faculty and students shared their experiences with us. Especially moving, an elderly Afro-Cuban man told us that only after the Revolution did he have the opportunity to attend elementary school and eventually become a professor. University enrollments increased during the 1970s, reaching over 10% of the population during the time of my trip. Like elementary education, higher learning was deeply ideological and oriented to meeting the nation's practical and technical needs. Although freedom of thought was an unappreciated value in Cuba's socialized educational system, I considered this necessary at this point in Cuba's economic and social transformation.

Our hosts wove a series of activities into our trip that highlighted the Revolution's commitment to cultural democracy and artistic diversity. At a Santiago nightclub, we enjoyed rum, danced and watched a traditional Afro-Cuban song-and-dance show with costumes, plenty of feathers and glittering sequins. The performance took us on a journey through many music genres, including *bolero*, rumba and *son*. The next day at Casa de la Trova, we drank *mojitos* while listening to two performers engage in a traditional *controversia*, an improvisational debate in song. I particularly liked a song, invented on the spot, about visitors from the United States in solidarity with the Cuban Revolution. At the Ballet de Camagüey, dancers rehearsed parts of an upcoming performance, showing us another aspect of Cuba's commitment to the cultural education of their citizens. After the ten-day tour, I was thoroughly impressed with the Revolution; it had without doubt found creative ways to meet many of Cuba's social challenges, providing both bread and social access to a society traditionally riven with inequality and lack of opportunity.

ꩠ ꩠ ꩠ

During my visit with Margo just before returning home, a young man, perhaps twenty-one years old, entered the house. He had been living with Margo while attending school and she introduced him to me as Juan. I learned he was Nana's sister Sara's grandson, that is, my second cousin. After a greeting, in rapid fire he directed questions my way. Why was I in Cuba? What did I think of Cuba? How long was I staying? When I began with some positive impressions of Cuba, he immediately told me not to believe the propaganda. He and Margo spoke in low tones and, after a while, I realized their whispers revealed a concern about who might be listening. I later learned this whispering was common in Cuba among those critical of the Revolution.

"What you saw is just a show," he assured me. "Cuba is a repressive place and not good for young people."

He went on to pelt me with questions about the United States. "Is it true that people can buy anything with special plastic cards?"

"Yes, credit cards," I said, "but they have to be paid back, of course."

"*Sí, sí*, but imagine, buying what you want whenever you want with a simple plastic card," he said.

Juan's attraction to consumerism called into question my stereotype about Cuban revolutionary youth fighting for equality and justice in the face of American imperialism and capitalist expansionism. This I experienced quite often in subsequent visits from people wanting to buy my shoes, pants and shirts.

My cousin's adamantly critical tone about Cuba took me aback. Children attended school, wore uniforms and received meals; citizens had the right to health care; and neighborhood bodegas distributed monthly rations to all citizens. Didn't Juan know that no country in Latin America—or even the United States, for that matter—could match that? But how could I argue after only ten days in Cuba? The implications of what I heard on this first trip sorted out in due time, but the instinctive family acceptance and trust Margo and Juan expressed gave me a sense that family still mattered. They knew nothing of me, and yet they spoke openly and critically of a government they knew could create problems for them. They didn't know my politics, but I imagined they knew blood protected them.

I returned home to ponder the contradiction between what I had perceived as revolutionary accomplishments and Juan's negative testimony. This disconnect between family narrative and my own ideological predispositions continued when Juan's sister Raquel moved to Miami the next year with her American husband, who had lived in Cuba for a couple of years. Nana gave Raquel my phone number when they moved to Houston sometime later, and Raquel called. They visited me in Austin during the summer of 1980. Her black hair, high cheekbones and warm smile reminded me of women I saw on the streets and in the stores of Seville, Spain. We established a strong bond that remains.

To my astonishment, my cousin Juan climbed out of Raquel's car on that same visit. We embraced excitedly, and he later told me an incredible story. His opportunity to leave Cuba came when a group of Cubans seeking asylum drove a truck through the gates of the Peruvian embassy, killing one of the soldiers guarding the entrance. Angered when the Peruvians gave the intruders political asylum, Castro withdrew the Cuban guards that habitually guarded all embassies to avoid just this kind of situation. Within hours, some ten thousand people crowded into the embassy grounds, at which point the Carter administration weighed in by criticizing the Cuban government.

A now even angrier Castro declared that all who opposed Cuba's revolutionary society were welcome to leave and could do so through the port of Mariel, which he opened to vessels willing to pick them up. Thousands of Cuban Americans in Miami lost no time renting boats of all sizes and sailing for the port to pick up relatives, but they also had to take as many people as their vessels would hold. During three months, some 125,000 Cubans left, including Juan, who managed to get the president of his local revolutionary committee to confirm in writing that he was an "anti-social" and should be encouraged to leave. Juan raced to Mariel and boarded one of the boats.

Facing a logistical and political nightmare, the Carter administration intercepted the refugees in Key West and Miami and sent them to processing camps around the country. Juan ended up at Ft. Chafee, Arkansas with 19,000 other refugees guarded by the National Guard, and a second layer of "volunteer" Klu Klux Klan vigilante guards who scouted the area for potential escapees. In cramped quarters and not sure what to expect, Juan feared what might happen. A riot did break out in mid-June. Two thousand heavily armed National Guardsmen and local police brought order, but not before beating and wounding dozens of detainees.

The government first processed and released those like Juan who had family in the United States willing to take responsibility for them. Raquel drove to Arkansas and secured his release within a couple of weeks. It took years to resolve everyone's status. Eventually, some were even forcibly returned to Cuba under a special agreement between the two countries. Juan's willingness to risk life and limb along with some 130,000 others awoke me to the desperation and deep troubles ailing the revolutionary project that seemed to contradict what I had perceived on my trip to Cuba the previous year.

When I returned to Cuba with my family in 1982, I knew I had a lot to learn. I started with Margo. At first, she had supported the Revolution, as had most Cubans. She was an elementary school teacher and believed that good public schools had to be accessible to all, and during the Bay of Pigs invasion, she even had volunteered for nursing-aid duty. She believed in the Revolution's goals, she said, until she saw how implementation produced unexpected and in her mind destructive results. Government propaganda and politics, she said, dominated school days. Atheism undermined efforts to cultivate the values of right and wrong, and children had no sense of cultural refinement and etiquette. She retired the first chance she got, lamenting that children had no respect for teachers. Margo then settled into a life that revolved around her home, church and a few friends of her generation in the neighborhood.

We scheduled our Sunday visits with Margo after lunch, since she had no way of offering a meal, and we left before dinnertime. I usually brought her ham and coffee from the *diplotienda,* which she enjoyed during the week with her housekeeper Emilia, an Afro-Cuban woman who had been with her since before the Revolution. Not much younger than herself, Emilia worked three days with Margo, including most Sundays. This continuity from the past gave Margo a certain comfort, and she enjoyed Emilia's company. Emilia earned a few extra pesos a week, which she may or may not have needed, but it seemed that she also enjoyed the continuing relationship with Margo. Each still played their pre-revolutionary social role, but it was relaxed, friendly and full of humor and laughter. At mid-afternoon, Emilia prepared a *merienda*, usually coffee and a *natilla*, a sweet cold custard-like dessert she made especially for Jeremy and Noel, but that we all enjoyed.

Luis and Nieves had their qualms about the Revolution too, and their voices lowered when making their criticisms. They even avoided uttering Castro's name, instead rubbing a hand off their chins as if pulling on a beard when referring to him. Never a political activist, Luis thought the Revolution a bad idea from the start and later was convinced. He told me about how at times in the 1960s they had to hunt all over Havana for something to eat. Nieves called herself a revolutionary and believed that Fidel Castro had taught the Americans a much-needed lesson, but also said that things had not gone as well as expected. She had wanted a Cuba fairer for all and conceded that initially the Revolution had done away with many injustices, but the socialist economy never gained traction. Nevertheless, the archive was their world, and they continued their work there, never seriously considering leaving Cuba in the early 1960s, when they had their chance. "The Revolution will pass, but the archive will always remain," Luis said. As archivists, they worked diligently with Cuban and foreign scholars, and with determination did what they could to promote research and writing about the history of Cuban.

❧ ❧ ❧

It was during this longer stay in 1982 and subsequent visits over the years that I figured out aspects of how Cuba worked and of the unanticipated implications and contradictions of the radical assault on poverty and social inequality that required total state control of politics, the economy and society. Equality seemed evident, and austerity stood out immediately. From the very beginning, Cuba's totally socialized economy faced severe production challenges and consumer shortages even during the early 1980s, the best of times under the Revolution. At first, Cuba experimented with Che Guevara's idea of a "new man" based on moral incentives, an exaggerated version of John F. Kennedy's "Don't ask what your country can do for you; ask what you can do for your country." Seeking maximum material equality across society, Guevara asked Cubans to work and sacrifice for the Revolution, as in an act of faith. He was convinced that enlightened socialist education could awaken people's consciousness to defer personal gratification in the cause of national solidarity.

The country's economic transformation began in earnest during May 1959 with the Agrarian Reform Law that most Cubans at the time considered a good idea. Originally designed to confiscate large holdings and distribute them to the *campesinos* as private lands, the second part did not happen. Instead, most of the nation's lands remained in the hands of the government and became state farms and cooperatives. The government regulated the small percentage of land that remained technically in private hands and during the 1960s completed the socialization of the entire economic system, rural and urban, and the abolition of capitalism.

The Revolution's original economic goals sought diversification of the Cuban economy away from sugar and toward the development of new industries and eventual economic self-sufficiency. Instead, the chaos of transition to socialism, along with its economic isolation in the Western Hemisphere thanks to the United States, caused plummeting production across the board. Cuba had little of the technology, human expertise or investment funds necessary to create a viable industrial sector in the short-run. Even the sugar industry ran into difficulties in the 1960s, and harvests declined throughout the decade until the economic crisis in 1970 forced a reevaluation and major adjustments. Guevara was wrong about moral incentives. Without economic and material incentives, worker productivity fell dramatically. Also, the United States imposed an economic embargo on exports to Cuba in October 1960 that has unfortunately persisted to this day.

In the 1970s, the government adopted a Soviet communist model more fully integrated with the eastern European economic bloc. This required abandoning efforts at economic diversification and doubling down on its sugar production in exchange for manufactured goods. The new system imposed economic order and allowed some limited market incentives, which yielded the best growth rates since the start of the Revolution. State farms allotted land for family use; some self-employment that did not involve hiring others created incentives; people were allowed to construct and swap homes; *campesino* markets in the cities provided more but expensive foodstuffs; wage differentials grew somewhat; and the availability of more consumer goods inspired harder work. It was better, but in the 1980s, the economy still failed to spark sufficient production and efficient distribution of goods to satisfy most Cubans.

Government employment guarantees for everyone seemed like a humane approach to economic development, but the havoc it played on the economy was easy to see. Over-staffed stores and offices ensured full employment, but also delinked salary from performance. I wandered through bookstores and ate at restaurants where the staff often seemed almost resentful at having to do their jobs. Few smiles greeted me at the bookstore cash registers. Some store clerks were helpful, but not out of incentive just good will. Even in hotel stores for foreigners, off limits to Cuban customers, employees had little interest in providing quality service. I imagined this lack of enthusiasm and consciousness rampant throughout the economy, including state agencies of all kinds. The overly centralized economic organization that was required to create the socialist project left the productive system impotent; this was the greatest challenge for all communist experiments, as it turned out.

~ ~ ~

Cuba's production deficiencies meant we shopped at the *tiendas para extranjeros*. The afternoon of our first day in Havana, we went to the *diplotienda* in Miramar, where we purchased groceries; it was quite far from our apartment in the embassy district of Havana. Catering exclusively to foreigners, mostly diplomats, the store had everything, much like a grocery store in the United States. To get to the store regularly, we had to take a bus, which required a transfer. Returning on the packed buses with people crunched shoulder to shoulder, with bags of food that most Cubans had no access to at all, was logistically impossible and rudely insensitive. We opted for a taxi.

On the street corner across from the store, we stood with our bags of groceries waiting. After about twenty minutes, a taxi stopped and asked where we were going. "Vedado," I said. "Sorry, not going that way," he responded and took off. After another while, a cab stopped and we repeated the conversation, almost verbatim. "What the hell?!" I said angrily to my wife, "Isn't the whole idea of a taxi to take us where we want to go, not where *they* want to go?" In the coming months, I would experience additional bouts of confusion and frustration, wondering why people did what they did.

Just then a light blue 1956 Chevrolet stopped. A middle-aged balding man with dark sunglasses in a white *guayabera* leaned toward the open window on the passenger side. He took off his glasses, flashed a friendly smile and asked if we needed a ride. It was not a taxi, so I hesitated.

"If you are going far and hoping for a taxi, you won't have much luck," said the driver. "Where are you going?"

"Vedado," I said.

"I'm going home and live in Vedado . . . happy to take you."

Seeing no other alternative, I nodded. He got out of the car and went around to the trunk, "Put the groceries in here."

About five-foot-six and well built, and with a bit of a beer belly, it was obvious he had experience with foreigners and knew how to put us at ease.

"My name is Pedro," he said.

From him I learned much about living in Havana. According to Pedro, *resolviendo* (improvising solutions) was a critical art in socialist Cuba. Facing shortages of everything and deficient transportation, among many things, Cubans used their creativity to provide for their daily needs and, unfortunately for them and the Cuban economy, they spent an inordinate amount of time doing so. The number of hours spent in lines for one thing or another represented a tremendous loss of productivity, whether as an office or hospital worker. Almost all Cubans had to *resolver* on a daily basis. Retired and with a pension, Pedro drove the streets transporting stranded pedestrians like us a couple of days a week to supplement his income. This was illicit, but, as long as he kept it to a minimum, police failed to notice, or at least left him alone. We arrived home, and he helped us carry the groceries into the apartment. He refused payment, but as a gesture of friendship, invited us to his home to meet his wife and have a coffee.

"Okay," I said, but knew something was afoot.

I soon learned that he had owned a gas station before the Revolution and became its manager when it was expropriated in the 1960s. He worked there until he retired early because of health problems.

"What do you think about the Revolution?" I asked him.

"Well, it works for me, but . . . I really don't believe in communism. . . . I'm a fan of the United States."

On visiting them, we learned that his wife Gladys had a stronger and more ideological commitment to the system. They lived in a nice apartment on the Avenida de los Presidentes, which they had owned before the Revolution. They managed quite well. He received good health care for his heart problem, and they went on vacation packages all over Cuba. They even traveled to East Germany and the Soviet Union, probably courtesy of Pedro's irreplaceable asset, his Chevrolet. For a time he had an agreement to drive a diplomat's family around Havana whenever needed, which gave him access to dollars.

By the end of the visit, Pedro made his motives clear. He offered to be available to drive us wherever we wanted, if in return I purchased for him \$10 or \$15 worth of items from the *diplotienda* on our weekly visits to the store. He usually wanted meat, which was very hard to get, but he also liked American cigarettes and whiskey and other products that simply were not available to the great majority of Cubans.

"Do not change any dollars into pesos," he warned. "I will give you all you need. There is little to buy in Cuba."

The only pesos I needed were to pay for buses, books, newspapers, cigars and restaurants, which were all very inexpensive. I often got coffee at the bus station down the street from the national library for very little, and at the bookstores, new and used books averaged a peso or two. An occasional meal at restaurants was our single-most expensive activity, which for us was not very much at that. Cubans especially frequented the cafeteria-style pizza parlors. Cheap and fast, they usually had long lines. We preferred quieter restaurants. We ate at the Conejito a few times, which served rabbit in a variety of ways. Not far from our apartment was an Italian restaurant, La Roca that served pasta dishes, and on the Malecón a small open-air place called-Pío Pío served roasted chicken and french fries. Jeremy and Noel especially liked going there. Ice cream at Coppelia every day did not break our budget either. We learned to contend with long lines, but the delicious ice cream certainly made it worthwhile.

Everything else we bought at the stores for foreigners in dollars. I could not pass up Pedro's offer and learned how Cubans were able to *resolver*. We became friends with Pedro and Gladys, enjoying occasional dinners at each other's apartments. On Saturdays, they often toured us around Havana, including Playa Santa María east of Havana, Antonio Maceo's tomb west of Havana, the poor dilapidated zoo and many other places. Pedro even ventured out one Sunday afternoon to pick us up at Margo's house after heavy rains from hurricane Alberto unexpectedly inundated Havana. He knew all the passable streets and took us safely home.

With so many shortages, Cubans "resolved" their needs through black-market transactions that undermined the socialist economy. One day while heading down the Malecón in Pedro's Chevrolet, a policeman pulled us over without apparent reason. He asked for identifications and instructed Pedro to get out of the car. The officer slowly walked around the car closely inspecting the vehicle, then had Pedro open the trunk. After that, Pedro lifted the car's hood. When we drove off a few minutes later, Pedro matter-of-factly explained that police routinely checked automobiles for black-market items, including car parts. Any consumer items had to be accounted for with a receipt, and the policeman even looked for newly installed parts in

Pedro's Chevrolet engine. Apparently, the police were on the frontline of trying to control a thriving trade in contraband auto parts, mostly stolen from government warehouses.

Constant and unremitting food shortages bothered most Cubans. As one put it to me, "How is it possible for Cuba not to have sufficient food? Go anywhere into the countryside and drop seeds," he seethed. "They will grow! Only the government makes this impossible."

People certainly weren't starving, but they consumed only modest calories that always left them yearning for more. Meals ceased to have the social function of bringing people together for conversation and community. Cubans are a social and generous people, and few things disturbed them more than not providing guests with hospitality and a meal. It tore at the very fabric of Cuban culture and sociability. On several occasions, we checked out a neighborhood grocery store near our apartment in Vedado. These were not monthly ration stores, but state markets with products at higher prices. Poorly stocked, the store carried mostly canned products from Eastern Europe. Sauerkraut, pickled beets, beans and eggplant lined the shelves. Cubans told me they ate this only when necessary.

Hoping to alleviate food shortages as well as the poor quality of offerings, the government allowed farmers at state farms and cooperatives to produce extra crops on designated plots at their leisure. They sold their crops at new farmers' markets in the cities. I visited the markets a couple of times and saw produce generally not available in the normal state stores, but expensive. A side effect of these markets was a great deal of corruption, causing Castro to take his people to task. In a televised speech in 1982, Castro explained that the government had allowed farmers to produce extra and sell at free markets in the cities as a way of easing shortages for the society in general. This had been a social decision, he said, not a policy to promote petty capitalism or enhance the wealth of some at the expense of others. He complained that police had arrested doctors who, instead of working at their jobs, had used their cars—given to them to facilitate their work as doctors—to transport produce from farms to the free markets. Some, he said, had thousands of pesos in their bank accounts. This was a corruption of Cuban socialism, he declared angrily. If people could not be responsible, he warned, market incentives would be eliminated.

Castro's ideological and inflexible response to the obvious consequences of inserting market mechanisms into the economy surprised me. Rather than providing *campesinos* with legal ways to get their produce to market, he simply threatened to return to previous policies. As it turned out, this speech was an early salvo in Castro's decision to back off the liberalization campaign of the 1970s. In 1986, Castro announced a campaign of Rectification of Errors and Negative Tendencies, known simply as *rectificación* to purify the system of *petite bourgeois* thinking. This campaign sought to eliminate the emerging social stratification that benefitted small farmers, middlemen, black marketeers and the small segment of self-employed who made money under the table.

Shortly after arriving in Cuba in 1982, I received a phone call from my cousin Raquel in Caimito del Guayabal. She had just arrived in Cuba to visit her ill grandmother, Sara, Nana's older sister, and would be in Havana the next day. I joined her while she ran some errands. First, we went to pick up her grandfather's food rations. Old and unable to care for himself, and although divorced from Sara, he had nevertheless moved into the family home in Caimito from his Havana apartment, but someone had to travel to his neighborhood bodega twice a month to pick up his food rations. The ration was indispensable, but the twice-monthly trip to Havana was too expensive in taxi and time consuming on the hopelessly crowded buses.

Raquel explained that if they transferred the ration card to a bodega in Caimito to avoid these trips, they would lose her grandfather's apartment. At the same time, they could not sell the apartment, only trade it in a process known as *permutar*. They had to find someone wanting to trade their house or apartment in Caimito for the apartment in Havana, which was not easy. Moreover, the trade had to be accomplished without money changing hands. Because two properties rarely shared the same value, a real estate black market developed to achieve a mutually agreeable trade. I began to recognize the economic distortions and inefficiencies inherent in the Revolution's one-dimensional insistence on absolute equality.

As she prepared to return to Caimito, Raquel encouraged me to visit her ill grandmother as soon as possible. I promised a visit the following weekend, but she quite suddenly died the next day. Not knowing what to expect, I left the family at home and set out for Caimito. Only thirty kilometers to the west, it should not have taken long to get there, but, with the difficult transportation situation, it may as well have been 150 kilometers away. I took a bus to the main station and waited an hour for another bus heading west to Pinar del Río along the *carretera central*. In the early afternoon, I arrived in Caimito and got off at the first stop in town, as Raquel had instructed.

I crossed the street and asked someone for the house. Just a short way up the highway, the house sat separated from the street by just a narrow sidewalk in typical Spanish style. "Nana was born in this house!" I thought. I climbed the steps to the porch, where half a dozen people, mostly women, sat on chairs. I asked for Raquel. She appeared, embraced me in tears and thanked me for coming. We entered a large living room empty of all furniture except for chairs around three walls, again occupied mostly by women. My great aunt lay in a casket against the fourth wall. Yolanda, Raquel's mother and my father's first cousin, then embraced me and thanked me for coming. Raquel's two sisters and their families also greeted me. Through a little window in the top of the casket, I saw Sara's old and wrinkled face for the first and last time. I had only ever met one other of Nana's siblings, her sister Concha in San Juan, Puerto Rico on one of our trips from Buenos Aires to New York. It was 1966, and I remember thinking how much alike the sisters looked and acted. I never saw Concha again.

Very close to her grandmother, Raquel suffered this loss terribly, but there was no clergy present to console, to help the family cope and process the pain. Somehow, the president of the neighborhood revolutionary committee had taken charge of the burial. When the moment arrived, several men picked up the casket and placed it in the back of a station wagon. I got into another car with Yolanda and Raquel, and we took a half-mile ride to the cemetery. As we pulled up, several men had already removed the marble top from an above ground burial vault, and we watched as they lowered the coffin into the tomb. They immediately returned the top to its place, and the president of the committee announced the burial ceremony finished. Raquel immediately broke into tears again and demanded to know how that could be. No words? No ceremony? No recognition of a life? The committee president told her matter-of-factly that death was normal and there was no God. He urged everyone to go home and get some rest. They would feel better soon. “A communist funeral?” I wondered.

Fortunately, not long after that sad internment, I returned to Caimito with the entire family so we could talk *con calma*. On that visit, Raquel showed me the house and the back patio with its orange trees. Behind the house were fields the family owned before the Revolution that they had rented to sugarcane companies. Although they had lost the lands, the family kept the entire house, for a time. In the years following my 1982 visit, the family lost the house in piecemeal fashion; it was divided to accommodate other families without homes. Eventually, it fell into the hands of the local committee and became its headquarters.

Yolanda dispatched her daughters to find a chicken to serve us an afternoon lunch. I felt embarrassed and guilty for this imposition and insisted that we had had a good breakfast and would eat when we returned to Havana. A café con leche, with the coffee I had brought them and cookies from the *diplotienda*, was sufficient, but they would not hear of it. No, she insisted, and, after a while, Raquel and her sisters returned with a chicken, which must have cost them a pretty penny. Yolanda prepared it with rice and beans. Standing in the kitchen with the women while they prepared the meal, I could see that they literally had nothing in their refrigerator. Each day they “resolved” that day’s meals. They knew how to do it, but nothing was easy.

ဢ ဢ ဢ

During our stay in Cuba, Betty Kay home-schooled the boys with texts and workbooks brought from Texas. I later regretted not putting them in a Cuban school, where they would have learned Spanish more fluently. They did, however, make friends in the neighborhood and got plenty of practice in the language. When the Cuban kids got home from school, eleven-year-old Jeremy would join them in the apartment parking area to play baseball. He also met a young girl—a few years older than he—who turned out to be the daughter of former United Nations Ambassador Ricardo Alarcón. They lived on the floor above us. She grew up in New York and, amusingly, spoke a fluent Brooklyn-accented English; she enjoyed practicing with Jeremy. Noel often accompanied Jeremy downstairs to watch the kids play, but they did not pay much attention to a much younger five-year-old.

When I returned home to the apartment at about three each afternoon, I stayed with Jeremy and Noel while Betty Kay walked a few blocks away to Spanish classes at the adult language school Escuela para Extranjeros. There she met students from Russia, East Germany, England and several African countries. The most interesting was Yonas, an Ethiopian pilot training in Cuba who spoke good English and had relatives in the United States. He often joined us at Coppelia for ice cream, and we exchanged stories about Ethiopia and Texas. An English businessman who painted ships for the Cuban government also took Spanish classes and visited us with his Cuban girlfriend, who mostly complained about the Revolution.

The existence of petty crime surprised me, especially since no one spoke about it. I learned of the "anti-socials" that roamed Vedado near the hotels and high-rise apartments inhabited by Eastern European advisers in an unfortunate way. In most places in the world, they are referred to as thieves, not "anti-socials," but the government in Cuba preferred a term that emphasized their criminality as a violation of the nation's shared social vision. One hot afternoon, we visited the Napoleonic Museum not far from our apartment. It held an extensive collection of Napoleonic artifacts, including weapons, jewelry, furniture, ceramics, paintings, books and even Napoleon's death mask. Displayed in an impressive replica of a Medici mansion with interior gardens, balconies and terraces, the collection reflected the wealth accumulated by some of Cuba's important sugar magnates, in this case the Julio Lobo family that had fled Cuba in 1959.

We returned to the apartment in late afternoon, and I headed for the shower, while Betty Kay laid down for a brief nap in the bedroom before dinner. Jeremy and Noel remained in the living room watching a television set we had purchased at the foreigners' store.

Suddenly, Betty Kay came into the bathroom and said, "Jerry! There's a strange man in the living room!"

"What? Who?"

"Don't know, better get out there, quick," she said. "He is asking about some family and using the telephone."

Jeremy had answered a knock at the door, thinking it was his friend. Somehow, I hadn't thought about dangers in Cuba and didn't think to warn him about opening the door without an adult in the room. The man had pushed the door open and slipped into the apartment, asking Jeremy for his parents. Frightened, Jeremy ran to the bedroom to alert Betty Kay. She rushed into the living room and confronted the stranger.

"I'm looking for the East German family that used to live here."

By the time I dried myself, dressed and made my entrance, he had planted himself on the sofa. Betty Kay stood watching him with her arms crossed and a stern face.

"What do you want?" I demanded gruffly.

He started with his story again, but I cut him off. "Leave now or I will alert the neighbors and call the police."

That convinced him. "*Bueno, no te enojes, mi hermano, sí, ya me voy*," he said and left.

Not immediately clear about what had just happened, I looked around the living room and discovered my Rolex watch gone. It was my father's retirement gift from GM that he had given me. I had taken it off on the way to the shower and placed it next to the telephone, as I always did. When Betty Kay went to get me, he had pocketed the watch. I told my father about the watch several months later, and with disbelief he said, "Why would you take it to Cuba?" I was too ashamed to tell him that I was naïve, but of course, he knew that.

I knocked on a neighbor's door to alert him, and he immediately called the police.

"Don't worry," he said, "if they catch him, you'll have your watch back in no time."

An officer arrived shortly. I described the man as mulatto with carefully cropped hair and dressed nicely in a white shirt and red slacks. The police officer, tall and mulatto also, asked that I walk through the neighborhood with him, because the thief was likely one of those who preyed on foreigners in the Vedado hotel district. Several blocks from the hotel near the Havana Libre Hotel, I saw a mulatto man perhaps thirty paces away walking in front of us and dressed exactly like the thief. I pointed to him. The officer blew his whistle and ordered him to stop. As we approached, I saw immediately that this was not the same man; he was shorter with an entirely different face. "No, no, that's not him," I said.

Ignoring my comment, the officer questioned him aggressively and with an authoritarian tone demanded his documents. Frightened to death, he handed the officer his identification card and meekly asked what the problem was. His eyes darted between the policeman and me, while the officer asked him where he worked.

"This is not the man," I repeated.

The questions continued, and finally the officer blew his whistle and motioned for a nearby patrol car. Now the man was beside himself. He had done nothing, he insisted.

I too became alarmed, and for a third time, with a stronger and insistent tone, I again said, "I'm sure this is not the man. There is no similarity other than his clothes."

This time, the officer impatiently turned to me, "Are you sure?"

"Yes, not the same man," I reassured him in a confident tone.

"Okay," he sighed, as if I had just wasted his valuable time. He handed the man back his document and said he could go.

"*Gracias, gracias, por Dios, gracias*," he said to me in a terrified tone as he turned to leave.

I had almost complicated this man's life in ways I could not imagine. The encounter reminded me of the militarized police in Argentina after the 1966 coup who dealt with citizens in arrogant ways. Everyone knew they had the power to arrest for the slightest offense or no cause at all, even picking up long-haired youths whose heads would be shaved at the police stations.

On our way home from dinner one Sunday evening in Buenos Aires, a police patrol stopped my father without cause and threatened him for a bribe. My father refused to pay, and after several angry exchanges, the officers realized they were dealing with a foreign executive and let him go. This Cuban officer acted in a similar way, except he had no interest in a bribe. His actions were about power and, clearly, the common citizen was at a disadvantage. People of color in the United States also knew exactly what this was like, and still do.

If petty crime was apparently alive and well, we also experienced Havana as accessible and safe. Cubans always greeted us in welcoming ways. On the crowded buses, men gave their seats to Betty Kay and the boys, especially little Noel. Women even offered to let the boys sit on their laps. We walked all over Vedado and Habana Vieja and, regardless the hour, never felt unsafe. Many dilapidated neighborhoods that would have raised cautions in the United States posed no threat in Havana. It took a while to shed the instinct we carried from the United States, linking a neighborhood's overall physical condition with the need for caution.

Figuring out how Cuba worked and how the people felt about the Revolution was not easy. For everyone I knew who condemned the Revolution, I heard from others who spoke of its many merits. I could not help feeling dismayed at the number of alienated youths seeking any opportunity to leave, but mass gatherings expressing popular support countered individual testimonials about problems and concerns. Betty, Jeremy, Noel and I attended the traditional labor day, *Día del trabajo* (May 1), gathering at the iconic Plaza de la Revolución, where Fidel Castro regularly spoke to his people with hours-long speeches defending the Revolution and lambasting the US-led systems of world capitalism and imperialism. Pedro and Gladys accompanied us. We arrived early, but thousands had already filled the plaza. Mesmerized by the spectacle, I did not notice the thousands more that over the next hour filled the streets behind us. Only when I turned around did I realize we were penned-in. "Don't worry," Pedro said. He had been to many such mass gatherings, but I could not help feeling a bit panicky for my family. We had no choice but to remain for the duration.

Speeches continued for a long while. As the heat set in, I looked up at the sky, hoping to see some clouds that might bring relief from the sun, but without luck. Endless thousands standing shoulder to shoulder listened restlessly, giving way to scuffles among some with bottles of rum and feisty attitudes. Here and there, brief fights broke out, and I saw the ripples of movement spreading through the crowd as people backed away from the violence. Frightened, I wrapped my arms tightly around Jeremy in front of me while Pedro put Noel on his shoulders. Ours were the only children in sight. Cubans knew not to bring small children, but we remained calm.

Initially disappointed that the Minister of Labor rather than Fidel Castro gave the main speech, I was thankful when I realized our situation. It would have been a long day had Fidel taken the microphone. The Minister of Labor spoke for about a half hour, and Raúl Castro followed and spoke even more sparingly, as was his custom. Then several other lesser dignitaries addressed the crowd. With the speeches completed, loudspeakers began blasting patriotic music. Betty Kay and Gladys grabbed onto to the rest of us to keep together just as the crowd began to move forward. Like the turbulence in water at the confluence of two rivers, we felt pushing and shoving as people from the various streets filed into the plaza. Tensions dissipated when we entered the plaza and marchers spread out.

People cheered and waved Cuban flags to the loud revolutionary music. They marched past the dignitaries' reviewing stand and the immense pensive statue of José Martí. Thousands applauded the revolutionary leadership as they walked by, and I caught a glimpse of Fidel smiling and waving. The iconic portrait of Che Guevara facing the plaza from high above or the Interior Ministry building ensured his presence at all of these revolutionary celebrations. After two hours, we finally emerged from the pressing crowds. I vowed to stay clear of massive public manifestations; to this day, they evoke claustrophobic feelings.

If as some claimed, Cubans in the main opposed the Revolution; there was no sign of it on that day. Certainly, the government facilitated the movement of people to the plaza, and communist functionaries at government offices directed people to go, but the crowds seemed genuinely joyous. Spectacle was at the heart of the Revolution. Mass mobilization and the leadership's constant reminder of the ideals at stake kept people engaged. There was no room for skepticism, only optimism. As Fidel Castro always said, "*Siempre seremos optimistas*."

I left Cuba in 1982 with a less romantic, more realistic understanding of the Revolution. Regular trips during the rest of the decade to continue my research, attend conferences and visit family gave me more opportunities to explore. Just as I completed my dissertation in 1983, I received my first invitation to present my research at an international conference. University College, London hosted a conference on José Martí with experts from Spain, England, the United States and Cuba. This led to an invitation to Havana the next year for another Martí conference, hosted by the Centro de Estudios Martianos. After this, I presented numerous papers at symposia sponsored by several academic and research centers in Havana. I enjoyed my interactions with Cuban scholars. Mostly serious and articulate researchers and writers, they taught me much about island's history and society, and I was especially impressed with their strong commitments to revolutionary ideals despite the many problems.

Overall, in the 1980s, Cuba seemed like a reasonable place to live, despite food and consumer shortages, especially when compared to the conditions for the majority of the poor across Latin America. Certainly, people with liberal democratic values found much to dislike about communist rule, as did many Cubans, but as a model for resolving the distressing poverty and malnutrition in Third World countries, the Revolution had much to commend it. Despite the problems Cubans faced, I believed the government would find ways to promote economic growth and provide the Cuban people with a more prosperous and personally satisfying existence, while maintaining their commitment to the social project. My continuing travels to Cuba also had a political dimension consistent with my personal opposition to the United States' unrelenting hostility toward Cuba: I believed that normal relations and dialogue offered a better future for both countries.

16
Inscribing a Maligned People

One day in late 1968, my roommates at the University of South Carolina invited me to eat at Taco Bell.

"What's that?" I asked.

"Tacos, man, you know, your kind of food, Mexican."

I had never eaten a taco; it was not part of my culture, I told them. They didn't believe me. At that moment, I instinctively embraced Argentina, the particular Latin culture I identified with. Mexico had rarely entered my consciousness growing up in Buenos Aires. Sometimes Mexican films ran on Argentine TV, and I especially liked Cantiflas. I enjoyed my father's records of Jorge Negrete and Agustín Lara, although I don't recall knowing at the time that they were Mexican. Unfortunately, and symptomatic of United States realities, the representations of Mexicans I most remembered were from television shows such as *The Cisco Kid* and *Zorro,* or from *The Real McCoys,* the show on which Puerto Rican actor Tony Martínez played a Mexican farmhand, Pepino.

It occurred to me later that the four unique Latin American nationalities that had formed my identity were part of a Hispanic hemispheric identity of sorts. These nations shared historical and cultural affinities that emerged from complex interactions among Spanish and Portuguese conquerors, African slaves, Native Americans and many other peoples over five centuries. Latin American communities included not only people with strong cultural attachments to specific ethnic and cultural backgrounds, but people who identified with social amalgams resulting from centuries of *mestizaje*, or mixing of races and cultures. They lived in colonial settings whose legacies remained visible in the region's politics, economies and society, even when I grew up there. These countries were marked by rich lands made poor through elite exploitation of the masses, economic inequalities and unequal social structures, but they were nevertheless vibrant, inviting and welcoming places blessed with great geographic diversity and extraordinary natural vistas.

While I recognized Cubans, Argentines, Venezuelans and Colombians participating in a Latin American identity, I realized Mexicans and all other Hispanic peoples of the region did so too. Simón Bolívar, José Martí and José Vasconselos, among others, had already thought of that, I later learned. I never imagined when I arrived in South Carolina in 1968, wondering how I would fit into the United States, that I would feel a sense of belonging as a Cuban American, and even less as a Latino. I embraced a calling as an activist-scholar intent on inscribing a much-maligned Latino people into the history of the United States. I wanted to vindicate the place and significance of Hispanics in a country that Anglo Americans generally claimed as uniquely their own.

In 1983, when I finally entered the academic profession as a historian, my research on Cuban American communities was not met with overwhelming enthusiasm on the job market. University history departments in the early 1980s were not much interested in Cuban historical communities in the United States. Departments looking for Cubanists wanted cutting-edge research on slavery and race, and those few looking for someone to teach US Latino history understandably preferred Mexican American rather than Cuban American specialists.

Fortunately, I saw an advertisement for a job at a museum and research center, the Institute of Texan Cultures at San Antonio (ITC). Originally founded as the Texas Pavilion of the San Antonio World's Fair in 1968, the ITC followed a similar model as the Smithsonian Institution museums in Washington, DC that combined exhibitions for the general public and academic research. I thought I had landed in heaven. The director of research suggested I spend a month reading and exploring the museum and deciding about what I wanted to research and write. I also explored the city with my family. What I saw inspired me to focus on the city's eighteenth-century origins.

I learned that San Antonio was among the largest cities in the United States and the result of Spanish colonization of the area beginning in 1718. Sharing a common history with St. Augustine that I was familiar with in Florida, as imperial outposts that eventually became part of the United States, the Spanish northern borderland communities were part of American history, although they were not traditionally interpreted as such. Any balanced history of the United States, I thought, could not avoid discussing communities like San Antonio, St. Augustine, Santa Fe and even later foundations such as and Los Angeles, in the same breath as Plymouth Rock and Jamestown. Others thought so too, and during the 1980s and 1990s many historians began interpreting these Spanish colonial communities as an integral part of the origin story of the United States.

This became the central theme of my work at ITC. I wanted to emphasize how Texas Mexican American or Tejano history had its roots in the eighteenth century. One of the great gifts of working at ITC was learning to transmit findings directly to the public through conferences and exhibitions. I began to think about history as more than an academic enterprise. Communicating with everyday people was different from the insulated conversations among academics. Mexican-American research buffs, members of local historical associations and genealogical enthusiasts crowded ITC's public events on the history of Spanish- and Mexican-era Texas. They appreciated a state institution publicly featuring their community histories, and without apology, they lamented loudly the systematic exclusion of their history. They were tired of hearing that Texas history began in 1836.

One elderly gentleman, Adolf Herrera, who visited ITC often and worked as a docent, descended from a prominent eighteenth-century San Antonio family. He often told me how much he resented that his great-grandfather, Blas Herrera, among the Tejano fighters for Texas independence from Mexico, had never received any recognition. A close friend and colleague to the legendary Juan Seguín, Herrera joined Seguín's military company during the conflict, only to be shunted aside along with his entire community after Anglo Americans took over San Antonio. Herrera's grandfather said that Texas history textbooks were a "pack of lies… no matter what they write."

One day I answered my office phone. "Hello, this is Emma Tenayuca."

Then silence. A bit taken aback that I was on the phone with this legendary figure in San Antonio, I waited for her to go on, but the silence persisted.

After a bit I said, "Yes, I know of you, Ms. Tenayuca. What can I do for you?"

When she was sixteen in 1933, Ms. Tenayuca joined women strikers on the picket lines at the Finck Cigar Company and was jailed. The following year she graduated from high school and helped organize garment workers at the Dorothy Frocks Company and two branches of the International Ladies' Garment Workers' Union. In 1937, she organized chapters of the communist Workers' Alliance of America and the next year led ten thousand pecan shellers in the largest strike in San Antonio history. She remained active with the Texas Communist Party until she was blacklisted and left San Antonio to study at San Francisco State College. She later returned to San Antonio and taught elementary school until retiring in 1982, just a year before I arrived at ITC.

"I saw in the newspaper about your conference and exhibit," she continued. "I would like to go, but I don't have any way to get there."

"Well, if you don't mind going early I can pick you up at your home on Saturday morning and bring you to the Institute," I offered.

"That will be fine. You can pick me up as early as seven in the morning. Thank you," and she hung up.

"What an odd lady," I thought to myself. But in subsequent months, I got to know her as a forthright, idealistic and endearing woman. She even consented to an oral history, which I still consider an important contribution in historical recovery.

I wanted to learn more about Tenayuca's years as a labor organizer and communist activist, but she was less interested in speaking of herself than about her ancestors, particularly a branch of her family that lived in San Antonio in the eighteenth century. "That is the history our kids need to know," she insisted.

Like Herrera, she complained that Mexican Americans were excluded systematically from the school curriculum. "Our people founded this city," she said often. "And our children need to know that."

Somehow never having been grounded in a local community, I had thought that people living their daily lives did not have time or energy to think about these things. Herrera, Tenayuca and dozens of others attending the events at ITC showed me otherwise. These experiences with the grassroots Mexican-American community in San Antonio further inspired my growing commitment to helping set the record straight about the historical role of Hispanic peoples in the history of the United States.

During the 1980s, as I added the history of Mexicans in eighteenth century San Antonio to my repertoire of research and writing, I wondered what if anything San Antonio and Key West had in common. Could these historically distinct and geographically distant communities share in a larger enterprise called Hispanic history? To what extent, I eventually wondered, could Latin Americans in the United States be understood as a coherent Hispanic presence of which I was a part? What in fact did *Latinidad* mean, if anything? The prospects for a historical understanding of *Latinidad* inspired me to learn about Chicanos and Puerto Ricans even as I continued to write about Cuban Americans. What would an Hispanic history of the United States look like?

At first, most Cuban American, Mexican-American and other scholars outright rejected the proposition of a shared history. And many still do. These experiences, they argued, were unique and had nothing to do with each other. It is true that their demographic differences were numerous, including class, race and education, and so were their politics. Cuban scholars viewed themselves as exiles, a unique identity that other Latinos in the United States could not hope to understand. Cubans were different, they insisted, and did not have much in common with Mexican Americans, who rejected them in any case. Mexican-American scholars viewed Cubans as right-wing elitists associated with US imperialist policies in Latin America. Chicano scholars related more to Fidel Castro, Che Guevara and the Cuban Revolution than to those who had fled the island. Since I was not a Cuban exile or a Mexican American, I looked past what I considered the reigning presentism and tried to envision a moment when their respective Latin American cultural heritages might inspire a sense of shared experience or historical affinity.

The Mexican-Cuban relationship was perhaps the most challenging example through which to consider the idea of Latino history, but historical affinities did express themselves more naturally among other groups. If I thought violence in Argentina was shocking and material conditions in Cuba lacking, neither country suffered the human distress that in Central America produced waves of immigrants from the 1980s to the present. As Central American refugees and South American exiles joined the already existing and migrating populations of Mexicans, Cubans, Dominicans, Puerto Ricans, Colombians and others, I began considering the implications for the United States as they coalesced—which I thought they were doing—into an identifiable national whole. Unlike Cuban exiles and Mexican Americans, working-class Central Americans and Mexican Americans found more in common, as did many middle-class Colombians, Nicaraguans and other Latin Americans with Cubans in Dade County. Puerto Ricans and Mexicans in Chicago often made common cause, as did Puerto Ricans, Dominicans and Cubans in New York. As Latinos of different backgrounds began to live in the same communities, many interacted with a sense of "we" and positive affirmations of community, culture and tradition. They advanced their political and socioeconomic agendas in coalitions, not without conflicts and challenges, as well as expanded their communal identities through cultural and civic activities.

I explored beyond the scholarship of historians who generally rejected such broad and integrated notions and discovered scholars in other fields not shy about tackling issues of *Latinidad*. The pioneers came from unexpected fields, particularly theology and philosophy, which made sense, since they worked at the conceptual level and were not required to ground their work in detailed historical documentation to make their case. But for me their conceptual work was extraordinarily important and foundational. Theologian Roberto Goizueta proposed that Latinos—whether Catholic or not—shared "a way of being," rooted in ancient Catholic culture and traditions, while philosopher Jorge Gracia proposed that only within an historical context is the idea of Hispanic at all intelligible. "The history of Hispanics," Gracia noted, was incredibly diverse and "there are no common properties to all those people whom we wish to call Hispanics." What is crucial for understanding the idea of Hispanic is history; the particular events of that history rather than the consciousness of that history. "A unique web of changing historical relations supplies the unity," he argued.

Of course, Goizueta's and Gracia's ideas are a challenge and must be approached with care. Historian Virginia Sánchez wrote that "the danger of seeking affinity within and across this enormously complex population lies in over-generalization, a blurring of distinctions and homogenization of these groups." The challenge to historians is to incorporate and balance the nuances and diverse experiences of Latinos without misappropriation, distortion or omission. Inasmuch as affinity may be understood as a continuum of related or shared historical experiences, then, I thought, a comprehensive narrative was surely possible.

An invitation in 1992 to join the Advisory Board of the national Recovering the US Hispanic Literary Heritage project at the University of Houston encouraged my thinking in this direction. Founded two years earlier, this community of mostly Latino scholars dedicated itself to the identification, recovery, preservation and publication of US Hispanic literary texts from their origin to 1960. At my first meeting and in subsequent years, I encountered a multidisciplinary group of literary critics, historians, linguists, archivists, librarians and more. For the first time I circulated among like-minded scholars willing to tangle with the idea of Hispanic history writ large.

I particularly appreciated that this field, increasingly called Latino Studies, was pioneered and developed by Latino scholars, which differed from my experience with the field of Latin American history. During the 1970s and 1980s, and before, very few Latino scholars entered the field of Latin American history in the United States, and I was always the only Latino graduate student in my MA and PhD courses. Anglo American scholars set the research and interpretative agendas, including my doctoral professors David Bushnell, Lyle McAllister and Neil MacCauley. Well-respected and published authorities in their specialties, they mentored me well. I took their courses in Colonial and Modern Latin America, the histories of Río de la Plata, Brazil, Nueva Granada and the Andean nations. But somehow, they had remained oblivious to the history of Latinos in the United States.

It took a long time before scholars of Latin American history even acknowledged that the story of Latinos in the United States was relevant to their field. On the other hand, Latino scholars knew instinctively that their history in the United States could not be interpreted effectively without an intimate knowledge of Latin American history and that scholars of US history would eventually have to confront the Latino reality. I ran into few Latinos at Latin American history conferences and was excited attending the Recovery conferences, which always exhibited a powerful sense of mission and solidarity.

As my personal and professional relationships grew with Mexican Americans, Puerto Ricans, Dominicans and others in the United States, especially in the Recovery Project, the affinities and shared experiences became clearer. Enjoying dinners, wine, cigars and good conversations, we learned of the many common elements of our histories, without denying the obvious and sometimes painful differences that required discussion.

An extraordinary thirty-year boom in Latino scholarship from the 1970s to the 1990s laid the foundation for the Recovery Project's work. That work revealed the intricate textures and layers of the political, socioeconomic and cultural intersections among the various nationality groups. Recovery scholars employed archives to the task of uncovering particular Latino micro histories, which also created the possibilities of connecting them across nationality, race, class, gender and other categories of analysis to incarnate the idea of Hispanic or

Latino. The Recovery Project reaffirmed my personal interest in thinking about the meaning of Latino.

The specific methodological challenge for historians, I thought, was to identify themes and processes in the histories of the various national groups that might provide frameworks for understanding diverse human experiences within a coherent whole. Should shared themes be eventually identified, they would emerge from the comparative study of local communities, which, of course, rested on the discrete histories of the various national experiences. Most historians spent little time thinking about Latino history at the conceptual level, but they did produce necessary narrative histories of Mexicans, Cubans and Puerto Ricans that helped others articulate the Latino idea. I felt certain that the specific histories, diversities and complexities of the various national groups could ultimately reveal experiences they shared that were distinct from those of European Americans, African Americans or Asian Americans.

Clues to these shared historical experiences appeared in a landmark Recovery publication, *Handbook of Hispanic Cultures*, in 1994. This four-volume compilation of writing about Latinos in the United States covered literature, history, arts, sociology, politics and other topics. It constituted an archive unto itself. These volumes and the overall scholarship of the era confirmed that Latin Americans in the United States had developed as ethnic communities within shared historical contexts. Life in the United States forced them to adopt a posture that was defensive and affirmative at the same time; Latinos shared a sense of exclusion caused by the racist assumptions of the dominant society, but they also shared experiences steeped in the practices of maintaining cultural heritage and adapting old and new ways in order to coexist and conform to US life and customs.

Taking the first point, racism, unflattering stereotypes and unfavorable labor market structures, and their related socioeconomic consequences and realities, created experiences of exclusion among Latinos. They faced the full reality of discrimination as they incorporated into the United States in the first half of the nineteenth century, which institutionalized economic disadvantage. Hispanic communities in San Agustín and Pensacola disappeared for all practical purposes. The inhabitants either left Florida altogether or were simply absorbed. In Louisiana, Hispanic communities remained isolated but began a slow process of absorption into the dominant society. Further to the west, the more numerous Hispanic communities did not face cultural annihilation, but suffered marginalization and subordination as second-class citizens.

In my readings, I explored the details of what happened to these provinces when they became part of the United States after the Mexican War (1846-1848). It was a war I did not even remember studying in high school history classes. Only vaguely familiar with US western history, I learned of the depth of the injustices Mexicans endured. Leonard Pitt's classic book, *The Decline of the Californios*, described how California's Mexican elites lost their lands and resources faced with the onslaught of American adventurers. The vast majority of Mexicans were pushed into the lowest economic rungs, which continued into the twentieth century, as militantly narrated in Rodolfo Acuña's *Occupied America,* which was another stunning revelation about the repressive legacy of conquest. Both these books gave me clues to why my friend Ignacio had been treated so badly by the fraternity boys at the University of South Carolina.

The racial stereotyping of Mexicans in the early nineteenth century pointed out in the Pitts and Acuña texts, and many others, was a precedent-setting development eventually imposed on most Latinos. The derisive stereotypes and prejudicial attitudes held by the dominant society led to historically debilitating and isolating discriminatory practices that resulted in severe implications for daily life. In the 1920s, Texas' economic and segregationist regime maintained Mexican Americans at the bottom of the social system. Dynamics differed from region to region, but Mexicans from Texas to California found it very difficult to move out of the traditional laboring classes. Only a handful of Mexican-American elites, usually with whiter skin tones, maintained position and status by disassociating themselves from their traditional communities and assimilating into white Anglo-American society. Puerto Ricans and Cubans found themselves in a similar reality as they established communities and entered employment markets in the United States. Twentieth-century pioneering memoirs of Puerto Ricans, such as Jesús Colón, Bernardo Vega and Piri Thomas, depicted the harsh conditions of the Puerto Rican barrios and the racism its inhabitants were made to suffer.

Cuban and Spanish workers entering the Florida cigar labor markets in the late nineteenth and early twentieth centuries also faced harsh attitudes that on more than one occasion led to deportations and even lynching. Later waves of Latin American immigrants including Dominicans and others were similarly rejected and subjected to discrimination and second-class citizenship. Historically, Latinos may not have rallied together as a group against this reality, and sometimes they even expressed racism against each other, but they did share a sense of rejection from Anglo-American society. Many Latinos recognized this long tradition of anti-Latino feeling based on language, culture and Hispanic civilization, which provided an intangible bond and a measure of mutual understanding.

Turning to the second point, the story's affirmative side is even more important. Specific cultural traditions and practices played a part in bringing Latinos together. Identification with the Spanish language was perhaps the most powerful affinity. Historically, Chicanos, Puerto Ricans and Cubans used language to defend their culture and identity. The Spanish language played an important role in connecting me to other Latinos, especially in Texas, since my skin is white. "Where did you learn to speak Spanish like that?' I heard often. "You don't look Cuban," people said in amazement. "What does a Cuban look like?" I would often answer. The language gave me a way to overcome those initial impressions that for some Latinos justified keeping me at a distance. Language often created solidarity, but not always.

Recovery research revealed that this was not new. Latinos in New York during the final quarter of the nineteenth and first half of the twentieth centuries were inextricably wedded to the use of Spanish in daily communication. They read Spanish-language newspapers, saw films from Mexico and Argentina, listened to Spanish radio, formed associations to promote Spanish, and danced and listened to Latin music. Cubans in Key West and Tampa and Mexicans in San Antonio and Los Angeles did the same. Language maintained connections to national cultures of origin and, in many cases, with each other.

Newspapers proliferated in Hispanic communities beginning very early on. From the earliest *El Misisipí* (New Orleans, 1808) and *El Habanero* (Phildelphia, 1824), to the myriad of newspapers even to this day, including *La Opinión* (Los Angeles), *El Nuevo Herald* (Miami) and *El Diario-La Prensa* (New York), these presses preserved language and culture. My own experience identifying and recovering Key West's *El Yara* newspaper was exhilarating. Not having grown up in the United States, this newspaper gave me a sense of belonging to this country that I had never imagined possible. All these newspapers reflected the basic identity of the communities they served, in the Southwest, Florida, Louisiana, New York and many other places, but also revealed a cosmopolitan vision, reflecting an awareness of Spanish and Latin American origins and connections.

Other activities amplified the sense of community promoted in the press. Theater had been part of Hispanic communities since the colonial days, not only for entertainment, but to celebrate traditions familiar to them. Nicolás Kanellos, founder and director of the Recovery Project, showed how Mexicans in San Antonio, Cubans in Tampa and Puerto Ricans in New York had distinct theatrical styles, content and genres mostly rooted in the Spanish tradition and language. Cross-group theatrical collaboration was frequent and a sense of Hispanicity infused their aesthetics.

Another landmark Recovery publication in 2002, *Herencia. The Anthology of Hispanic Literature of the United States* speaks to a shared literary tradition. A literature of exploration and colonization including chronicles, diaries and testimonials, administrative, civil, military and ecclesiastical records, as well as oral traditions, chronicled multi-faceted life in colonial settlements, from the sixteenth to the early nineteenth century, from Florida to California. A Hispanic native literature by Mexicans, Cubans, Puerto Ricans and many others included English, Spanish and bilingual texts with themes reflecting the experiences of people of Latin American descent as citizens. The literature of immigrant's frequently explored racism and ethnic or national identity, conflict, pride in culture of origin, and appealed to justice. It was about adapting and reaching out to the broader society from an existing cultural tradition. An exile literature spoke to forced departures, yearning for the homeland and seeking balance between new and old places.

Grassroots cultural expression in Latino communities provided the rationale for resisting their marginal place within the broader society. After annexation into the United States, Mexican-American communities reorganized themselves and slowly created political movements and ideas that allowed them to resist and challenge the hostilities they faced within the United States. Politics sometimes took on a nationalist and ethnic character and other times a separatist or insurrectionary character prevailed, but mostly their political goals emphasized integration and accommodation.

Nationalist and ethnic politics usually emerged when the possibility of legitimate involvement within the American system seemed out of reach, or when the communities simply were not interested in integrative politics. In Nuevo Mexico, organized armed groups known as Gorras Blancas resisted Anglo American domination. Tejanos in Nacogdoches rebelled against Texas Republic authorities soon after the province's independence from Mexico, when it seemed clear that local Mexicans were unable to defend their interests. The famous separatist and revolutionary Plan de San Diego in Texas during 1917, that conspired to form a Mexican-American nation in the South Texas free of Anglos, revealed the extent to which some would go to destroy the Euro American dominated economy and society of the Southwest. In the late nineteenth century, Cuban and Puerto Rican nationalist politicians in New York and Florida chose not to focus on domestic US politics. Instead, they worked primarily to rid their homelands of Spanish rule.

For the most part, however, political struggles emphasized Latino determination to participate in electoral politics of the United States. In the late 1830s, Mexicans elected to office in the Texas legislature defended the rights of their people, and whenever possible maintained their involvement in the political system. In the late nineteenth century, Cubans served as mayors and aldermen in Key West and Tampa and went to the Florida legislature. Puerto Ricans in East Harlem elected one of their own to the New York State Assembly in 1937. Latinos struggled for inclusion, giving birth to such civil rights organizations as the League of United Latin American Citizens (LULAC) and, among Puerto Ricans in New York, El Congreso del Pueblo.

After that came the civil rights movements of the 1960s and 1970s. Though often separatist in tone, the Chicano Movement kicked in the doors and integrated the system, not only benefitting Mexican Americans but also Puerto Ricans, Cubans and other Hispanics. Throughout the 1970s and 1980s, Latino participation in the US political system became routine as voter registration campaigns spread through Mexican-American and Puerto Rican communities. Despite their different political orientations, even Cubans who arrived in the United States after 1959 learned from these movements to promote their own agendas, resulting in their integration into the electoral and political system. Ironically, their exile status and their reaction to the political situation in their homeland motivated them to become involved in the US political system.

Latinos also struggled to advance their position within the economic system. In the nineteenth century, Latinos in annexed communities in the Southwest initially experienced a collapse of their class structures. In some places, they remained a permanent underclass. This prolonged into the twentieth through the continuous funneling of immigrants from Latin America into the lower rungs of the economic structure without much possibility of advancement. Globalization and deindustrialization of the US economy beginning in the 1970s further aggravated economic distress.

More than not, Latinos and African Americans' opportunities were limited to low-skill, low-pay, high turnover jobs. Their options were confined to construction work, manual labor and service-sector jobs as domestics and as hotel and restaurant workers. They experienced high rates of poverty. Not willing to accept their secondary socioeconomic status within US society, Latinos, as part of their political struggle, worked to overcome employment barriers by organizing around ethnic views of the world and radical ideologies. Latinos organized immigrant unions and mutual aid societies to defend their interests until they managed to break into the US union movements, such as the AFL-CIO.

In general, the various Latino national groups organized and acted independently of each other, but often worked together in coalition to advocate for themselves. In the late nineteenth century, for example and as noted earlier, Cubans and Puerto Ricans worked together in revolutionary clubs, publishing exile newspapers and raising money to promote the independence of their homelands from Spanish rule. In San Francisco in 1871, Hispanic Catholics proposed the establishment of a national parish. Although most of the Spanish-speaking residents were Mexican American, representatives from the consulates of Spain and various Central American and South American countries provided leadership. These various groups gathered in the parish Our Lady of Guadalupe, reflecting their desire to worship together within Hispanic religious traditions. Puerto Rican and Mexican communities in Chicago understood their common condition and came together during the 1950s to defend their interests by forming Latino institutions. While their socioeconomic conditions triggered the need to build political coalitions, language and culture determined their decision to act together.

They shared struggles for bilingual education in the 1960s through the 1980s. The need to gain access to college and university education cut across regional and ethnic borders and became a rallying point of cultural affirmation and self-determination. As Latinos of various backgrounds interacted directly within communities, the unifying force of language was clear. Latino politics in the United States developed a coalition dimension that brought groups together on a number of political fronts. In 1977, the Congressional Hispanic Caucus formed to monitor legislation affecting Hispanics and increased Latino possibilities for participating in and contributing to the political system of the United States. Political scientists observed that the diversity of Latino racial, class and national origins ensured disagreements in Latino political thinking and action, but fundamental socioeconomic realities and cultural factors offered a basis for political coalitions and cooperation among Latinos.

As people of Latin American backgrounds in the United States increasingly embraced the idea of Latino, my conviction remained that historians would eventually produce broad and comprehensible historical narratives of this experience. A real sense of belonging requires historical memory, which intellectual cadres, now several generations in the making, are providing from the spaces they've carved out in the nation's teaching and research institutions of higher education. This historical memory is also filtering down into high school and middle school classrooms, and even elementary schools, not to mention museums and other public history sites. Latino children are growing up with a claim to their ancestor's important role in shaping US history and culture as never before, which not even the most retrograde of Anglo-American chauvinists can effectively deflect.

17

No Longer Home

For a very long time, Buenos Aires remained home, and a nostalgic need to return remained in my psyche. Finally, in 1988, the opportunity arrived. I received a four-month Fulbright Fellowship at the Universidad de Luján, just outside Buenos Aires, to teach US history. A mixture of excitement and nervous anticipation accompanied my departure with Noel in early August on our ten-hour American Airlines flight across the hemisphere to that faraway place. I took a deep breath, fought back tears and joined dozens of Argentine passengers clapping and cheering when the plane touched ground at Ezeiza International Airport. Together we passengers, strangers to each other, celebrated our shared experience of returning after many months or many years.

From the very start, I searched for that place I called home. Our first week in Buenos Aires was in a modest downtown hotel not far from *calles* Florida and Lavalle, the first known for shopping and the second for its dozens of movie theatres. We dined the first evening at the famous Palacio de la Papa Frita on Lavalle, where I ate frequently as a teenager on Saturday afternoon excursions to the movies. "Let's see if the steaks are as good as I remember," I told Noel. "Maybe I romanticized them." Walking along packed Calle Lavalle, there was no sign of Argentina's economic crisis. Settling back in his seat fully satisfied after consuming a *bife de chorizo,* Noel assured me that I had not romanticized the steaks. In a couple of days, after arranging schedules and other fellowship-related obligations, we began searching for a place to live.

After seeing several apartments, we settled on two bedrooms in the home of Señora Muller, an elderly German-Mexican widow, who lived in the suburban neighborhood of Vicente López, not far from my old barrios. She had immigrated with her Austrian husband to Argentina from Vienna immediately after World War II. The location and situation suited us well, and I enrolled Noel at Lincoln School. He had access to the school bus each morning, and when he arrived home in the afternoon, Señora Mueller greeted him with a snack. I fixed dinner for the two of us when I returned to the house in the early evening from my teaching obligations. Living in a large house by herself, Señora Mueller was happy to have us there and particularly enjoyed Noel's company. Every Saturday she had a group of women her age over for canasta and tea in the afternoon. They spoke a mixture of Spanish and German, although they preferred the latter, and I wondered about their lives and the particular histories that brought each to Buenos Aires.

∽ ∽ ∽

At the University of Luján, an hour and a half bus ride from Buenos Aires, I taught a course on US history. I also gave five seminars on the Cuban Revolution at Universidad Católica, where I had wanted to study in 1968, and taught another US history course (in English) at a language school. While I kept up with this busy schedule, Noel learned from my former teachers, Profe Laurita and Mr. Czarnik, at the Lincoln School, and he saw where I had spent my adolescent years. It reminded me of the way that I had explored my father's and grandfather's origins in Havana. In Vicente López, we had easy access to the train that ran from the central downtown Retiro Station to the various suburban stations. We explored the Acasuso, Olivos and La Lucía neighborhoods, where my family had lived. The neighborhoods had not changed very much. The difficult economic conditions of the previous twenty years had prevented growth and redevelopment, the neighborhoods were exactly as I had remembered them and I showed Noel the houses where we had lived as well as the bowling alley, the ice cream parlor and even the bar I frequented most often.

To my surprise, I did not experience the feelings of connection and belonging I had expected to feel as we walked the streets. Those were no longer my neighborhoods. I knew no one. The houses remained but nothing more. That is when it dawned on me that home was less about place than it was about community. From the very start, home for me was the artificial expatriate communities that had simply dissipated over time. The only live connection to my past, besides the two teachers, an office worker and a housekeeping staff member at Lincoln School, were Mary and Ricardo, and seeing them was at the top of my agenda. Over the years, we had stayed in touch, after my parents had departed they were my only strands of continuity with Buenos Aires. We corresponded and I always considered their comments to be a barometer of how Argentina was doing, they were not usually optimistic. In 1979, with the military government in full throttle, Ricardo wrote, "Unfortunately, our country has changed a great deal. Not the fault of the country, but of bad governments." With a sense of helplessness, he said, "Well, Gerito, there is much to say, but it's not worth it."

Sometime in 1980, my father telephoned from Detroit one day. "Guess who's here visiting?" he asked. Some long lost family member, I thought. After several guesses he finally said, Ricardo and Mary. I shouldn't have been surprised. In one of their letters, they had said in passing, "Don't be surprised if one day we appear in the United States." Although I had not thought they were serious, Ricardo's sister did live in Chicago and, as the Argentine economy continued its meltdown, she had offered to pay for their travel. Ricardo did not have steady work in Buenos Aires, he hoped that at least in the United States they could earn enough to send something back to Mary's family, especially for the nieces' school. They arrived in Chicago with tourist visas, and Ricardo's sister rented them a small basement apartment while Ricardo found work as a taxi driver.

From Detroit, my father did what he could to help them adjust, and Ricardo was optimistic that he could make it, but Mary grew homesick and missed her family almost immediately. She spoke no

English and was not able to find work. She found the city too impersonal, the apartment perpetually cold, and felt terribly lonely at night when Ricardo drove a friend's taxi. They had arrived just in time for Chicago winter and, by the end of that season, she was ready to return home. In Buenos Aires, she could find steady work as a housekeeper, and despite their very modest life, she preferred that to the hectic and uninviting conditions in Chicago. Mary admitted that she had not really given the city a chance.

I rang the doorbell. After a few minutes there Mary stood. I had the address of a German family, *los alemanes*, as she referred to them, who she worked for near our old neighborhood in Olivos. Since I had no phone number, Noel and I appeared unannounced. She had not changed much, but she did not immediately recognize me.

"*Soy* Gerito," I said.

She screamed. "*No lo puedo creer*," she said and gave me a tight hug. "This is your son?!" she exclaimed and hugged him just as tight.

Mary led us to the kitchen table, where we talked for a long time, catching up with each other's lives and families. We met her and Ricardo the next evening at a restaurant, and they invited us to their house, the one they had been building when I first saw it over twenty years before. Living in her own house had made things better. She no longer worked as a live-in housekeeper and made more money working for several families on an hourly basis.

The next Sunday, Noel and I caught a *colectivo* and when we got off, there she was. The empty fields of two decades before had become a densely populated working-class community with houses of every size and shape facing onto narrow and only partially paved streets. We walked through the neighborhood for several blocks and arrived at the house where the entire family lived. Ricardo greeted us as did Mary's brother, wife, two daughters and mother, and they proudly showed us around what was now a concrete block house with a living room, kitchen and two bedrooms. Outside the back door, two additional bedrooms faced onto a small patio, and there I saw what was perhaps the same grill for *asados* they'd had before building years ago. They also pointed to the refrigerator, kitchen table and chairs, and a few other pieces of furniture my parents had given them in 1974 when they moved to Uruguay. As I talked excitedly with everyone, somehow Noel slipped out of the house and in a few minutes was playing soccer with the neighborhood kids in a dirt field just in front of the house.

Mary's neighborhood was not a *villa miseria*, but it was certainly modest, and its organic development had proceeded in similarly haphazard ways to the development of the *villa miseria*. There were no squatters; people held legal titles to their lands and enjoyed municipal water and sewage service. But only those who could afford electricity received service; the rest connected illegal lines to the electrical poles. Telephone service was limited to public phones near the bus stops. Mary and Ricardo had shown me love and care as an adolescent, without even knowing it they had kept me grounded, attuned to Argentina's social realities and inequities. I was in awe of their persistence and commitment to family solidarity. The whole family just worked hard to build a future for their two nieces. I never forgot their admirable way of being.

∽ ∽ ∽

In addition to Mary and Ricardo, and the Lincoln School, the excitement surrounding Argentina's national sport, *fútbol*, warmed my heart and made me feel nostalgic. I continued to play when I left Argentina in 1968. At the University of South Carolina I joined the university soccer club and learned that my soccer skills, mediocre in Buenos Aires, were considered decent in the United States. I later enjoyed playing in men's leagues in Austin and then coaching my sons when we moved to San Antonio at the end of 1983. Over the next decade, with friends, I coached Noel's soccer team and we even adopted Argentina's national team uniform as our own. In Buenos Aires, Noel and I took a long and complicated bus ride to a FIFA store to buy official Argentina *fútbol* uniforms for the entire soccer team and other coaches back home. We wore them with pride for many years, and I am satisfied that I was among an early generation of parents in the United States who introduced their children to soccer and enjoyed watching the sport gain popularity throughout the 1980s and 1990s.

When we arrived in Buenos Aires, I was determined that Noel experience a first-division soccer match. The Fulbright Commission secured tickets for us, and I expressed special delight when they announced it would be for the River-Boca classic. Despite my memories of news coverage of the terrible events twenty years earlier, we caught a train from Vicente López station to Belgrano. In the packed railway car, River fans chanted, sang, waved flags and jumped up and down in unison, as the train rocked and rumbled toward its destination. As we got off the train in Belgrano, another train from the opposite downtown direction pulled into the station and several dozen Boca fans debarked, also chanting, singing, waving flags and jumping in unison.

So far, everything seemed friendly enough, but Noel and I kept some distance from the crowds, knowing that the fierce rivalry could spark a problem at any time. At the stadium, military personnel with dogs checked bags for weapons and whatever else. We made our way to box seats the Fulbright office had secured, safely shielding us from the sixty-five thousand excited arm-waving fans, singing nonstop their club songs. Despite their segregation on opposite sides of the stadium, Boca and River fans found numerous opportunities to cross the lines and pick fights while the police struggled to maintain order.

A roar of enthusiasm and approval from fans on both sides signaled the start of the game. After a terrific match that Boca won with a spectacular goal at the last minute, fans began to exit the stadium and another kind of excitement began. People in the upper stands threw plastic cups full of urine on the people below—this was a common prank. Others filled cups with newspaper and lit them on fire before throwing them into the crowd below. The people below expected these antics and kept an eye above to be able to sidestep the falling debris. Noel and I sat for a long while and waited for the most unruly folks to move on before we headed to the gates.

Once out of the stadium, tensions were clearly on display. We fell behind people walking down the middle of the street toward the train station and soon figured out they were Boca fans. Fortunately, Boca had won. Their fans were joyous or I wouldn't have wanted to be in their midst. Some fans carried large duffle bags on their backs, while others opened them and pulled out rumpled newspapers. Others yet sprayed the papers with a liquid, and a last group set them on fire. The street was ablaze, and winds blew the burning newspapers under some of the canvas awnings hanging over closed and barred stores.

A large military riot-control vehicle followed the chanting fans, spraying water on the burning newspapers and the canvas awnings that had caught fire. When fans turned around, stopped and hurled invectives at the military, the water truck also stopped until the fans continued. Clearly, the goal was to extinguish the flames without provoking a riot. At this point, I grabbed Noel and moved in the opposite direction. We avoided the train filled with disappointed and angry River fans and walked back to Vicente López. The long trek passed quickly with the bag of *empanadas de carne* we had bought at a little store along the way.

On the evening before our return to San Antonio, we had dinner with Mary and Ricardo at a restaurant near the corner of Calle General Roca and Avenida Maipú. Somehow, we all knew this would be our last meeting, although I assured them I would return one day. It hasn't happened. Ricardo suffered from a liver ailment and had spent time in the hospital earlier that year. "Probably too much wine," he said. "I'll probably be in the Charcarita next time you come," he laughed, referring to Buenos Aires' working-class cemetery. We ate steak, drank red wine, laughed and finally cried. I left them with as many dollars as I could; the difficult times in Argentina did not seem likely to improve any time soon. In fact, during the next decade, things went from bad-to-worse. Argentina's governments experimented with neoliberal economic policies and eliminated more programs of the social safety network that had survived earlier cuts.

Revisiting the past usually highlights how much people change, even without realizing. I had changed. Despite the vivid and imposing memories, I realized Buenos Aires had ceased to be my home. The American corporate community I had been raised in was gone. I didn't even try to track-down Argentine friends I had not communicated with since leaving. Some of them had left Argentina for university and never returned, while others quietly moved on with their lives. I had even lost my Argentine accent, which provoked people to ask where I was from. As I've said before, I am good at moving on, but this was hard. I heard no more from Mary and Ricardo. I had sent correspondence to the address of *los alemanes*. When Mary no longer worked there, I lost touch with them. Sadly, life pushed that relationship aside, and, in some way, writing this book has helped me to grieve that loss. I continued to remember that place, Buenos Aires; it was no longer home, but remained deeply embedded in me.

18

The Worst of Times

I traveled to Cuba in 1990, before the catastrophe, and again in 1994 as Cuba descended into the depths of depression and darkness. I set out, not knowing what to expect as the Revolution embarked on what Fidel Castro had designated the "Special Period." Though I was not keen on visiting, I traveled there with trepidation to honor a personal obligation to Nieves, my cousin Luis Alpízar's widow. After her husband's death in 1987, Nieves discovered a bundle of sixty-seven letters from José Martí to José Dolores in an old trunk that had belonged to Luis' mother. Nieves surmised the letters had passed from Luis' grandmother América (daughter of José Dolores Poyo) to Luis' father, Bolívar. Despite working at the National Archive, Bolívar kept the letters at home. Nieves told me about them during my 1990 trip, and we agreed that the safest place for them was the Centro de Estudios Martianos. She offered to donate this collection if the center published them in Luis' memory, and she wanted me to attend the official book presentation.

The collapse of the Soviet Union had changed everything for revolutionary Cuba. The 1990s was the worst of times. For the first time, Cuban economic impotence had become clear. Everyone knew Cuba received massive subsidies from the Soviet Union, but only when this help ended did it become obvious just how unproductive Cuba actually was. As the United States pushed Soviet President Mikhail Gorbachev to reduce and then eliminate trade and aid to the island, austerity measures and new rationing schedules left most Cubans nearly starved. In 1989, Soviet aid amounted to about a quarter of Cuba's gross national product. The next year, Cuba's gasoline supplies declined by a third and electrical use fell ten percent. Within two years, the average daily caloric consumption, already austere, dropped about a third. During the decade, thousands fled the island any way they could. People launched boats and rafts held afloat with inner tubes. Some even hijacked a ferry in the Havana harbor, an escape that ended tragically when a Cuban coast guard vessel rammed and sank it. One enduring image of the mass emigration was of a truck loaded with refugees driving across the Straits of Florida kept afloat by an ingenious array of tires, inner tubes and whatever else. The United States increased its political and economic pressure on Cuba, but at the same time negotiated an immigration agreement, hoping to slow down the flood of migrants fleeing across the Florida Straits.

As usual when I traveled, I made plans to visit the various scholars and archivists at research centers and the José Martí National Library. There was tension in the air from the moment I arrived at José Martí airport. Usually someone met me at the airport, but not this time. Gasoline shortages had made this difficult. There were very few cars that roamed the streets during my taxi ride to Hotel El Presidente on the Avenida de los Presidentes in Vedado; there were mostly motorcycles and bicycles. The bus system was crippled, and people without transportation stood on corners trying to hitch rides.

At the Martí Center the next morning, I had just greeted the staff when a smiling and excited Nieves arrived. After the event, I invited Nieves to lunch at the hotel restaurant. Her upbeat attitude turned serious as she gulped down her food, it was as if she had not eaten in a week.

"I haven't seen chicken in months," she said.

"Prepare more chicken for her to take home," I told the waiter, but he had nothing to wrap it in. Impatiently, I emptied books from a cloth bag and handed it to him.

Then she delivered stunning news: "I am not giving the letters to the center."

"But you promised them," I reminded her.

"I had intended to, but if I give them up, I won't have anything," she insisted. Her miserable pension left her chronically short of food. "I just told them!" she said.

The exasperated director hoped she would reconsider and left it at that, certainly understanding her situation.

The next day, one of the staff from the Martí Center took me in the sidecar of his motorcycle to see Nieves. I took her a couple of bags of aspirins, soaps, chocolates, clothes, vitamins and other supplies from the United States. We talked, and I carefully reminded her of how my great-grandfather's family archive had disappeared after his death in 1961. She understood, but her mind was made up. The letters were her only insurance, she said. The economic crisis that she lived with daily required her to have something to fall back on. I did understand, and spoke about it no more. I was awkwardly caught in the middle, on my departure I simply told the center's director that I too hoped she would reconsider at some point. I left Nieves with as many dollars as I could and returned home.

Some months later, I read in Miami's *Nuevo Herald* that an unknown Martí letter had surfaced in the city. I recognized it as one of the recently published Alpízar letters. On my next trip to Havana, Nieves pleaded with me not to be angry. She was desperate. I knew how heartbreaking it was for her to sell the letter. To avoid doing that again, she deposited the letters with a friend for safekeeping. Again, I gave her money, but knew that when her resources ran out, the documents would be at risk. Fortunately, no more letters that I know of appeared in south Florida's illicit and thriving trade in Cuban historical documents and other national patrimony treasures. Only a decade later, I learned that Nieves had promised the letters and her home to a family on the condition that they cared for her until she passed. Fortunately, a facsimile collection survives at the Martí Center, and the letters are in the new editions of Martí's *Obras Completas*, but the location of the original documents remains a mystery. I did not blame Nieves. She struggled for everything in an impossible environment, especially for the elderly.

Feeling depressed after my visit with Nieves, I walked through the neighborhood where my hotel was located wearing slacks and a white *guayabera*. Even though the sun was about to set, my shirt was quickly soaked with perspiration. Along the Avenida de los Presidentes, the same deteriorated buildings cried out for new coats of paint. They dominated my line of sight one after another on each side of the broad *avenida*. These vistas had changed little from my previous visits, but everything felt different. A few people stood on their balconies, bored and staring blankly, even sadly; it was too hot to be indoors. The proud Cuban defiance I had known in the 1980s was replaced by a silent desperation that permeated the air. Tempers flared easily. I passed a bodega where people argued about their places in line. They feared that food would run out. There were preoccupied faces everywhere, smiles were rare. As if threatened by some unknown force, my own body filled with anxious tension, which I can only attribute to a sense of the unpredictability of this place.

As I continued my slow amble down the sidewalk, an elderly woman walked toward me. There was a terrible anger on her drawn face that was apparent from at least thirty paces away. She walked, like me, seemingly without a destination, lost in her particular trauma, but suddenly she noticed me. Her eyes looked intently at mine; she sized me up. As she was about to pass, she suddenly stopped, and with a rage she could barely control, she accused me: "*¡Tú no vives el periodo especial . . . estás muy gordo! Tú no vives el period especial. . . . Estás muy gordo*," she mumbled and walked on. (You are not living the Special Period. You are very fat!) She probably thought I was a *dirigente* (communist official), but, in any case, I was not fat at all by American standards.

After my walk, a cousin María from Caimito arrived at the hotel with her two teenage sons. Someone had driven them the thirty kilometers, and they had very little time. I was afraid to ask how much the ride cost her. Not having seen them in several years, they looked emaciated, just skin and bones, and terribly anxious.

"How is everyone in Florida?" my cousin asked.

"Fine," I said. "How are you?" I knew the answer was not well, but hadn't know what else to say.

We talked for a while on the hotel's porch chairs, as the driver sat waiting impatiently in his car.

María then said, "Need to go."

I hugged her and the two boys. She took the money and two bags of items from her family in Florida. Desperate to get out of Cuba, within a couple of years, she and her children managed to get to Miami. The Revolution had come to this.

A friend arrived for a drink at the hotel bar before my departure the next day. Finishing his whisky, he inhaled his cigarette one last time before snuffing it out in the ashtray at the bar. Cubans smoked a lot. They still do. I sensed our conversation was at an end. We had spent a couple of hours discussing Cuba's dilemma, as well as his own. My friend was a committed revolutionary who I had first met in 1982. A talented intellectual and writer, he now seemed at a loss about what to do next. His intense gaze seemed to go straight through me.

"It's up to us now," he said. "We have to find new ways, our ways, ways that work. No more Soviets, we cannot return to the Americans or the Spaniards, as some apparently want. For the first time, we have the opportunity to be on our own. This darkness gives us the freedom to do what we want. If we don't make it, we have only ourselves to blame."

His eyes shifted to meet mine as though they were returning from a faraway place, as if mourning the loss of the ideal and feeling the painful birth pangs of the limited alternatives.

"Have a safe trip home." He gave me an *abrazo* and left.

I never saw him again; he died of a heart attack not long after our meeting.

I felt relieved leaving Havana; it was the first time I had ever felt that way. Looking out the window at the men loading luggage onto the airplane, I sorted through the experiences of the last few days that had frayed my emotions. The tension in my body eased. Then a man approached with a little girl, about twelve, and settled her in the seat next to mine. I could smell the rum on his breath as he leaned over to secure her seat belt. He patted her on the head and moved forward to another seat, where he settled his wife and an infant child. Even further to the front of the packed airplane, he found his own seat.

The nervous young girl looked at me, and I smiled. She shyly returned the smile and quickly looked away. Her bright but sad brown eyes projected fright and worry. When she looked back, I asked if she was okay.

She nodded, then said, "We are leaving Cuba forever."

I nodded.

"We are flying to Miami. Grandpa will be waiting," she said. Apparently, he had visited Cuba only several months earlier for the first time since leaving Cuba many years ago. "He will take us to Disney World."

Feeling more comfortable now, she launched into nervous, excited talk about her grandfather's home in Hialeah and the school she would attend. She looked ahead trying to soothe the moment's hurt. "The school in Hialeah is full of Cubans," she reassured herself.

Then she thought about her school in Cuba. Her friends envied her, she boasted. Then she realized the significance of the moment: "*Pero, por Dios*, I will never return to Cuba."

"Yes, you will," I reassured her. "Look at me, I travel to Cuba. You will do the same."

She then arched her back and neck and spotted her mother and sister. "I'm worried," she told me. Her little sister had a fever. "Is there a doctor on the airplane?" she asked.

"I don't know, but don't worry," I said. "We will land in Miami in only forty-five minutes, and the stewardesses have aspirins. Don't worry."

She seemed satisfied with my answer, especially the part about the aspirin.

"You will see how easy the trip is," I added, hoping to settle her fears. "We will go up and come right back down.

"*Parece mentira*," she said looking at me intently. "Miami is so close?"

The plane moved down the runway, and I asked her if she had ever flown.

"Yes, five times," she said proudly. "To Ciego de Avila, but never away from Cuba, over the water."

The plane paused, turned and after a moment the engines roared, the plane lurched forward, the cabin shook and the landscape rushed past as the chartered Lloyds Bolivian aircraft rose into the sky. She grasped the armrests tightly and smiled nervously.

"Come sit in my seat so you can see the coast," I offered.

We exchanged places, and with her face glued to the window, she said quietly, "I see the coast, and the water." She settled in her seat and again looked for her mother and sister. They were settled and quiet. Smiling, gazed out the window once more. "*Parece mentira*," she repeated quietly to herself.

~ ~ ~

Despite observing the many creative efforts to overcome the crisis during several vists to Cuba in the 1990s, I helplessly watched the terrible toll the situation exacted on family, friends and many ordinary people. Throughout the decade, Cuba's people survived by their wiles and their hustle, and as such the least mobile suffered the most. On each trip, I continued to bring Margo and Nieves money, medicines, clothes and even insignificant gifts to lift their spirits, but they died. They were elderly, but not necessarily ready to die under normal circumstances. Other younger friends lacking food and medical attention, living in constant fear and anxiety about what might come next, and unable to maneuver under the prevailing circumstances, also succumbed. They all passed away, alone, disillusioned and disappointed with the Revolution. As younger people, they had been indispensable to the Revolution, but that had changed.

As I thought about the Revolution at the millennium, several conclusions seemed to me inevitable. The popular enthusiasm and expectations of the 1960s withered in the face of the economic stagnation that slowly culminated in the 1990s, created by the very same economic centralization needed to provide continuing social improvements. Cuba's economic reliance on the Soviet Union blocked incentives to conceive of practical and effective economic and social reforms needed for improving long-term productivity. This was the Revolution's Achilles heel. Che Guevara's belief that under the proper circumstances people could be persuaded to work for the collective good had seemed reasonable to me, but it hadn't worked out. Cuba lacked the economic productivity necessary to support the regime's social promises, once Soviet trade and aid had disappeared. Without sufficient wage incentives and creative opportunities, the society simply failed to produce. The social experiment seemed to confirm what my father had always said: "Don't be so naïve."

The Revolution badly underestimated the capacity of Cubans to resist uniformity and conformity when the system was no longer able to help them rise to meet their personal aspirations, especially for the new generations. Castro's ideological inflexibility—his need to maintain a classless society at any cost undermined the social project more generally. Any practical market-based solutions to people's problems were deemed counter-revolutionary; too many citizens found their creativity blocked. Eventually, a majority of Cubans had concerns and priorities that the Revolution could not or would not address. They included non-conformists of all kinds uninterested in the Revolution's Marxist ideology: people without any sense of solidarity, people who wanted consumer choices in their lives, others who wanted to travel and many who just wanted to be left alone to fix up their houses or own a neighborhood bar or pizza place. Some wanted to practice their religions without stigma, others just wanted to be beach bums. Societies include all kinds, but the revolutionary leadership refused to recognize this. Fidel Castro remained insistent on defining everyone within one framework and a set hierarchy of values. The creativity of the next generation remained cooped up, their energy bottled, their contributions blocked, their genius unfulfilled. People produced little, and the economy collapsed.

At first, Cuba's authoritarianism was not a deal-breaker for me. I was familiar with dictatorships across Latin America, especially that of Argentina's military, but the Cuban form was different. If a country was to endure a dictator, I thought, at least it was better for them to promise the people social good, but the inability of Cuba's leaders to rein in their own grandiosity and act with some measure of humility made me question my benign assumptions about authoritarianism. A lack of empathy, compassion and generosity for those who failed to meet expectations or resisted the rigid political and economic policies ultimately hurt the Revolution. A leadership that had originally claimed that revolutions only remained relevant with constant change (revolutions within revolutions) became caretakers of a difficult-to-transform bureaucratic system that failed to produce economically, that remained totalitarian long after it was necessary and that denied the existence of social tensions. The revolutionary generation refused to retire and to cede its place to new leaders. While they horded power, they failed to escape the internal contradictions that had plagued other communist experiments around the world. Thirty years of revolution had remedied many social inequalities, but created new forms of injustice.

Despite a decade of unimaginable suffering, the Revolution survived the 1990s. Inevitably, the revolutionary course began to shift, very slowly, but surely. The future would soon be in the hands of a new generation, I thought, less ideological and more concerned with solving the everyday problems of Cubans. Perhaps these leaders would have less grandiose goals and by making practical economic and political decisions would create in time a genuine social democracy and unleash the skills and talents of a well-educated and socially aware population. Building on the social achievements of the revolutionary generations within a new context might harness the nation's enthusiasm for justice in new ways. Processes of change and adjustment that harmonized tradition with new generational perspectives had the potential to make things better. That was worth hoping for, and would certainly be more achievable if the United States abandoned its aggressive, pompous and heartless policies against a country intent on deciding its own path. José Dolores Poyo, over a century ago, struggled so that Cubans could determine their own destiny, which was not to be. Perhaps now it was possible.

19

Bread, Spirit and Community

Adjusting one's perspectives and expectations in light of accumulated experiences, disappointments and insights about life becomes inevitable at a certain point. On returning to Cuba from Key West, José Dolores realized that his vision of an independent and nationalist Cuba was not to be. He withdrew from political life and served his country as director of the National Archive. A disillusioned Pancho adjusted to his less than ideal civic life in Havana, but never forgot what he considered to be grave insults to his father's memory. José Francisco perhaps died too young to have been aware of his limitations and life's inevitable transitions. And my father, whose family history warned him against having unrealistic expectations, learned to adjust when necessary without much complaint.

I too adjusted, less gracefully, and with many complaints. Like my grandfathers, I learned that grandiose ideas and revolutions usually fall short, that human frailties and selfishness are often more powerful than good intentions and noble goals. The study of history at first caused me to become angry as I discovered the many injustices that societies cover up with self-serving whitewashing and boosterism, but history also revealed age-old human brokenness and the difficulties of finding justice and the common good.

Disillusionment with Cuba in the early 1990s, as well as my awareness of the difficult social realities in Venezuela, Argentina and United States, challenged my belief in the capacity of human societies to act for the common good. My profound conviction remained that most people in liberal democracies would always vote for their selfish interests rather than for the general welfare of their society. The spectacle of American democracy systematically dismantling the New Deal after the 1970s suggested that its nod to the greater good had been a historical anomaly. The New Deal failed to instill the solid social democratic ethos that emerged in many European nations after the war. American liberal capitalists bided their time and returned more powerful than ever since the Gilded Age and the Roaring Twenties.

I also became less sanguine about the viability of wholesale revolutionary social restructuring and the wisdom of forcing people to live in total conformity. Fidel Castro influenced me profoundly when it came to thinking about fixing entrenched socioeconomic inequities. He inspired my thinking as I looked south during the 1970s and early 1980s. Not just to Cuba, but to Latin America as a whole. The Cuban Revolution delivered on egalitarianism, health care, education, basic nutrition and other things, but, after thirty years, the social project seemed at the end of its rope. I fell prey to an emerging cynicism that tempted me to think of humanity's self-centeredness as simply too powerful to overcome.

Matters of a more personal nature also left me further disoriented. Betty Kay and I had grown apart. Despite our love for one another, our marriage could not survive our different temperaments, cultures, interests and hopes for the future. It seemed like it should have been easy to go my separate way, but it was not. An overwhelming sense of failure haunted me for a long time. As a good historian friend of mine was always fond of saying, "*La vida es muy cabrona*."

One day, shortly after my divorce, I spontaneously removed from the wall an image of Nuestra Señora de la Caridad del Cobre, the patron saint of Cuba, that had belonged to Nana. In ways that I can't explain, the image became the centerpiece of a home altar on the dresser where I then placed the icon; it slowly ceased being simply a cultural artifact. Over time, the space took on a devotional character, and for the first time I glimpsed the way in which a sacred image could provoke a sense of transcendence and awareness of humanity's compelling need to live with heart and spirit.

Nana suffered a stroke at the Detroit airport right before Christmas in 1982. Waiting to board an Atlanta flight to visit Aunt Judy and family after a month with my parents, she fell ill. I arrived at the hospital to find her in and out of consciousness, mostly incoherent. "*Rotando y rotando, rotando y rotando*," she repeated in agitated tones over and over. "Are you dizzy? What do you mean, 'revolving'? What do you need?" I asked her, as I sat at her bedside, frustrated with my inability to comfort her. Each day I visited her, she seemed to improve until I finally had to return home. On my way to the airport, I stopped at the hospital for a last visit. To my surprise and relief, she had gotten out of bed for the first time. Sitting in a wheelchair in the hospital's large Florida room, she was enjoying the sight of the sun shimmering on the freshly fallen snow. Clear headed, Nana smiled, gave me her hand and said she loved me. The only thing I could muster was tears. They rolled freely down my cheeks. In a strong voice, she said that the worst had passed, "*Nos vemos en Miami. Allá te espero y hablamos de Cuba.*" We had not talked about Cuba since my return in June. Frugal to the end, she had avoided spending money on the telephone, hers or mine. We'll talk in person, soon, she said. I went home, but she died a week later, never having left the hospital.

She lived simply each day without fanfare or preaching, and throughout her modest life she modeled respect and empathy for everyone around her. Attentive to her family and her neighbors, Nana's presence made the world better. Perhaps the most genuinely faithful person I knew, she did not attend church regularly but instead expressed her spirituality privately through her personal devotion to the Virgen de la Caridad del Cobre and by reciting the rosary daily. Nana had always celebrated the Virgin's Saint Day on September 8, the day before her own birthday. When she fell ill, Nana asked Uncle Jorge, who traveled to Detroit from Miami, to bring her the plaster image of the Virgin that hung on her bedroom wall; it had consoled her.

My father gave me the image after Nana's death.

"Don't you want it?" I asked him.

"What would I do with it?" he responded. "Nana would want you to have it."

The gift inspired me to learn more about this devotional tradition. A slave named Juan Moreno in 1687, at the mining village of Cobre near Santiago de Cuba, first narrated the apparition of the Virgen de la Caridad. As a boy of ten, he had accompanied two Indians in a canoe on the Bay of Nipe on Cuba's north coast through rough weather, where they traveled to collect salt. They encountered what at first looked like a bird hovering above the roiling sea. As they rowed closer, they recognized instead a sculpted image of the Virgin. It had remained dry despite the rain and the splashing waves. They had hurried back to Cobre with the image and gave it to the administrator of the mines, who had placed it in a chapel. The Virgin then became the protector of Cobre's Indian and African slaves and eventually provided the rationale for their freedom. In time, she became the protector of Cuba itself, officially proclaimed as such by Pope Benedict XV in 1916.

Writing eluded me during those troubled times in the early 1990s. Scholarly interests faded, and I wrote nothing for a while except some poetry. Somehow, I went to a place I had not been to since I was fourteen, when I was fond of sketching the agonizing Christ hanging on the cross. Unwittingly, my artist mother had inspired the drawings, but eventually my obsession with drawing the crucified Christ passed, and I stopped drawing. Now, that long quieted artistic impulse had returned. But anxiety got the better of me as I sat paralyzed in front of my sketchbook in my first drawing class. Then I took a painting class and encountered the same problem, when the teacher put an apple, orange and banana on the table and said, "Paint that!"

"I don't know how to paint," I protested.

"You can do it." he insisted.

I struggled through that session and several others but found the experience to be draining and disheartening.

I gave up on the whole idea, but then one evening at home, I began swirling paint on the canvas without any preconceived notions. I had no goal in particular—a novel idea for a history professor who placed much stock in methodology, reasoning and training. Surprisingly, swirling the paint without purpose, without a goal in mind, had eased my anxiety. I applied the paint spontaneously until visions suggested themselves and forms emerged of their own accord. Ocean water smashed against coastlines, palm trees of all sizes and colors appeared, and I painted lots of sky, all in loud and bold blues, reds, yellows, oranges and browns. José Martí appeared, as did Antonio Maceo. Some canvases evoked dark omens and symbols of hope while tropical themes with bright colors recurred on others. Paintings often reflected or contradicted my moods and produced unexpected surprises. Where these images came from eluded me, but, surely, their tone expressed something deeply embedded in me. These paintings pointed to aesthetics inside me only accessible through emotion and spirit, not training and logic. My disappointments, the Virgin, and this new aesthetic provoked existential and metaphysical questions and inspired readings in philosophy and theology.

I slowly revisited Catholicism and learned about social change from a very different vantage point. Even after giving up attending Mass in Argentina in the mid-1960s, I had never abandoned my Catholic identity. Whenever official questionnaires of one kind or another asked about my religious affiliation, without much thought I checked the box marked Roman Catholic. It just seemed to be a part of me. When I felt lonely or anxious, I occasionally found myself in church. On one such occasion during my first semester at the University of South Carolina, I went to Mass with a roommate. The radically informal attire of T-shirts, shorts and sandals of the students contrasted with my conservative slacks and collared shirt. Congregants clapped their hands and sang loudly to lively guitars and tambourines as they waited for the service to begin.

"My God," I thought, "this isn't a Catholic church." Somehow, I must have stumbled into a Protestant service, which I had seen on television in Columbia—their services were like this! For some reason, perhaps a need to relieve my nervous anxiety, I began laughing uncontrollably.

"Why are you laughing?" asked my roommate.

"Are you sure this is a Catholic church?"

"Yes, of course," he assured me.

How to explain my laughter? The service seemed like some kind of spoof on the solemn Catholic Masses attended by well-dressed congregants with humble and respectful demeanors I had been accustomed to in Buenos Aires. Even women's heads remained uncovered here in the United States. In a few minutes the Mass started, and the music got even livelier as the priest proceeded down the aisle toward the altar with a bit of a bounce in his step. He began the service, and to my astonishment, the priest said the Mass in English instead of in Latin and stood on the wrong side of the altar facing the congregation. This was some renegade offshoot of the Catholic Church, I thought. It all seemed too strange. My brief experiment with returning to church ended.

I did figure out that I had indeed attended a legitimate Catholic service. During the next couple of years, I learned that Pope John XXIII had convened a Vatican Council and brought about great changes to the Catholic Church, reinventing the liturgy, among many other things. Liturgical changes in Argentina had proceeded so slowly and conservatively that I had not even noticed. Or perhaps they were implemented as my attendance at Mass was dwindling. Whatever the case, I had known nothing about these dramatic changes until that Sunday in South Carolina.

These changes in the liturgy did not impress me much at first. As a former altar boy, I loved the pomp and mysticism of the Latin Mass. The liturgy now seemed so ordinary and undignified in comparison, but I liked other innovations of Vatican II, especially the renewed focus on the problems of the poor. Besides concrete references in the council's documents, Pope John XXIII issued two encyclicals, *Mater et Magistra* (1961) and *Pacem in Terris* (1963), and Pope Paul VI followed with *Populorum Progressio* (1966). Like Jesus, the encyclicals spoke firmly about the temporal problems in the world that needed urgent attention, especially the fate of the poor and vulnerable in the world. These documents reinforced an already established tradition of papal encyclicals I had never heard of dedicated to social justice dating from Pope Leo XIII's *Rerum Novarum* (1891). Activist and theologian John C. Cort wrote in the 1980s that Jesus "spelled out certain basic principles that a contentious Christian should look for in any economic and political system. . . . First among these was an active, practical, effective concern for the poor." The encyclicals teach, in effect, that it is hard to be a principled Catholic without making this concern for the poor a top priority.

Published in response to the exploitative nature of liberal capitalism and the rise of socialism during the nineteenth century, *Rerum Novarum* advocated reformed capitalist solutions to deepening social tensions and divisions in Europe. Pope Leo wrote that capitalism overemphasized individualism to the detriment of the common good, causing dissention and radicalism among the working classes. At the same time, Pope Leo viewed communism and the abolition of private property as contrary to natural law, traditional ideas of hierarchy and authority, and an even greater threat than liberalism to society and the common good. He condemned materialistic systems of the right and the left that repressed individuals in different ways that he perceived as sins against human dignity.

To ensure the survival of a capitalist order, Pope Leo urged social reforms aimed at relieving exploitation and misery. Charity would no longer suffice; structural changes ensuring social justice were deemed necessary. These changes could be effected through an ethic of social justice, along with state action and corporate social forms. According to the encyclical, associations that encouraged capitalist-worker cooperation within a decentralized capitalist system guided by a benevolent state could advance justice. The twentieth-century encyclicals followed in the same tradition but became increasingly radical. Although recognizing that human society could never be perfect, at their heart the encyclicals taught that spiritual renovation could awaken individuals to the imperative for social good and inspire them to work to improve conditions for the poor and vulnerable.

Rerum Novarum inspired very practical temporal responses across Europe in the 1920s and 1930s in the form of Catholic Action movements dedicated to social reforms for workers, youth, women and peasants. Catholic Action movements spread to Latin America and Cuba, where they spawned Christian Democratic movements seeking reforms especially in the agrarian sectors. I did not know it, but during my last year in Argentina, in 1968, Latin America's Roman Catholic bishops met in Medellín, Colombia with Pope Paul VI at the Latin American regional council of bishops. The meeting placed the issues of poverty and inequality at the top of the bishops' agenda for Latin America.

The Catholic action tradition in Latin America foreshadowed the Medellín meeting, which gave visibility to an increasingly systematic theological movement known as Liberation Theology. First formally articulated by a Peruvian priest, Gustavo Gutiérrez, in the late 1960s, Liberation Theology called on Latin Americans to take a stand against poverty. Unlike the more traditional approaches in Catholic theology that drew inspiration from Thomistic reliance on reason and natural law, the liberationists' pointed to Christ's concrete advocacy for the poor in scripture and compared the context of his life to the dire inequalities of the late twentieth century. They read scripture in light of sociological and anthropological realities, concluding that conditions of overwhelming poverty in Latin America required Christians to take an affirmative posture of advocacy in favor of the poor. Liberationists found it impossible to separate the church from the daily lives of its faithful and unapologetically and affirmatively endorsed an activist posture in support of the poor majority in Latin America. They called on Christians to form small base communities (*comunidades de base*) to read the Gospels, learn of liberation and seek solutions to their everyday problems.

This "option for the poor" became a central inspiration for many activist Christians in the 1970s. I was attracted to the Christ of the poor, the afflicted and the excluded. For me this was the essence of Catholicism as expressed in the Gospels. The idea that the church could organize local communities for social change reminded me of that visit to the *villa miseria* in Buenos Aires with the seminarians. The *villas* were good places for liberationist activism. In theory, this activism contemplated universal structural transformations, often along Marxist lines, but in reality liberationists worked for incremental local changes accomplished step-by-step through faith, activism and solidarity. Some grew frustrated and turned to violence, but, as a matter of religious principle, Liberation Theology rejected violence and inflexible ideological solutions to human problems. What was needed were communities acting together locally for their own welfare, for the poor and in the name of hope for a just world. I had never heard Catholic social activism preached from the pulpit expressing concern for human dignity, freedom from dire poverty and spiritual aesthetics beyond personal piety. But Catholicism now seemed more attuned to helping people cope with earthly matters than the Church I remembered from my childhood. Throughout the 1970s, I kept a close watch on this movement.

Unfortunately, the Vatican disappointed me. After the death of Pope Paul VI in 1979, liberationist thinking came under attack from conservative dogmatists and ideologues. Newly elected Pope John Paul II viewed these theological developments in Latin America with suspicion. The Pope's long struggle against communism in Poland blinded him to the radically different social conditions in Latin America, and he did what he could to discredit Liberation Theology. Especially unforgiveable was his refusal to support Archbishop Oscar Romero's challenge of military brutality and impunity against the Salvadoran people in the late 1970s. As far as I was concerned, Romero's assassination in 1980 left a dark scar on Pope John Paul II's legacy, even though later, as the Pope traveled throughout Latin America, he came to appreciate the real challenges people faced in this part of the world because of systemic inequality. Even so, when the Pope visited San Antonio in 1987, I could not bring myself to attend his Mass.

Revolutionary Cuba circa 1982 had seemed like a perfect place for a flourishing liberationist church. During the 1930s and 1940s in Cuba, Catholic social doctrines had inspired at least two generations of religious leaders and intellectuals to move beyond their pastoral traditions and engage pressing social and civic problems. Most Catholic activists backed the Revolution, and some even joined the rebel forces in the mountains. They celebrated the victory in 1959, but ultimately rejected the Revolution when the government took a clearly inflexible communist path. Catholics faced a devastating defeat in their confrontation with communism, and most fled to safety in the wake of the suppression of the Church in the early 1960s.

Despite the Revolution's rejection of Catholic activism in the early 1960s, I thought Fidel Castro might be persuaded to reconcile with the church by Vatican II's very clear openness to dialogue and the emergence of Liberation Theology. During a month-long visit to Chile in 1971, Castro met with leaders of the Cristianos por Socialismo organization and publicly stated that there were many compatibilities between Catholicism and socialism, but that narrative did not prosper. A new Cuban constitution in 1976 reaffirmed the Revolution's atheism and, although people had the right to practice religion, the government unapologetically discriminated against people of faith.

I saw the effects of this animosity toward religion. One day while visiting the Cuban maritime museum at the Castillo de la Fuerza, near the docks at the harbor, a young boy perhaps twelve asked us if we were tourists. I nodded yes, and to my surprise he pointed to the large figure of Cristo de Regla across the harbor and said, "Do you know about the *bruja de* Regla?"

"Witch?" I said.

"No, that's a Christ figure," I told him.

"No," he assured me, "it's a witch and bad luck."

The twenty-meter tall statue inaugurated on December 24, 1958, just a week before the triumph of the Revolution, is visible from many vantages in the city. Although it was not disturbed after the Revolution, it remained off-limits to visitors until recently.

We attended church just a few times in Havana in 1982, but one memorable occasion was Easter Mass, which began at about six o'clock in the evening. As we walked into church in Vedado, a group of teenagers milled around, presumably curious about what was happening inside, but they also taunted people as they entered. Their tone was not especially hostile; rather, they intended to ridicule the faithful. "Don't you know religion is just superstition?" shouted one boy. Relatively few people between the ages of twelve and sixty were attending Mass; most Cubans either had accepted the state's official atheism or feared losing tightly controlled state jobs and other benefits. The liturgy proceeded without a problem, but I could understand how Catholics, and all religious people, thought themselves under assault.

The solemn and traditional Mass in the dark church full of flickering candles reminded me of the pre-Vatican Masses in Buenos Aires, although the service in Havana included the reformed liturgy, of course. Easter Mass in the United States usually lasted about two hours, but this Mass was just getting going after two hours. There was an intensity to this celebration of faith I had never experienced in a Catholic church. The readings were endless and, after each recitation, the faithful joined in song and in candle processions inside of the church, since the government prohibited processions outside the building. I asked a parishioner how long Easter Masses lasted, and he said until about ten o'clock. Not used to a four-hour Mass, we left at eight o'clock.

There was nothing liberationist about the parish church in Vedado that evening. The conservatism and deep piety suggested a church in retrenchment, a return to the basics in the face of a hostile society; the parishioners found inspiration in their shared sense of solidarity with the persecuted early Christians. The Cuban faithful, at least at the grassroots, seemed to know little or nothing about Catholic theological trends coming out of Latin America and instead focused on spiritual consolation. The Revolution did not appreciate the wisdom of accommodating the spiritual sensibilities and needs of many Cubans. This ideological stridency, and the anger and resentment it bred in the people ate away at the Revolution.

When I moved to San Antonio in 1983, I discovered how Catholic social thought could inspire action for change in the local community. My family and I attended San Antonio de Padua church, originally a mission to Mexican immigrant workers at the Alamo Cement Company quarry and factory. The workers had lived on the quarry property in their Cementville community, as it was known, and attended the small church just off company grounds. In 1957, the mission became a parish with a new larger church architecturally resembling the Alamo downtown. Descendants of the original workers settled in a neighborhood just north of the church that bordered the affluent white suburb of Alamo Heights. Working-class Mexicans and Mexican Americans remained a majority at San Antonio de Padua through the 1980s until the cement factory and quarry grounds were redeveloped into a vast upscale neighborhood and shopping mall. The parish became gentrified, more ethnically and economically diverse, and lost its humble character.

In this welcoming community, I made friends, and my sons attended Catechism. The Irish priests of the Missionaries of the Sacred Heart brought an international sensitivity to their local ministry. They were clearly committed to the Mexican-American community where they worked. I too enjoyed my first grassroots experiences within this community, including managing the *raspa* stand at the annual parish fundraising bazar. At the festival, Father Bill Collins walked the grounds after Mass with a large hat protecting him from the hot Texas sun, he checked all the stands and welcomed everyone with his Irish broage.

I frequently attended services at San Fernando Cathedral in downtown San Antonio, the city's original parish church founded in 1754. It became a cathedral in 1874 with the creation of the Archdiocese of San Antonio. I heard the preaching of two extraordinary pastors, Archbishop Patricio Flores and Father Virgil Elizondo, rector of the cathedral. Adopting the logic of the civil rights struggles and the inspiration of Liberation Theology, in the 1960s and 1970s, they promoted greater Hispanic influence in the US Catholic Church. They and those they inspired demanded greater acceptance and inclusion of Latinos in parish communities and in national church governance, including Spanish-language Masses, respect for their devotional customs and traditions and naming Latino bishops. Both regularly spoke of the church's social mission, unlike most priests I had encountered in my life whose traditional homilies were limited to messages of individual piety and personal salvation.

Just two years after his appointment the first Mexican-American bishop in US history in May 1972, Flores joined with Elizondo in establishing a specialized pastoral institute, the Mexican American Cultural Center, in San Antonio, to focus on theological education and promotion of a culturally specific mission to train laity, priests and seminarians in Hispanic ministry. Elizondo took the basic sensitivities of liberationist ideas and applied them to Latino cultures in the United States. But he recognized that given the deeply racist traditions in the United States, breaking political and cultural barriers to Latino empowerment had to precede tackling economic struggles. Unlike in Latin America, where jobs simply did not exist, in the United States jobs existed but racial discrimination made the good ones off limits to Latinos. The ethnic poor needed access to decent-paying and inspiring work that could become a career, and making this a reality required strategies consistent with the civil rights agendas of the day.

During the 1990s, my own scholarship turned toward exploring Latino Catholicism. The Virgen de la Caridad del Cobre took on even deeper meanings for me as I became aware of Father Virgil Elizondo's writings about La Virgen de Guadalupe and his take on the relationship between culture, religion and social justice. I finally came to know him personally in the 1990s and had the privilege of occupying an office next to his at the Institute of Latino Studies at the University of Notre Dame, where I spent two years as a research fellow writing a book on Cuban Catholics in the United States.

After many hours of conversation with him, I came to appreciate that while God may be universal, as human beings we think about the divine and worship within specific communities, with specific languages and through specific cultural contexts. It is especially important for minority groups to recognize this, because dominant groups will always tend to declare themselves and their traditions to be the vehicles for reaching universal truths.

After a brief stint in Miami at Florida International University, in 1992, I joined the faculty of St. Mary's University, one of three-sister universities of the Society of Mary (Marianists). I'm not sure if I could have joined the faculty had I not first discovered the Church's social teachings. I was excited to learn that Marianists took their social commitments and sense of community seriously. The challenges inherent in grand societal transformations that I had learned about gave me respect for Marianist initiatives across the world, as well as for the long-standing work of such organizations as Catholic Charities, Catholic Relief Services and other worldwide efforts to fight misery and despair. I also gained a deeper respect for the individual actions of mercy and charity that made life easier for people in their local communities, which I had always considered to be generous but piecemeal gestures, inconsequential for resolving deep systemic social problems. Systemic solutions it turned out were not so easy, and while I still believed in social democratic solutions, it seemed that genuine change in local communities could also evolve from individual action inspired through empathy, spirit and heart. Giving immediate relief to burdened individuals required personal action and commitment beyond rhetoric and good intentions.

The social justice ethos of Marianist projects around the world inevitably bled into their high school and university missions to educate students for the common good. I was gratified to learn during the 1990s how many of San Antonio's Mexican-American community activists, civil rights advocates and political leaders had graduated from St. Mary's University. One particularly extraordinary person, Willie Velázquez, who founded the Southwest Voter Registration Project, educated and registered Mexican-American voters in San Antonio and then Latino voters across the United States, helping them transform American politics. Velázquez was the essence of what it meant to be an agent of change in a local community.

I learned the craft of history through books and in the archives, but discovered my vocation in the classroom. Besides a place to teach history, liberal arts and professional skills, St. Mary's classrooms also provided a place to speak openly and frequently of social justice, as well as to teach mostly Mexicans-American students about the difficult historical struggles in Latin America and the challenges Latinos faced in claiming their place in the United States. Latino students comprised some sixty-five to seventy percent of the student body, and very few of those I encountered had much consciousness of the history of Latin America, Mexico or even Mexicans in the United States. I urged them to learn their own histories, as I had had to do. Only in that way would they genuinely define their own manner of belonging in the United States and remain cognizant of the continuing need for social struggle.

At St. Mary's University, I have come to believe that encouraging charity, acts of mercy and distributive justice on a personal level often opens people up to thinking of the common good at the local, national and international levels. The Church's social teachings challenge Catholics to see the links between personal salvation and attention to the welfare of their neighbors. To understand the Church as a vast tent where voices in support of the common good might one day convert even one-dimensional pious Catholics who regularly pray for their own souls each Sunday without thought for the vast majority in the world on the margins of their societies. Social teachings seek to change hearts and minds and in so doing encourage the work of caring for the most underserved, both on a personal level and through permanent structural social transformations.

I learned much about the importance of concrete community action one day at a time from Miryam Bujanda, whom I met in 1993 when she visited St. Mary's University for a conference. Her upbringing in El Paso and her Baptist faith produced in her an understanding of the imperative to help the most vulnerable in the community. She committed her professional and personal life to helping the least advantaged, or those in emotional or spiritual need, and making a difference in people's lives every day. She, like I, believed in the power of bread, spirit and community—values that have defined our relationship and marriage.

My reengagement with the Church, which in many ways remains an unending struggle, also helped me think about Cuba's future. Despite the hardships of the 1990s, Cuba would have to find its way, as my Cuban friend had said. I was hopeful when Fidel Castro invited Pope John Paul II to visit Cuba in 1998 and allowed him to hold public Masses and address the Cuban people. His call for the world to open to Cuba and for Cuba to open to the world set the tone for what might follow. While this visit did not lead to immediate changes in Cuba, it signaled a softening of its long-standing ideological rigidities. The Pope's visit seemed to symbolize the possibility of new directions. Economically, the country had already begun to experiment, and people spoke more boldly of their discontent and even let the government know.

20

We Shared the Sign of Peace

My parents' move to the United States in 1978 signaled the end of the family's nomadic life. The five generations' journeys back and forth from Cuba to the United States were complete, at least for the time being. Only my younger brother Jeffrey remained in Latin America. Like I had wanted to do, he returned south after university, to Santo Domingo. While I had remained in the United States, always thinking about the south but unable to find a way to return. Jeffrey, a developmental economist, was better equipped to return than an historian. Over the generations, some members of the family resisted the forces that had determined our northward trajectory, but political and economic realities had won the day. We were like the countless millions of immigrants who for over two centuries had ended up in the United States.

∽ ∽ ∽

My father felt bittersweet about his return to New York in 1978. His first consideration was defeating my mother's illness, but he thought his reassignment probably spelled the end of his career. In fact, the corporation soon encouraged him to step down. Determined to stay on, he turned down several attractive retirement packages and spent the next two years in an office, feeling depressed, without much to do. One of the benefits of corporate life at that time was a reciprocal loyalty that kept him employed even when the newly created overseas division in Detroit did not have an immediate need for his expertise. In some ways, this downtime worked for him, considering my mother's health, but he complained that the corporation, now employing dozens of young MBA's with sophisticated theories about business, had little interest in what he had learned during his thirty-five years of practical experience in Latin America.

But he went to work each day until something finally came his way. As the integration of the overseas division into the larger corporate structure proceeded, his stubbornness finally paid off with an appointment as Director of Marketing Services for Latin American and South African Operations in the newly formed General Motors Overseas Distribution Corporation. He worked closely with the Vice-President for Latin American and South African Operations, John McCormack, and traveled regularly across Latin America and sometimes to South Africa. Mostly, he spent time in Colombia and Venezuela, the site of GM's newest investments.

He also participated in an initiative with Isuzu Motors in Japan, of which GM owned a third of its shares. GM had made this investment in 1971 in a widely publicized move to enter the perennially protected Japanese market as well as Asian markets beyond Japan. A decade later, GM also acquired shares in Suzuki, making it the largest single shareholder, in hopes of developing a competitive minicar. In 1980, my father accompanied McCormack to the Annual GM-Isuzu Export conference in Fujisawa, Japan, and attended for the next four years. The meetings brought together executives of the two corporations to discuss strategies for advancing Isuzu and GM in world markets. They formalized a GM-Isuzu joint venture, entitled the Isuzu Motors Overseas Distribution Corporation, to sell vehicles in Southeast Asia, the Middle East, Africa and Latin America.

In 1984, my father was promoted to vice president of General Motors Overseas Distribution Corporation and that same year my mother did something quite uncharacteristic, which my siblings and I enthusiastically applauded. Having grown tired of the cold winters in Michigan and convinced she had done her part in supporting my father's career, she declared, "I am ready to retire." She had hoped he would also retire within a couple of years of moving to Detroit. However, he was only sixty-one and still enjoyed the work. With my father's reluctant acquiescence, she established their retirement home in Savannah, just a few hours' drive from Atlanta, where my brother Sergio lived. My father in the meantime rented a furnished apartment in Farmington Hills, another Detroit suburb. For the first time since her marriage in 1943, my mother placed her own interest first and made a decision for herself. In Savannah, she made new friends, took her art more seriously than ever before and seemed relaxed for the first time in many years. This time, my father paid the price. He had not lived alone since his years at GMI and had never learned to cook. "I even burned the water!" he exclaimed. After living alone for two years, my father had had enough. At the end of 1986, after forty-years with General Motors, he retired at the age of sixty-three. With a hard and stressful career behind him and with a comfortable pension, he joined my mother in Savannah.

~ ~ ~

After a decade of retirement, my mother lay dying with a recurrence of throat cancer that had spread to her lungs, diagnosed two months before Miryam and I visited her and my father in Savannah for Thanksgiving, 1996. For fifty-eight of her seventy-three years, she had smoked at least one pack of cigarettes a day. Her weak and dehydrated body signaled a quicker demise than the six months the doctor had predicted. I sat in her bedroom watching her sleep for a long time, when she suddenly woke with a startled cry that four terrorists had broken into her room and tried to drag her away. She knew that Death had come for her. Anxious to talk, she demanded I bring my father into the bedroom. My normally passive mother announced to him, "It's time to purchase a gravesite."

"There's plenty of time for that," my father told her. "The doctor says you've got at least six months."

"No," she persisted, "I'll be gone soon."

Then, she shifted to another more pressing matter: "I don't want to die knowing that you two will fight forever. Please, please, love each other."

"But we do," my father insisted. "We can disagree and still love each other."

"Then tell your son you love him. Give him a hug," she pleaded.

"Gerald knows that," he said as he leaned awkwardly toward me and we embraced.

"For years, I have listened to you argue and yell at each other for no good reason. Stop it, please!"

Just before the Christmas holidays, my father, my three siblings and I gathered around her hospice bed and held her hand as the priest administered the last rites. She raised her head off the pillow and watched us with wide-open eyes, happy to see us all together, and then after the prayers, she settled back into a deep sleep from which she never awoke. Early the next morning, December 12, 1996, my mother went peacefully.

My mother's passing forced a transformation in my normally less-than-reflective relationship with my father. Once my parents had settled in the United States, I had interacted with them much more. But my relationship with my father had remained contentious throughout the 1980s as the last years of the Cold War played out. He never shared my grandiose wish to transform the world and saw himself as just one person working hard within the world of impersonal capitalist development that he could neither control nor influence. From his perspective, populists and communists had brought Chile to its knees in 1973 and had done the same to Argentina throughout that same decade. He was a great fan of Ronald Reagan and supported the administration's aggressive stance toward Cuba and the Soviet Union. We agreed on very little, but our reconciliation began after the funeral, when we stood together in his bedroom and he sobbed in my arms. It was a show of vulnerability without precedent.

Some days later, my siblings and their families returned home, and my father and I sat in front of an impromptu altar to my mother's memory. It appeared around a devotional candle of Nuestra Señora de la Caridad del Cobre I had placed on a bookcase near the breakfast table. My father had placed next to the candle a photograph of my mother in a green flowing silk robe as she stood on a staircase in a grandiose pose with an arm outstretched against the wall like a Hollywood star. She could be playful and outgoing, which my father adored in her. Others in the family took his cue and added their *ofrendas* to the sacred space.

He had rarely engaged me as an adult, but more often as a rebellious son. Sitting quietly at the kitchen table next to this altar, we reminisced about her life. As usual, the conversation turned contentious when we moved on to other topics. I said something harsh. He turned to me, offended, and judged me to be disrespectful.

"Never would it have occurred to me to speak that way to my father," he hissed.

"You were eighteen years old when your father died," I reminded him. "I'm forty-seven!"

We both fell into an awkward silence.

After a while he said, "I take your point."

"Tell me about your father," I said to him.

That question opened the way forward for us. My father's idealized image of his father, who died in Havana at age forty-six, had remained frozen in time. He was the prototypical Cuban patriarch: loving and dutiful, but distant and generally uncommunicative. He did not speak to the children much, and before bedtime they filed into the living room to say goodnight with a peck on his cheek. After a hard day at the office, he relaxed by reading mystery novels. The family gave him purpose, and he provided well. In turn, the family looked to him as its main source of security and authority, as I had done with my own father as a child. My father embraced his own father's image of fatherhood, but he never experienced the transformation of their relationship that would have been inevitable if he had lived.

Not until then did we see the truth that my mother had so insistently demanded we recognize, the truth of our inability to talk. We remained mostly silent for months after that, but eventually we began to have new kinds of conversations. Over the years, I had pieced together a family genealogy, and I now asked about the many personalities composing the family tree. He remembered, and, in time, his brothers chimed in. They provided the clues, textures and pathways that made this book possible. It took some time to eliminate politics and defuse the arguments, but we made an extra effort to listen and understand each other's experiences and points of view without bluster and judgement. As our conversations deepened, we learned to trust and be open, although sometimes we slid back into fruitless jousting. These conversations led to greater mutual understanding, intimacy and affection, as well as respect for each other's careers and accomplishments and challenges we'd faced.

❧ ❧ ❧

As we both grew older, the sharp lines drawn years earlier had softened. Life is complicated, my father and I finally agreed, and so is history. I admitted that my hopes and wishes for Latin America had been overly idealistic, and he agreed that too much self-interest, poverty and violence had ultimately created unacceptable havoc in the region. Despite my continuing skepticism of capitalist modernization and American corporate engagements in Latin America as the best economic solution, I listened to my father's stories and appreciated his sincere belief that his work had improved the region's future. My criticism of his career as a corporate executive in Latin America ceased to be so strong, as I began to understand the complex relationship between foreign corporations and nationalist mostly military governments, and learned about the unanticipated difficulties inherent in a fully socialized Cuban economy.

My father wanted me to understand his life with General Motors, but even more importantly, he hoped I would appreciate his life's work dedicated to our family's financial security and his children's education and future. I did, but I told him there was more. He was a Latino pioneer in the American corporate world overseas, an idea he had never considered. Few US Hispanics like him worked for General Motors in an executive capacity; the only others I had encountered in my research were his brother Jorge, and his colleague and friend Joseph Sánchez.

He in turn said he was proud that I had blazed my own path, honoring my own instincts rather than his. Despite our fierce disagreements, he respected my choices. He remembered me heading to graduate school in Austin from Atlanta in January 1973, wearing long hair, a T-shirt and jeans in a rattrap Volkswagen. With a few dollars in my pocket, my itinerary had taken me through Alabama, Mississippi, Louisiana and northeast Texas, which had seemed like an uninviting place to both of us at the time. I imagined it would be like South Carolina, and he, having trained briefly in San Marcos, Texas in 1944, during the war, said I should watch out for "rednecks" who would not much appreciate how I looked. When I told him I would sleep in the car at rest stops along the highway, he offered money for motels. No, I said. I had vowed not to accept more money. He had put me through college, and I would do the rest myself, although there were times I stumbled and he and my brother Sergio had, again, helped.

"It must have been quite an adventure," he said. "I never had the opportunity to do anything like that."

"Of course not," I responded. "You had nothing, and you had to build a future. I had a safety net that I knew would be there if needed."

He smiled and was happy.

As Cantiflas always said, "*¡Y allí está el detalle!*"

"Why didn't you raise us with an appreciation for Cuba?" I asked him.

The dramatic difference between my father's experience on arriving in the United States in 1942 and my own in 1968 had always remained with me. I rejected having to conform to someone else's idea of how I should be American. Multiculturalism, pluralism and tolerance of difference gained ground in the United States, and that is how I grounded my American identity, even though my fondness for the United States did not grow quickly. The USA's essentially imperialistic and aggressive nature was determined by exaggerated capitalism, and I had difficulty with that. As I uncovered remnants of our family's origins in Florida, and Argentina slipped away from my everyday experience, my sense of identity as a *Cuban*-American grew. Eventually finding a Latino place within the United States gave me a stake in an American future and a sense of belonging, but I had to dig, and it was the work of a lifetime.

My father simply moved on when he left Havana and did not dwell on the past. He had some pleasant memories of Cuba, especially of family life, time spent with his father at the car dealership and with his grandfather, whose enthusiasm for baseball always stayed with him. But memories were mixed, at best. The pain and trauma of his father's death and subsequent family economic crisis also remained burned in his psyche. In a revealing aside, my father resented his uncles in Mexico who never contacted the family after his father's death. He thought this was an unforgiveable betrayal of their moral obligation to stricken relatives. Throughout his life, my father pointed to their behavior as an example of how not to treat family and constantly reaffirmed the need for siblings to support each other without question, regardless of differences they may have. My siblings and I have always followed that advice. Despite his resentments, in this spirit he took time to see his uncle Luis Poyo and wife Ruth in 1965, when they called on us while on a vacation tour in Argentina. He received his uncle and aunt graciously, and that was the only time I ever saw any of my grandfather's brothers. My great-uncle Luis at least provided a visual sense of what my grandfather might have looked like at about age seventy had he survived.

Like his father's generation, my father had also recognized the family's dramatic divergence from its nineteenth-century nationalist ideals. José Dolores, the revolutionary, was a noble man but with unattainable aspirations, my father and his brothers said. They neither knew the details of the family's life in Key West nor much about their reasons for returning to Cuba at the end of the nineteenth century. It was only their grandfather's tales of political corruption and the tenuous economic realities in Cuba that framed their family history. My father came back again and again to his father's experience in the early 1930s, when he spent nights at the distributorship with a gun to protect the cars from insurgents intending to overthrow the government. Somehow, all of this had soured him on Cuba, and he did little to instill in us an appreciation for his land of origin.

Cultural immersion in the United States during the 1940s convinced my father of the need to express his loyalty according to the definitions of the dominant society. Once in the United Sates, my father perceived strong pressures to abandon his Cubanness, and his military service produced in him a patriotic zeal for the United States that I never acquired. At his homes in Birmingham, Michigan and Savannah, Georgia he liked to fly the American flag on the front porch and he constantly reminded me of his belief in the greatness of the United States presence across the world. He embraced assimilation whole-heartedly and aspired to a comfortable suburban life in the United States. That aspiration did not work out, but he had no regrets and was thankful that unexpected barriers disrupted his initial craving for a conventional career in the United States. His life with General Motors consolidated his sense of national belonging, and his Latin American postings were eminently more exciting and interesting than what he might have experienced had he remained in the North.

All of this meant masking his Cuban background and keeping the Spanish language a private matter. At most, sometimes he referred to us as Latins, but never Cubans. Latin probably sounded more respectable, a term he preferred to Latino, because it was English. I never asked him exactly what Latin meant to him, but the term certainly spoke to his cultural self-consciousness as a person somewhere between Latin American and American. As American Latins, he believed, we lived with certain values that mainstream Americans did not understand or care about and that we could honor only privately. We are different from them, he would always say. Our task was to live within that careful balance, but, at the same time, he never doubted our Latin ways would eventually be lost; it was the price to pay for the political and economic security and opportunity the United States provided. For him, it was an acceptable trade-off.

Ironically, despite his willingness to assimilate and reject Cuba, I don't believe he ever felt truly accepted in the United States. He remained sensitive to what he thought others felt about his place of origin. Even living in Latin America, he was often wary of the American executives he worked with and did not develop social relationships with Argentines for fear of being accused of being a turncoat.

Quite a few General Motors and other corporate retirees lived in his Savannah golfing and gated community, where he and my mother happily lived out their retirement. He had never considered retiring in Florida: "Too many Cubans," he said only half in jest. Even in his last years he felt uncomfortable letting non-Hispanic friends and neighbors recognize our Latino roots, despite their growing influence in our family. I married a Mexican American as did a niece, my younger brother married a Dominican, another niece married a Colombian and my son Noel married a Guatemalan American.

At one family reunion, we had all gone to a field not far from his house and organized a soccer game. My brothers and I had raised our children playing the game, so we had a multigenerational match. To keep us in a spirited mood, my brother, who had spent most of his career in the Dominican Republic, put on music: *merengues* and *bachata.* After a while, my father arrived to watch, but first he had furrowed his brow and had turned the music way down.

I'd run over and said, "Come on, we can't hear it," and had turned it back up.

Visibly bothered, "I don't want it so loud," he had insisted, and had turned it down again, even lower.

I had shrugged and gone back to the game, but knew exactly what had bothered him.

Another time, much later, he had taken Miryam and me to brunch with a group of his friends. One of the guests included a real estate agent who happened to be Cuban and who had immediately begun to speak with us in Spanish. My father responded in English.

As we sat down, he had whispered not to speak with her in Spanish. "She always wants to speak in Spanish. It's rude," he said.

"We'll only speak Spanish in private conversation, between us," I said.

"But the others might think you're talking about them."

That was his public face; he still dreaded being perceived as a foreigner by his Anglo-American friends. At home, however, he listened to Latino music and used Spanish expressions with us.

Still, he was aware of the growing Latino influence in the United States, and this intrigued him. When I first visited my parents in

Savannah in the early 1980s, the city was composed of the typically segregated white and black communities, but, within a decade, a distinct Mexican-American community had appeared, with their own restaurants and an eight-o'clock-Sunday-morning Spanish Mass at my father's church. My father began to "get" what I was up to in 1989, when I published my first book on nineteenth-century Cuban-exile nationalism, which contextualized our family's experience in Key West. He was delighted that I had connected our family with the United States. As I continued writing about Cubans and Mexicans in the United States, he recognized that now—unlike his experience in the 1940s—Hispanics could live in the United States as Americans without necessarily negating their identities of origin.

One Sunday after Mass, I had suggested we have brunch at a Mexican restaurant.

"Okay," he'd agreed.

The owner, not much over thirty, met us at the door. "Welcome," he said with a thick accent.

"Gracias," I responded.

Much surprised at hearing a Spanish response, he attended us at the table, and we enjoyed a nice meal. Along the way, we learned that his uncle had opened several restaurants in Atlanta many years earlier and that the family had extended franchises to various cities in Georgia. On our way home, my father had said that these Mexicans were entrepreneurs and would do well in the United States. He had admired their hard-working determination to make new lives for themselves in the American south. Perhaps it had reminded him of his own family's experience in Atlanta some decades back.

"Who would have thought it?" he said.

I had never heard him complain of the growing presence of Latin Americans in the United States, and he never expressed any animus toward their presence in Savannah.

"As long as they learned English," he said.

∽ ∽ ∽

In 1999, I learned something about my father I had not known: he had maintained one ongoing relationship from his Cuban past. In 1947 while living in New Jersey, a high school classmate, Ignacio "Nacho" Tamayo, had arrived in New York on his honeymoon with his wife Yvonne. Tamayo, who was the only friend he had kept up with from Cuba with occasional letters, had looked up my father. They had met for the first time in seven years since graduating together from Belén high school in Havana, where they had belonged to the same study group and played together on sport teams. Then he heard from him again in 1960, when Tamayo had fled the Revolution to Miami. "I called Sergio from Miami to ask for advice about finding a job. He suggested I travel to New York, which I did," Tamayo wrote to my siblings and me when he heard of my father's death. "At General Motors I was offered a very interesting job," he said, but he could not take it until he had received his permanent residence. In the meantime, he had found another job in Puerto Rico, but he had always remembered the strings my father had pulled for him at General Motors.

Eventually, Tamayo had moved to Miami and remained in touch with my father. In 1997, Tamayo had invited him to a Belén school class reunion. The Revolution had closed all private schools in 1960, but Belén had transferred its operations to Miami, where many alumni lived. In coordination with the school, Tamayo had organized the event and had urged my father to go. My father was a bit nervous about attending because he had not kept up with any classmates except Tamayo. Most of them lived in Miami and had interacted over the years. Would I accompany him? he asked. In the midst of completing my research for a book on Cuban Catholics, I jumped at the opportunity.

Perhaps a dozen former high school classmates had attended. At a tour and Mass at Belén school and later at a reception and dinner, I had seen my father's interactions with his old schoolmates. They had been genuinely excited to see him and had immediately launched into their *choteo cubano*, Cuban-style verbal jousting, as they had in their youth. They had reminisced about sports, teachers and academics, and had lamented that they would never return to Havana and visit the sites of their youth. Lively stories had filled the air, laughter had rung out and several had even shed a few tears. The many years of separation were of no importance, and my father felt genuinely moved at this reception. Later, he had reminisced with me about his baseball and basketball teams, his many friends, especially those in his study group, and he had told me what he remembered about each of his former classmates who had attended the day's events.

During the next couple of days, I had driven him around Cuban Miami, especially Little Havana. We had eaten at La Carreta, had visited the monument to the Bay of Pigs invasion and Nana's grave. He had known about Cuban Miami only from afar and through its reputation, which was not always very flattering, but he had enjoyed what he saw. For the first time ever, I had seen that he was genuinely comfortable with his Cuban origins. My own faith had helped me become more compassionate and understanding, and I had persuaded him to accompany me to Mass at the Basilica of Nuestra Señora de la Caridad del Cobre.

In 1961, exiles had smuggled a statue of the Virgin from a parish church in Guanabo, east of Havana, to Miami. Placed in a local church, the image attracted thousands of faithful. During the following years, the community had built the Basilica to house the image, which Cardinal John Krol of Philadelphia consecrated in 1973. It had become an important devotional space and place of pilgrimage not only for Cubans in Miami, but from across the United States. I had first visited it in the mid-1990s during research trips to Miami. I usually visit whenever I am in the city.

We had entered the Basilica and saw behind the central altar a thirty-six-foot high mural, which depicted Cuban geographic, religious and patriotic symbols. At the very center of the work stood the Virgin holding the Christ child, while at the top a Cuban flag, representing a suffering nation, was draped over a cross held by two angels. Just below the flag, my father had picked out Father Félix Varela, the historical figure who symbolically unites the themes of faith and nationality. Around the Virgin were important historical figures who had traditionally defined Cuban nationality. My father had also pointed out independence heroes Carlos Manuel de Céspedes and José Martí he had learned about in school; he had even identified Archbishop of

Havana Manuel Arteaga Betancourt, whom he had recalled meeting at Belén school one time. He had recognized the Morro Castle at Havana harbor and Pico Turquino, the highest peak in Cuba. Attached to the mural was a pedestal supporting the statue of the Virgin.

My father normally attended Mass at a rather homogeneous middle-class Anglo-American church in Savannah. He had seemed surprised as the Basilica filled with Cubans and other Latinos of every age, color and class. During the Spanish-language Mass, we had shared the sign of peace and received the Eucharist together. My mother would have been ecstatic—maybe she was!

My father's long-distance relationship with Tamayo over so many years had finally brought him to Cuban Miami, where he had seemed to reconcile with his Cuban past. This gave me a strong sense of well-being for him and for myself. Maybe he had sensed that it was okay to be Cuban in the United States. I remember that after Mass at the Basilica that day, we had stood together at the edge of Biscayne Bay, looking south toward Havana.

∽ ∽ ∽

On Saturday evening, March 10, 2005, my father died of a massive heart attack, just ten days short of his eighty-second birthday. One is never prepared for this kind of news. I cried when my brother called. I had spoken with my father just the day before, but now he was gone. A friend who witnessed his death said that he died in an instant, without awareness of what was happening. Later I thought, "Not a bad way to go." He had heart problems, had carefully prepared his estate and often said he did not want to die a long, painful death. He got his wish; perhaps it was a reward for the dignity with which he cared for my mother in her last months.

The family gathered during the next few days, and we buried him. Funerals are sad occasions of final farewell, but may also be happy times, as it was in this case. We remain a geographically scattered family, and his death brought us together to remember, but also to deepen our bonds with each other and the next generation that was already grown. Close and caring family is what he always advocated for, more than anything else. He was an emotionally distant father for most of his life until retirement, when he opened himself to me, but this had not distracted from his insistence on the centrality of family. His legacy—and that of my mother—was evident at the funeral gathering, where together we mourned, laughed, reminisced and toasted, as they would have liked.

Within weeks of my father's passing, I set out to tell our family's story. It fell to me, and my uncles José and Jorge shared generously their time and their stories. They both passed in 2018 as this book went to the editors. I had no choice but to tell this story. I had an obligation to write what I had learned over so many years. Years of accumulated family history needed recording, or the time spent satisfying my own curiosities would have been for naught. Anyway, this was the only way that my granddaughters Isabella, Gabriela and Alexandra would come to know the Cuban part of their family's Latino story.

Sources

This story also owes its existence to the many authors who have written about Cuban, Latin American and US Latino history and provided the contextual settings for my family story. Here I highlight some of the sources most directly related to the family's story as well as my own. I also reference my published and unpublished work reflected in this book. In preparation for this writing, I read numerous memoirs but two especially relevant for my project were Ariel Dorman, *Heading South, Looking North. A Bilingual Journey* (New York: Penguin Books, 1998) and Edmund de Waal, *The Hare With Amber Eyes. A Hidden Inheritance* (New York: Farrar, Straus and Giroux, 2010).

I worked for many years on a biography of my great-great grandfather José Dolores Poyo entitled *Revolution and Exile: José D. Poyo, Key West and Cuban Independence* (Gainesville: University Press of Florida, 2014) that served as the basis for his treatment here. The biography built on an earlier work of mine, *"With All, and for the Good of All": The Emergence of Popular Nationalism in the Cuban Communities of the United States, 1848-1898* (Durham, NC: Duke University Press, 1989). The first sources I consulted on José Dolores Poyo were Raoul Alpízar Poyo, *Cayo Hueso y José Dolores Poyo. Dos símbolos pátrios* (Havana: Imp. P. Fernández y Cia, 1947) and Fernando Figueredo Socarrás, *José Dolores Poyo. Conferencia*, (Havana: Imp. P. Fernández y Comp., 1912). I first learned of the role of Poyo women in helping organize Key West in Juan J.E. Casasús, *La emigración cubana y la independencia de la patria* (Havana: Editorial Lex, 1953); Gerardo Castellanos y García, *Motivos de Cayo Hueso* (Havana: UCAR, García y Cia, 1935) and Manuel Deulofeu,

Héroes del destierro. La emigración. Notas históricas (Cienfuegos, Cuba: Imprenta de M. Mestre, 1904).

Two works that my great-grandfather Francisco A. Poyo y Camús compiled gave me insight into aspects of his life are *Acuerdos del Ayuntamiento de la Habana* (Havana: Imprenta "El Figaro," 1923) and *Álbum del Estado Mayor del Cuartel General del Ejercito Libertador Cubano* (Havana: Imprenta El Score, 1912). My maternal grandmother's hometown is described in Ireneo Díaz y Valdés, *Memoria de Caimito del Guayabal. Memoria de los trabajos realizados por la administración municipal del alcalde Miguel Angel Castro y Camps, con datos geográficos e históricos del término 1923-1928* (Havana: Imprenta y Librería "La Propagandista," 1931). Material on Francisco Poyo's baseball career is drawn from my article, "Baseball in Key West and Havana, 1885-1910: The Career of Francisco A. Poyo," *Florida Historical Quarterly* 87:4 (Spring 2009), 540-564.

The context for José Dolores and Francisco Poyo's lives in early twentieth-century Havana relied on Louis A. Pérez, Jr. *Cuba under the Platt Amendment, 1902-1934* (Pittsburgh: University of Pittsburgh Press, 1986). Our family's Americanization is better understood after reading Louis A. Pérez, Jr. *On Becoming Cubans: Identity, Nationality and Culture* (Chapel Hill: University of North Carolina Press, 1999). A childhood friend of Uncle Jorge in Havana wrote a memoir with interesting details about their life as children in the Almendares neighborhood, Bob Tippett, *Never to Return: A Tale of My Two Worlds* (Xlibris Corporation, 2010).

To better understand my maternal grandmother's and mother's lives in Flint, Michigan, I consulted John Barnard, *American Vanguard. The United Auto Workers during the Reuther Years, 1935-1970* (Detroit: Wayne-State University Press, 2004) and Sidney Fine, *Sit-Down: The General Motors Strike of 1936-1937* (Ann Arbor, MI: University of Michigan Press, 1969). Material on my father's career in the military is drawn from my article "Seeking 'America': A Cuban Journey through the United States and Beyond During the World War II Era," in Maggie Rivas-Rodríguez and B.V. Olguín, eds. *Latinas/os and World War II: Mobility, Agency and Ideology* (Austin: University of Texas Press, 2014).

Sources that contextualize my paternal grandfather's and father's careers with General Motors include Frederic G. Donner, *The World-Wide Industrial Enterprise. Its Challenge and Promise* (New York: McGraw Hill Book Company, 1967); Maryann Kelly, *Rude Awakening. The Rise, Fall and Struggle for Recovery of General Motors* (New York: William Morrow and Company, Inc., 1989); Thomas O'Brien, *The Century of U.S. Capitalism in Latin America.* (Albuquerque: University of New Mexico Press, *1999);* and Richard P. Scharchburg, *GMI: America's Co-Op College-The First Seventy-Five Years* (Flint, MI: The GMI Press, 1994).

Books that helped me make sense of the difficult political and social realities my family encountered in South America during the 1960s and 1970s include Paul H. Lewis, *Guerrillas and Generals. The "Dirty War" in Argentina* (Westport, CT: Praeger, 2002); Jonathan Brown, *Cuba's Revolutionary World* (Cambridge, MA: Harvard University Press, 2017); Jon Lee Anderson, *Che Guevara. A Revolutionary Life (*New York: Grove Press, 1997); and Thomas C. Wright, *Latin America in the Era of the Cuban Revolution* (Wesport, CT: Praeger, 2001).

In my attempt to make sense of our family life in Latin America also took me to the following sources: Harlan Cleveland, et. al. *The Overseas Americans* (New York: McGraw–Hill Book Company, Inc., 1960); Ariel Dorfman and Armand Mattelart, *Para leer al pato Donald: Comunicación de masa y colonialismo* (Buenos Aires: Siglo Veintiuno Argentina Editores, 1972); Robert Seidenberg, *Corporate Wives—Corporate Casualties? (New York: AMACOM, 1973);* and Paul T. Luebke, *American Elementary and Secondary Community Schools Abroad* (Arlington, VA: American Association of School Administrators, 1976).

As I recalled my experiences with race relations in South Carolina, I consulted Jack Bass and Jack Nelson, *The Orangeburg Massacre* (Macon, GA: Mercer University Press, 1996); Henry H. Lessner, *A History of the University of South Carolina, 1940-2000* (Columbia: University of South Carolina Press, 2001); and *The Gamecock*, The University of South Carolina student newspaper. Scholarly accounts I came across of Anglo Americans' negative attitudes about Latin

Americans are John J. Johnson, *Latin America in Caricature* (Austin: University Texas Press, 1980) and Philip Wayne Powell, *Tree of Hate: Propaganda and Prejudices Affecting United States Relations with the Hispanic World* (New York: Basic Books, 1971).

Richard Crossman, ed. *The God that Failed* (London: Hamilton, 1950) and Lee Lockwood, *Castro's Cuba; Cuba's Fidel: An American Journalists's Inside Look at Today's Cuba* (New York: Vintage Books, 1969) raised interesting, exciting and troubling issues that helped me think through my first experiences traveling in Cuba in the late 1970s and early 1980s. The following sources provided background as I recalled my travels to Cuba in the 1980s and 1990s: Luis Martínez-Fernández, *Revolutionary Cuba: A History* (Gainesville: University Press of Florida, 2014); Carmelo Mesa-Lago, *The Economy of Socialist Cuba: A Two-Decade Appraisal* (Albuquerque: University of New Mexico Press, 1981); Marifeli Pérez-Stable, *The Cuban Revolution: Origins, Course, and Legacy*, 2nd edition (New York: Oxford University Press, 1999); and Archibald R.M. Ritter, *The Cuban Economy* (Pittsburgh, PA: University of Pittsburgh Press, 2004).

My reengagement with the Catholic Church in the 1990s grew as I researched my book *Cuban Catholics in the United States, 1960-1980: Exile and Integration* (Notre Dame: University of Notre Dame Press, 2007). Edward L. Cleary, *Crisis and Change. The Church in Latin America Today* (New York: Orbis Books, 1985) and Virgilio P. Elizondo, *Christianity and Culture: An Introduction to Pastoral Theology and Ministry* (San Antonio: Mexican American Cultural Center, 1975) helped me think about Catholicism in Latin America and among US Latinos during the same time.

Two seminal books that introduced me to the Mexican American experience in the United States in the late 1970s were Rodolfo Acuña, *Occupied America: The Chicano Struggle toward Liberation* (San Francisco: Canfield Press, 1972) and Leonard Pitt. *The Decline of the Californios: A Social History of the Spanish-Speaking Californians, 1846-1890* (Berkeley: University of California Press, 1966). My chapter on the Latino experience is drawn from an unpublished historiographic essay I wrote mostly in the mid-1990s and completed in 2002 entitled "Thinking about Latino History." The essay's broad conceptual frame was inspired by Jorge J.E. Gracia, *Hispanic/Latino Identity: A Philosophical Perspective* (Malden, MA: Blackwell Publishers, 2000) and Roberto S. Goizueta, ed., *We Are a People! Initiatives in Hispanic American Theology (*Minneapolis, MN: Fortress Press, 1992). Among the important source materials for that article were Nicolás Kanellos and Claudio Esteva Fabregat, eds. *Handbook of Hispanic Cultures in the United States (*Houston: Arte Público Press, 1993-1994); Nicolás Kanellos, *ed. Herencia. The Anthology of Hispanic Literature of the United States* (New York: Oxford University Press, 2002); Nicolás Kanellos, *History of Hispanic Theatre in the United States: Origins to 1940* (Austin: University of Texas Press, 1990); and Nicolás Kanellos, with Helvetia Martell, *Hispanic Periodicals in the United States. Origins to 1960. A Brief History and Comprehensive Bibliography* (Houston: Arte Público Press, 2000).